666 DAYS OF METAL

Chip McCabe

Dedication

This book is dedicated to metalheads worldwide who keep the spirit of heavy metal music alive and well.

So what will you find in these pages? You'll find albums and bands from every corner of the metal universe – traditional metal, power metal, death metal, black metal, grindcore, doom, stoner rock, hardcore, and everything in between. All 666 albums are listed in descending order, and at the end of the list you'll find further examination into how it all breaks down. You'll also find my suggestions for some albums worth listening to from the years 2013-2016 – 25 albums per year, 100 albums total. Being the original list of 666 stopped in 2012 it was only fair to include some recent classics for you to investigate.

This project was written with many different readers in mind. For those who are new to heavy metal or are 'metal curious' consider this your introduction to the genre. For long-time fans, I hope you discover something new or re-discover your love for an album that was lost over time. Regardless of your knowledge of the genre, you're heartily encouraged to search out bands and albums which aren't included in these pages as well. There is a massive world of music out there waiting to be explored.

Yours In Metal
Chip

I. The List of 666

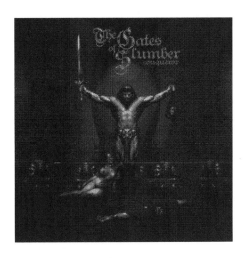

666. The Gates of Slumber – Conqueror

The Gates of Slumber were a doom metal band from Indianapolis, IN. In 2008, ten years after their formation, they unleashed the album *Conqueror* on Profound Lore Records. It was easily one of the best doom albums of the year upon its release and has remained one of the better doom albums of the last decade. *Conqueror* was their third full-length album, and it could be argued that up to that point it was easily their best. If you're looking for a doom metal reference point, the legendary Reverend Bizarre is a good place to start. This album is as heavy as a rhino busting through a brick wall, mixed with twinges of old-school, traditional heavy metal for good measure.

Recommended Track: "Conqueror"

665. Corporation 187 – Perfection In Pain

Corporation 187 was a thrash/death metal hybrid hailing from Sweden. This will be the first in a lot of albums in these pages from Sweden. Corporation 187 often stylistically fell in line with fellow Swedes, At The Gates (as well as early Arch Enemy and early Soilwork). When you remove the unfair comparisons to the above mentioned compatriots this album often received, what you find is that it stands on its own merits. This was the band's second album, released in 2003 by Earache Records imprint Wicked World. The vocals on this album are sick as hell and there is some great Slayer-esque soloing at certain points. Fans of thrash and melodic Swedish death metal will find a lot to like on this album.

Recommended Track: "Strange Is Strong"

664. Darkmoon – Seas of Unrest

In 1999, North Carolina's Darkmoon would unleash their second and final full-length album through Music For Nations. In 1999 black metal was still a predominantly European export. North America had a few, seminal bands playing black metal or black metal hybrids, and doing it successfully, but not in the droves we have now. So when a band like Darkmoon came slithering out of the hills of North Carolina a lot of people initially assumed they were from some country that gets a lot more snow than NC, especially being signed to a UK label. This is a an exceptional black metal album similar in style to what Dissection had done a few years earlier. Definitely worth a hardy listen or two if you're a fan of corpse paint.

Recommended Track: "From The Moon's Mist We Arise"

663. Children of Bodom – Something Wild

In 1997, Finland's Children of Bodom released their debut album on Nuclear Blast here in the U.S. The vocals have a distinct Hypocrisy meets Dissection vibe to them, the guitar playing is solid, and I really don't mind the upbeat tempo that a lot of the songs carry forward. This is the album that first put this metal juggernaut on the map. Despite stylistic changes over time it would seem they have grown exponentially in popularity, and in turn the number of new bands cropping up that count these guys as an influence has also grown. Love them or not there's no denying their influence on the current metal world.

Recommended Track: "The Nail"

662. Crisis – Deathshead Extermination

Although they deftly mix in elements of doom and death metal, New York's Crisis weren't the heaviest band in the world (they were as heavily influenced by a band like Swans as any other metal band). The amazingly unique vocals of front-woman Karyn Crisis are all over the place: from pleasant, clean vocals to gruff growls to basically just some high-pitched screaming…all in the same note sometimes. In 1996 they released their second full-length album, and first for Metal Blade Records. Upon its release this album was seriously unlike anything else being released at the time. Karyn Crisis was a trend-setter in the metal world and doesn't get enough credit for helping to influence all the bands today who employ gruff-vocal, female singers.

Recommended Track: "Working Out The Graves"

661. Fudge Tunnel – Hate Songs in E Minor

Fudge Tunnel is one of those bands that some diehards will chastise me for. Cries of "they aren't really a metal band" will cascade down from the mountains. Yes, they are actively categorized as "noise rock" and often bands of that ilk (i.e. The Melvins) are not always considered part of the metal pantheon. They are supposed to be in their own little corner of the rock world. But there's so much more going on with this album than just jangly, down-tuned guitars playing what seems like, at times, random notes. This was Fudge Tunnel's debut full length released on Earache Records in 1991. There are some very distinct sounds at play here that a lot of doom and stoner rock bands would actively rip off over the course of the next decade.

Recommended Track: "Bed Crumbs"

660. Ipsissimus – The Way of Descent

It was sometime in the mid to late '90s when I first heard the expression "Christ-raping Black Metal" used to convey just how grim, nasty and evil a black metal album could be. However by the time 2011 rolled around I don't think I had experienced that expression in several years...until I listened to this album by Connecticut's Ipsissimus. I know, what the hell is so grim about Connecticut? Maybe it's because CT has been dubbed "the most haunted state in the country?" Maybe it's the often Nordic-like winters they have to endure? I like to think though that the reason a band from Connecticut put out one of the most brutal and blasphemous black metal albums of the last decade is because things like 'grimness' or 'blasphemy' are a state of mind. If that is truly the case, then the trio in Ipsissimus have some seriously warped states of mind. But that's exactly how you want your black metal, no? This was the first official full length album for Ipsissimus, released on Metal Blade Records.

Recommended Track: "The Third Secret of Fatima"

659. Saviours – Into Abaddon

Saviours is an Oakland based doom/stoner rock band that plays around with sweeping, epic hard rock and a touch of NWOBHM influence. They are reminiscent of High On Fire only not as heavy and pummeling, or The Sword only slightly less polished in the studio. 2008's *Into Abaddon* is the second full length album from Saviours and the first to be released on Kemado Records. It really is one of those albums you put on, sit back and just rock out to. There is little to no predictability that seemed to plague a lot of stoner rock bands in the mid-2000s. Saviours has been an integral part in revitalizing a sub-genre that was starting to grow a little stale around the seams less than a decade ago and this album is a big reason why.

Recommended Track: "Cavern of Mind"

658. Burst – Prey On Life

Although I would not call this a hardcore album, nor would I dub Burst a hardcore band; there are certainly elements of hardcore that are ever present. However, Burst always were much too progressive to simply wear one label or tag. This album is a unique example of a band being able to successfully combine progressive elements with hardcore and then integrate in everything from blast beats to stoner rock inspired guitar riffs. At the time of its release in 2003 this album stood tall amongst a sea of bands attempting to fuse hardcore with various other styles and coming up woefully short. This album was their debut full-length for Relapse Records

Recommended Track: "Sculpt The Lives"

657. Circle of Dead Children – Starving the Vultures

Circle of Dead Children were a death metal/grindcore band from Pittsburgh, PA who released their debut album on Willowtip Records in 1999. First off, this really was one of a handful of albums that helped put Willowtip on the map for a lot of metalheads. This album includes their four-song demo and a handful of new material. They mix in elements of crust punk and doom giving them a style that probably more closely resembles death metal than grindcore, but grind fans can rest assured that they're going to find plenty of blasting goodness on here. This album really is the perfect example of a band at the top of their genre just making music that's sick as hell.

Recommended Track: "Return To Water"

656. Witchery - Restless & Dead

In 1998 thrash was pretty much a loaf of stale bread. Sure there were still the classic bands of the genre that were mostly clinging to past glories. But there were very few "new" bands doing thrash justice. There were death metal and black metal bands that retained or started to utilize thrash elements but when Sweden's Witchery unleashed their debut album on Necropolis Records thrash fans could rejoice. Now, tagging this band simply as "thrash" is actually kind of a misnomer. The vocals are so dirty sounding that they are almost black metal in their delivery and there are certain mid-tempo songs that incorporate elements of both Swedish death metal and black metal. However you want to classify this band there was no denying their pedigree. Band members on this album counted the likes of Mercyful Fate, Satanic Slaughter, and The Haunted, among others, as projects they had been involved with.

Recommended Track: "The Reaper"

655. Cavity - Drowning

In the late '90s and early 2000s Florida's Cavity was arguably one of the most important sludge/doom bands around. In fact there was so much talent in this band that upon their demise members would go on to form Torche, Black Cobra, and Floor. In 1996 they released this compilation album featuring material originally recorded in 1994 and 1995. It represents some of their earliest recorded material and what that means is you get Cavity at their most stripped down. At certain points this album has the same tenacity as one of their live shows. Cavity broke up in 2003 but over ten years later the importance of this band still can not be understated. Drowning is a good start both sonically and chronologically for anyone looking to check this band out.

Recommended Track: "Marginal Man Blues"

654. Immolation – Dawn of Possession

In 1991 Roadrunner Records released the debut album from New York's Immolation. This would also be the last album Immolation would do for Roadrunner as the label decided soon after that they were apparently over the whole death metal thing. By the late '90s death metal would become a pretty watered down genre with a lot of pretenders to the throne, so to speak. But in 1991 the U.S. was churning out some seriously awesome death metal albums and this is absolutely one of them. This album gives you the best of both worlds when it comes to death metal – from the mid-paced, somewhat atmospheric variety to the pummeling blast beats and all out aural blasphemy. It's a solid example of just how rich and talented the death metal scene was in the States in the early '90s.

Recommended Track: "Those Left Behind"

653. Black Tusk – Taste The Sin

I'm not really sure what's in the water in Georgia, specifically the greater Savannah region, but the amount of great metal coming out of The Peach State over the last decade has been immense. 2010's *Taste The Sin* is the second full length album from Savannah natives Black Tusk and also happens to be their debut for Relapse Records. Rising out of the ashes of various crust punk bands, Black Tusk incorporates a punk rock aesthetic to the sludge/doom formula. The album fluctuates between straight ahead hardcore punk rock and the driving, rhythmic elements that so many other bands from that area have utilized. All three members contribute vocals and the heaviness of it all is as oppressive as a wet blanket on a humid July night.

Recommended Track: "Red Eyes, Black Skies"

652. Dimension Zero – This Is Hell

Sometimes a band will forever be tied to another band based on shared members. But rarely are the comparisons justified. Such is the case with Sweden's Dimension Zero. Formed by two former guitarists from In Flames this band seems to forever be tied to their Swedish counterparts. This is the second full length album for Dimension Zero, originally released in 2003 on Regain Records. Think back to 2003. In Flames had just released their *Reroute to Remain* album and was well on their way to further polishing their sound. This album is infinitely heavier and rawer than anything In Flames was doing at this point. So really, besides their country of origin the comparisons should cease there. Dimension Zero was still experimenting with adding thrash to their sound and even drawing a little bit from black metal at certain points on this album as well.

Recommended Track: "Dimension Zero"

651. Damaged – Token Remedies Research

Coming out of Australia in the mid-90s, playing a sort of death metal/grindcore hybrid was a band called Damaged. Damaged would find a following here in the U.S. with their second full length album, released in 1997 on Rotten Records. Damaged were not a straight forward death/grind band though. In fact, on this record especially they borrowed quite a bit of "groove" from bands like Pantera. However, behind some serious drumming and vocals that sounded like a rabid dog tearing into raw meat, Damaged was able to put together an album that transcended the divide between great underground metal and more accessible mainstream metal. To be honest if Pantera decided to put out a grindcore album this is probably what they would have attempted to accomplish. This album was recorded after the bands first extended hiatus and is the last album recorded with this vocalist (replaced at one point by Brutal Truth's Kevin Sharp).

Recommended Track: "Change"

650. Holy Terror – Mind Wars

Rising out of the L.A. metal scene in the mid-80s, Holy Terror released their debut album in 1987 and followed it up with this gem in 1988 on Roadracer Records. The first thing you notice about this band is their ability to shift gears at the drop of a hat, going back and forth from mid-tempo thrash to all-out speed metal madness. The vocals alternate between Tom Araya-esque yelling to full-on unholy screams. The guitar work is absolutely top-notch and the production is pristine. This album and this band are criminally underrated by any standards. The easy reasoning as to why lies in the fact that *Mind Wars* was also the last album that Holy Terror would release. Luckily for us though this album has been reissued multiple times, including by Candlelight Records in 2009

Recommended Track: "Judas Reward"

649. Winterfylleth – The Mercian Sphere

Winterfylleth play a sort of pagan black metal hybrid that utilizes everything from first and second wave influences such as Bathory, Immortal, and Satyricon to progressive elements that quite frankly would have had Euronymous shitting a Satanic brick. Winterfylleth prove you don't need corpse pain, gauntlets, and fake blood when every song you write is an absolute sweeping epic. Plain and simple, every song on this album is mesmerizing – perfectly executed, blasting black metal that grips you by the throat and then lets go just long enough for you to catch your breath during some exceptionally beautiful progressive interludes. Released in 2010, *The Mercian Sphere* was the second full length album from Winterfylleth and their first for Candlelight Records.

Recommended Track: "The Honour of Good Men on the Path to Eternal Glory"

648. Black Anvil – Time Insults The Mind

What happens when some dudes who made their name as part of one of the most successful hardcore bands in the world decide they are going to play blackened trash metal mixed with Motörhead worship? You get New York's Black Anvil that's what. After the demise of NYHC band Kill Your Idols three members got together to form Black Anvil and in 2009 released their debut album on Relapse Records. While the punk rock aesthetics of their former project are often pervasive (in a good way), the transition to something a whole lot darker and nastier was certainly a successful one.

Recommended Track: "I.t.h.I.t.k."

647. Black Pyramid – Black Pyramid

Sometimes it's just all about the riffs. The sweet, sweet riffs laid forth by the masters of Satan's favorite instrument. Stoner rock in general is a genre predicated on Black Sabbath worship and the ability to craft songs that rock a little bit harder or weirder than the last one. Enter Massachusetts' Black Pyramid, who released their self-titled debut album in 2009 on Meteorcity Records. They are a power trio of the highest order mixing in elements of doom and cobbling together lyrical content revolving around all things mystical and occult. Stoner rock and doom have expanded and evolved over the years but the essence of what makes up a good stoner rock/doom band has not and that essence lives on in Black Pyramid.

Recommended Track: "Visions of Gehenna"

646. Carnal Forge – Who's Gonna Burn

The one time I saw this band live their vocalist looks up at a huge sign on the wall in the venue that read NO MOSHING. He points to the sign and yells, "You see that sign? It says 'no mosh'…well too bad because THIS SONG IS FOR MOSH!" That about sums up Sweden's Carnal Forge. In 1998 they released their debut album on WAR Music (distributed by Relapse Records here in the U.S.). The songs on this album really are "for mosh." They are thrash-infused, Swedish death metal that play out as an intense, high-octane thrill ride. Most of this album comes off as fast and pissed but what melodic parts they do throw in totally work.

Recommended Track: "Who's Gonna Burn"

645. Life of Agony – River Runs Red

1993 was right around the time that the music press started using the term "Alternative Metal". Clearly, because of the rise of bands like Nirvana and the whole "alternative" movement in rock music it was a label that was used to attempt to sell more records. At one point, one of the poster child bands for the whole "Alternative Metal" thing was NYC's Life Of Agony. Originally rising out of the New York hardcore and metal scenes, (they shared a drummer with Type O Negative at one point) Life Of Agony dropped their debut album in 1993 on Roadrunner Records. Genre labels aside, at the end of the day they did a great job of combining the aggressiveness of the New York hardcore scene with some seriously doomy riffs. If you can embrace the unique vocal delivery this should appeal to fans of varying forms of heavy music.

Recommended Track: "River Runs Red"

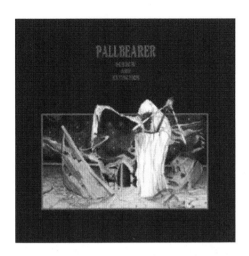

644. Pallbearer – Sorrow and Extinction

Every now and then an album comes along and just blows…your…mind. In 2012 that album was *Sorrow and Extinction* from Little Rock's Pallbearer. This is their debut full length, released through Profound Lore Records. It is, frankly, some of the most epic and beautiful doom metal you will ever hear. This band has somehow managed to take progressive elements and deftly combine it with old school doom metal (not unlike Candlemass and Trouble). Between the soaring, clean vocals and the lumbering, dirty riffs this plays out as one of the most unique and stunning doom albums to be released in the current decade.

Recommended Track: "Foreigner"

643. Wodensthrone - Loss

The U.K. has certainly had their shining moments in black metal history, but it's rare that they have given us black metal as epic and well played as this. *Loss* was the debut full-length for Wodensthrone. It was originally released in 2009, but it wasn't until Candlelight signed them and re-released the album in 2010 that a lot of people started to pick up what this band was putting down. What they were putting down was folk-tinged black metal that in certain respects pays great homage to many of the classic second wave black metal bands. This album is not unlike the early outputs from the likes of Emperor, Satyricon, and Enslaved. But this is definitely not some random copycat band just trying to recreate past glories. These guys definitely went out of their way to successfully carve out their own niche in the genre.

Recommended Track: "Those That Crush the Roots of Blood"

642. Cretin - Freakery

Released in 2006, *Freakery* is the full length debut from Cretin, released on Relapse Records. It's actually the culmination of almost a decade worth or work this band put in, including an extended hiatus so their bass player could "go insane" (their words, not mine). Featuring the drumming of Col Jones (formerly of Exhumed), Cretin play a throwback version of grindcore, not unlike early Napalm Death or Extreme Noise Terror. But also mixed in is some classic California crust punk, and even a little old school death metal for good measure. Every song runs right around the two minute mark so you really have no excuse for not spending at least 10-15 minutes with this album, which is more than enough time to convince you of its brutality.

Recommended Track: "Mannequin"

641. Black Label Society – Stronger Than Death

This is the second full length album from stoner rock/sludge metal outfit, Black Label Society, released in 2000 on Spitfire Records. It's probably the last BLS album that mainstream hard rock radio stations would ignore, as commercial stations would spend the next decade paying more and more attention to this band. The first thing you notice about this album is the trademark Zakk Wylde lead guitar. You could probably pick out a Wylde solo/riff from a million miles away but that's not an awful thing. The dude can occasionally write riffs that are as heavy as cement. Love or hate Wylde and his sometimes off the mark opinions, there is no denying Black Label Society's musical influence on the rock and metal scenes over the last decade or more.

Recommended Track: "Stronger Than Death"

640. Dystopia – The Aftermath

From one of the heaviest crust/d-beat bands around, *The Aftermath* was the second full-length album (CD version only as the vinyl was an EP) from Dystopia. Released in 1999 it would also be the last full album they recorded until almost a decade later. The album consists of four new tracks and then culls together a bunch of stuff from various splits and their Backstabber 7". Members of Dystopia can count bands as varied as Phobia, Mindrot, Noothgrush, and Ghoul as acts they performed with as well. That should give you some semblance of a reference point. These guys play a sludgy brand of crust that was head and shoulders above a lot of bands playing a similar style at the end of the '90s.

Recommended Track: "Socialized Death Sentence"

639. Satan's Wrath – Galloping Blasphemy

No new band, in a long time, has taken me back to the days of the 1980s Satanic Panic quite like Satan's Wrath. Here's a quote from the accompanying press release: "Satan's Wrath deal in a style of heavy metal music which harkens to the times when the death, black and thrash genres were all considered one in the same, and only leather, spikes and bullets were real!" Think Possessed, early Bathory, Venom, Sodom and Kreator all rolled up into one brutal package and you get their debut album, released through Metal Blade. You hear the terms "throwback" and "retro" used a lot these days but I don't know if I've come across a band in recent memory that fit those terms so perfectly. This album is a serious homage to a great era of metal music and if the 700 Club was still interested in inadvertently turning kids from the sticks on to metal they should absolutely start with this album.

Recommended Track: "Between Belial and Satan"

638. Darkane – Rusted Angel

Sweden's Darkane released their debut album, *Rusted Angel*, on WAR Music (distributed by Relapse Records here in the US) back in 1998. Darkane play a thrash/death metal hybrid mixed with some progressive elements. You'll often find comparisons to both their melodic death metal contemporaries, as well as acts like Strapping Young Lad. Neither of those comparisons would be wildly off the mark. Interestingly though, when you look at the metal landscape today, especially the more mainstream stuff that litters various summer festivals in the States, you can't help but wonder if that's the influence of a band like Darkane you hear, especially this album. The similarities are sometimes there for the taking.

Recommended Track: "A Wisdom's Breed"

637. Lord Belial – Enter The Moonlight Gate

Lord Belial was one of the more unheralded bands during the second wave of black metal in the early to mid 90s. That could be because they were more of a hybrid band that played the "blackened death" sound that Dissection would perfect. *Enter The Moonlight Gate* is the second full-length album from Lord Belial, released in 1997 on No Fashion Records (licensed in the U.S. by Metal Blade). One thing I always liked about this band, and this album in particular, was that they weren't afraid to take chances and mix it up a little bit. Whether it was the addition of a cello or a dark acoustic interlude, for example, this band did a great job of keeping your interest from beginning to end.

Recommended Track: "Lamia"

636. Exit 13 – Don't Spare the Green Love

When people make a list of all the early grindcore bands that helped make the genre what it is today you don't hear Exit 13 mentioned very often. Maybe it's because of the somewhat goofy nature of their songs? The messing around they did in the studio sometimes comes off like kids who first find out that their Casio keyboard can make cool sound effects. I'm not really sure though why these guys often get ignored but when your line-up consists, at one point, of the rhythm section of Brutal Truth you should probably pay attention. *Don't Spare The Green Love* was released in 1993 on Relapse. It's actually a compilation record consisting of three EPs and demos the band recorded between 1989 and 1991. It's an interesting mix of brutal grind with a whole lot of experimentation.

Recommended Track: "Terminal Habitation"

635. Executioner – Break The Silence

Sometimes a band is best known for who was in it and what it spawned instead of the music itself. In this case Boston's Executioner are probably best known for having the late Seth Putnam of A.C. fame on bass. But if you are expecting the type of schizophrenic grind that A.C. specialized in you're a little early for that. This was the second full length from Executioner, originally released in 1987 on New Renaissance. Executioner play an extremely raw form of thrash metal and could be lumped into the category of thrash bands who helped pave the way for death metal. What I think makes this album unique is what a lot of people think is their downfall – the stripped down, almost garage rock recording quality. There's a definite element of punk here that stands out. I could have totally seen these guys sharing a stage with an old school punk band like Verbal Abuse and being right at home.

Recommended Track: "Break The Silence"

634. The Crown – Hell Is Here

If you couldn't tell by now there are a lot of great bands and albums that have come out Sweden. If you also couldn't tell there were a bunch of them in the '90s playing various forms of death metal, dominated by the melodic variety and the thrash/death metal hybrid. With the exception of the last track, there is very little about this album that you could dub as melodic. This one is a ripper for sure. This was technically The Crown's third full length album, released in 1999, and their first for Metal Blade Records. It's their first album under the moniker The Crown, as their first two albums were released under the name Crown of Thorns. However there was already a U.S. band with the same name so they were forced to make the change. If you like your death metal spitting nails then this album is probably one you want on your wish list.

Recommended Track: "The Poison"

633. Kalmah – They Will Return

Kalmah play a unique style of blackened death metal heavily influenced by prog rock and NWOBHM bands, especially Iron Maiden. (Listen to the opening of the track "Kill The Idealist" if you're looking for Maiden influence.) Normally a band that relied so heavily on keyboards to fill out their sound would be a misnomer in death metal circles, one subject to ridicule by those trying to keep it 'true.' But Kalmah is able to maintain their brutality alongside successfully blending their prog influences with virtuoso playing. *They Will Return* was their second full length album released in 2002 on Spikefarm Records (a subsidiary of Spinefarm).

Recommended Track: "Principle Hero"

632. Sacramentum – The Coming of Chaos

Although labeled and marketed as a black metal band the closest comparison Sacramentum has is probably Dissection or early Rotting Christ. So there is definitely a black metal current running through this band but they also mix in slower tempos, the occasional well-performed clean vocal passage and even some thrash elements. But there are still plenty of blast beats and tremolo picking to go around as well. *The Coming of Chaos* was the second full length album released by Sacramentum, originally in 1997, and their first for Century Media. This album is actually a slightly more melodic affair than their debut, which was a more primitive, yet less dynamic, form of black metal.

Recommended Track: "Awakening Chaos"

631. Watchmaker – Kill. Fucking. Everyone.

Boston's Watchmaker played a very similar brand of grindcore to bands like Assück, whereas they often blur the lines between grind and death metal. They even tossed in some thrash-tastic riffing while they were at it. No matter how you slice it though this band tears it up something fierce. They are a violent, brutal aural assault and their sound is just completely uncompromising. *Kill. Fucking. Everyone.* was their second full length album, originally released in 2003, and their debut for Willowtip Records. It could be argued that Watchmaker, for a brief period of time, was one of the best grind bands in the world and this album is an absolute testimony to that notion.

Recommended Track: "Conference Call Immolation"

630. Primordial – A Journey's End

Ireland's Primordial often get lumped into the black metal genre, partly because their early sound really did borrow from the burgeoning black metal scene emanating from Scandinavia. However these guys were also one of the first bands from that second wave of black metal to successfully merge their sound with the folkloric traditions of their homeland, not just in lyrical form, but in sound and style as well. *A Journey's End* was their second full length album, originally released in 1998, and the first album where they started to deeply integrate the folk elements. Flutes, mandolins, clean vocals, Irish folk music rhythms - it all starts to really come together with this collection of songs and in turn this album helped to make Primordial a pioneer in the new wave of folk metal.

Recommended Track: "Graven Idol"

629. God Dethroned – The Grand Grimoire

God Dethroned played a blackened form of death metal with lots of anti-Christian songs and the occasional symphonic touches. It's a brutal slab of '90s death metal, mixed with melodic elements. This Dutch group was heavier than many of their European counterparts at the time but at the same time where more melodic than a lot of their U.S. counterparts. *The Grand Grimoire*, released in 1997, was their second full length album, and first for Metal Blade. Their first album was essentially a glorified demo so you could argue that this is their first proper release. This band would continue to grow more and more melodic as they went along, so this is also arguably their heaviest release. Needless to say, there's a lot on this record that will appeal to fans of all forms of death metal.

Recommended Track: "Under A Silver Moon"

628. Ed Gein – It's A Shame...

The full title of this 2003 album is, *It's a Shame a Family Can Be Torn Apart By Something As Simple As a Pack of Wild Dogs*, and was taken from an old Saturday Night Live sketch (Deeps Thoughts With Jack Handy). But don't think for a second that you are about to listen to some goofy, A.C. styled joke band. This album is a 100% full-on scissor-kick to the face. Ed Gein are from Syracuse, NY, and where born out of the immense hardcore scene there, however they should probably be considered a grind band above all else. This album does a phenomenal job of blending the fierce hardcore of bands like Deadguy and early Converge with the pummeling grindcore of bands like Nasum and Rotten Sound to create a beautifully manic listening experience.

Recommended Track: "You Suck At Life..."

627. Old Man's Child – The Pagan Prosperity

Released in 1997, *The Pagan Prosperity* is the second full-length album from Norway's Old Man's Child and their first for Century Media Records. Old Man's Child is the brainchild of Galder, who most people know these days as a member of Dimmu Borgir. But before joining Dimmu he created a band that borrowed as much from traditional and NWOBHM as it did from any other bands in the black metal scene. Symphonic black metal is absolutely at the heart of this project but you can't help but listen to those galloping rhythms and some of those soaring riffs and not hear the influence of bands like Iron Maiden, Angel Witch and Saxon. As far as black metal was concerned this was a fairly unique album at the time of its release.

Recommended Track: "Soul Possessed"

626. Dark Funeral – Vobiscum Satanas

Sweden's Dark Funeral have proven to be one of the most prolific and accomplished bands to come out of the storied second wave of black metal. *Vobiscum Satanas* was their second full length album, released in 1998 on No Fashion Records. It's also the first album to feature former Hypocrisy vocalist, Emperor Magus Caligula, on vocals (and he would remain with the band until 2010). Dark Funeral really play no frills, straight ahead, black metal, fairly close to its purest form. This album is fast, angry, and full of Satan, exactly what you would expect out of a classic, second wave black metal band.

Recommended Track: "Thy Legions Come"

625. Deceased – Fearless Undead Machines

You really don't get much more "metal" than a concept record about a zombie apocalypse. That's exactly what Virginia's Deceased gave us in 1997 with their third full length album, released on Relapse Records. It's a fantastic mix of thrash and early death metal. Despite the band often being lumped in with other death metal bands in the eyes of some fans and critics these guys were really one of the pioneers of the retro-thrash movement. At a time when thrash had become an after thought to a lot of metal fans Deceased continued to fly the flag of the old school, doing their best to remind people that thrash would never die. You could say, in a way, that Deceased were actually ahead of their time and this album is easily one of their best efforts.

Recommended Track: "The Psychic"

624. Grand Magus – Grand Magus

Some bands just know how to write riffs. They know how to write down-tuned, dirty, sexy riffs. They know how to channel the great forefathers of heavy metal. This is one of those bands. Grand Magus released their self-titled debut album through Rise Above Records in 2001. By this time the stoner rock scene had absolutely exploded and Grand Magus' arrival on the scene further cemented the idea that you can be as heavy as a ton of bricks and still rock out. This band would continue to release great albums while also expanding their sound and experimenting even more on future releases. If you are looking for bluesy, doom-laden, balls out rock though this album is the one you should start with.

Recommended Track: "Wheel of Time"

623. Incantation – Diabolical Conquest

Diabolical Conquest was the third full length album by Incantation, released in 1998 on Relapse Records. It was the only album to feature the bass playing and sick as hell vocals of Daniel Corchado (who is also the front man for his own band, The Chasm). Incantation play brutal death metal with hints of doom, not unlike a band such as Autopsy. It's a fairly straight forward, no frills approach to death metal but at the same time it's a nasty aural assault. It could be argued that the reason Incantation has never gotten the same attention as some of their Northeast death metal contemporaries is because they could never keep a semi-permanent line-up together. It should then come as no surprise that their best album came out of arguably their best line-up.

Recommended Track: "Disciples of Blasphemous Reprisal"

622. Iron Angel – Hellish Crossfire

One of those lost gems of the early thrash scene is the album *Hellish Crossfire* from Germany's Iron Angel. This was their debut full-length album released by SPV/Steamhammer in 1985. Germany has had a long and storied history in heavy music. The late '60s and early '70s brought us all the great "Kraut rock" bands that would prove to be so influential on the world of heavy music, and of course the '80s brought us a lot of great metal. But mention metal and Germany in the same sentence and you usually hear about all the great Teutonic thrash giants. Rarely, if ever does anyone mention Iron Angel. These guys played a sort of speed metal/thrash hybrid. They could go like a bat out of hell, combining double bass rhythms with pseudo-tremolo picking, but could also play it more atmospheric as well. Regardless of what the history books say, this band and this album absolutely deserve your attention.

Recommended Track: "Wife of the Devil"

621. Agalloch – The Mantle

Agalloch hails from Portland, OR, which is a town known for its vibrant metal scene. *The Mantle* is the second full length album released by Agalloch and their second for The End Records as well. This album has a decidedly more mellow tone than their first full-length. Clean vocals, acoustic guitars, and the occasional "post-rock" element all find a home here. But make no mistake, this is a dark record and maintains a lot of the black metal aura that they had perfected on their first effort. This band really pushed the boundaries of what was acceptable to be considered "black metal" by taking their sound into, what was at the time, almost uncharted territory.

Recommended Track: "You Were But A Ghost In My Arms"

620. Bloodlet - Eclectic

Florida's Bloodlet were signed to Victory Records, whose marketing team decided to pitch these guys as "evil-core," which is a truly silly moniker, but it's somehow fitting nonetheless. Bloodlet were dirtier and nastier than the vast majority of hardcore bands, owing as much tribute to doom metal as they did anything else. They wrote thick, sludgy riffs and constantly slowed it all down a couple notches. Sure there were still 'dance parts' for those kids who liked to pretend they were Bruce Lee in the pits but these guys were heavy enough to play alongside some of metal's biggest names and not miss a beat. *Eclectic* is the first full length album Bloodlet released and is comprised of songs that appeared on various 7"s from before they signed with Victory.

Recommended Track: "Husk, The Art"

619. Deeds of Flesh – Path of the Weakening

Originally released in 1999, *Path of the Weakening* was the third full length album from Deeds of Flesh, and first for their own label, Unique Leader. Deeds of Flesh play it one way: death metal. Brutal, technically proficient, hammer to your skull, death metal. There is no other way to describe it, but one could argue that this album is criminally underrated. While their label has moved towards releasing more progressive (and often times more polished) death metal bands, at this point in their careers Deeds of Flesh themselves would never be mistaken for either. If you're a fan of no-nonsense death metal, a la Deicide or Suffocation, then this is one band that also belongs in your record collection.

Recommended Track: "Summarily Killed"

618. Toxic Holocaust – An Overdose of Death

One of the bands today that absolutely could have held their own within the original 80s thrash scene is Portland, Oregon's Toxic Holocaust. Originally a one-man wrecking crew, by the time these guys released their third full-length, *An Overdose of Death*, in 2008 they had a worldwide deal with Relapse Records and were ready to take the metal world by storm. Toxic Holocaust were born out of both the metal and punk scenes and borrow as much from bands like Discharge and Broken Bones as they do Slayer or Kreator. Mix in a love for Bathory and what you get is a band that has rested firmly at the top of the most recent thrash revival.

Recommended Track: "In the Name of Science"

617. Priestess – Hello Master

Every now and then a major label gets it right. In this instance what RCA got right was picking up Canada's Priestess and re-releasing their debut album *Hello Master* in 2006. Make no mistake, Priestess were a live band above all else. They toured the world with some of the bigger names in metal – Black Label Society, Mastodon, Clutch, GWAR, etc. But if ever an album took a live band and was able to encapsulate at least part of what they do on stage this album might be it. Priestess were one of a very small handful of bands around the time of this release to revive the fledgling stoner rock genre and help usher in all of the retro-70s, occult/doom rock that you are hearing today.

Recommended Track: "I Am The Night, Color Me Black"

616. Behemoth - Demigod

Originally started as a pure black metal band in the early '90s, Behemoth would eventually, over the course of nearly two decades, morph into a pure death metal band. But somewhere in the middle they would become masters of propagating the combination of the two genres into a 'blackened death metal' style. It was during this sort of transition period that they unleashed their *Demigod* album. Released at the tail end of 2004 this was the album, thanks in no small part to it being their first on Century Media, that would propel this band to the forefront of the metal world. Besides being their first album easily accessible to the U.S. market this is also, arguably, their best produced album. The songs walk that aforementioned line of black and death metal, and add to the mix a distinct Middle Eastern vibe in both song structure and lyrical components. It was quite the mélange of unholy sounds.

Recommended Track: "Demigod"

615. Orange Goblin – The Big Black

Orange Goblin hail from the UK and they play loud, riff-oriented stoner rock…and they are really good at it. Orange Goblin has always been in the Kyuss/Monster Magnet school of rock. Much like those bands they aren't afraid to mix things up, sometimes putting the foot on the proverbial gas pedal and other times tapping the brakes. To put this into perspective a bit, when this album was re-released it included covers of songs from Black Sabbath, Motörhead and Leaf Hound as bonus tracks. *The Big Black* is Orange Goblin's third full length album and was originally released in 2000 on Rise Above Records and licensed here in the U.S. by The Music Cartel. 2000 was a great year for the stoner rock/doom scene and this album was one of the reasons why.

Recommended Track: "The Big Black"

614. 1349 – Beyond The Apocalypse

Norway's 1349 are "fronted" by drummer Frost who is most famous for banging on the skins in Satyricon. It makes total sense to me that Frost would join this outfit. As Satyricon would continue to evolve into this sort of black n' roll hybrid, 1349 remained straight ahead, evil as sin, uncompromising, black metal. *Beyond The Apocalypse* was 1349's second full length album released by Candlelight Records in 2004. As one of the best and brightest bands of this newest wave of European black metal they draw equally from the first and second waves for inspiration. There is as much Celtic Frost and Bathory influence on this album as there is Darkthrone or Mayhem. This album still stands as one of their best and one of the best examples of how good truly merciless black metal can be.

Recommended Track: "Blood is the Mortar"

613. Dark Tranquillity – The Gallery

There are a small handful of albums that really epitomize what melodic Swedish death metal was in the 90s. One of those albums is *The Gallery* by Dark Tranquillity. Released in 1995 through Osmose, this was the second full-length album from Dark Tranquillity. It really is one of the archetype albums of the genre – screamed/growled but understandable vocals, twin-guitar leads, the occasional acoustic interlude and classical music elements, a distinct NWOBHM influence, etc. If there was a blueprint for the "Gothenburg sound" this album would have to be considered one that people should reference. Although this band would morph and tweak their sound, what seems like, a million times over the course of the next two decades, *The Gallery* stands the test of time for sure.

Recommended Track: "The Gallery"

612. Gorgoroth - Antichrist

When you include the term "True Norwegian Black Metal" right there on the album cover for all the world to see you better be ready to deliver the goods. *Antichrist* was originally released in 1996 before any of the prison terms, inter-band lawsuits, or other extracurricular activities that have followed this band like an albatross throughout their careers (and prior to Gaahl joining the band). It was the second album released by Gorgoroth on Malicious Records out of Germany. This album was reissued multiple times, including 1999 by Century Media, who gave this album its first proper intro here in the U.S. Six songs (two of which are instrumental) are all this band needed to put their blackened mark on an already powerful Norwegian black metal scene.

Recommended Track: "Possessed By Satan"

611. Hypocrisy – The Fourth Dimension

The Fourth Dimension, released in 1994 on Nuclear Blast, was the third album by Sweden's Hypocrisy. This is the first album that Peter Tagtgren does the vocals for after their original vocalist left the band. Hypocrisy, at this point, were playing a pretty brutal and often doom-laden style of death metal. Their brand of death metal more closely resembled their Floridian counterparts such as Obituary and Massacre than what any other Swedish bands were doing at the time, thanks in part to Tagtgren living for a time in the U.S. before returning to Sweden. Although their name is not often invoked with as much reverence as say Deicide or Morbid Angel, Hypocrisy have had their hands all over influencing the modern day death metal scene, and this album is a great example why.

Recommended Track: "Apocalypse"

610. S.O.D. – Speak English or Die

Stormtroopers Of Death, or S.O.D. for short, were formed by Anthrax guitarist Scott Ian in the first half of the 80s basically because he was a fan of the hardcore/punk scene and wanted to experiment with something a bit different. However, instead of just writing a punk record what he did, along with bass player Dan Lilker (Anthrax, Nuclear Assault, Brutal Truth and about 8,000 other bands), drummer Charlie Benante (Anthrax) and vocalist Billy Milano, was create one of the most influential crossover albums of all-time. The album was originally released in 1985 on the mighty Megaforce label, and was their only studio album up until 1999. Despite the fact there is no way this album would get made today because of its extremely non-P.C. humor, it still puts them on the map, alongside bands like Suicidal Tendencies, D.R.I. and Cryptic Slaughter as pioneers of the thrash crossover sound.

Recommended Track: "Kill Yourself"

609. Soilwork – The Chainheart Machine

In 2000, Soilwork unleashed their second full-length album, *The Chainheart Machine*, on Listenable Records (later distributed by Century Media here in the U.S.). This was the album that 'broke' them here in the States and made them a household name in the metal underground. And for good reason. This album is chock full of great riffs - both the grinding and melodic kind - and solos, violent vocals, and accompaniments (i.e. keyboards) that are used to perfection. It's an all-around stellar record and deserves all the acclaim its gotten over the years. It could be argued that it is possibly their finest hour to date and one that they have yet to match in intensity and power.

Recommended Track: "The Chainheart Machine"

608. Nevermore – The Politics of Ecstasy

The Politics of Ecstasy was the second full length album by Nevermore, released in 1996 on Century Media. This was the first album where the band would really start to experiment with their sound and thus the first album that really brought them out from the shadows of Sanctuary – the band which they formed out of in truly "Epic" fashion. (Their origin story is legendary, as they decided to give their label the proverbial middle finger and break up the band instead of being forced to change styles to cash in on the grunge phenomenon.) By this time they were becoming a huge force to be reckoned with in the U.S. metal scene and their ability to successfully blend multiple genres into this almost indescribable brand of metal was second to none.

Recommended Track: "Next In Line"

607. Strapping Young Lad - City

Strapping Young Lad originally started as a solo project but by the time their second full length album was released in 1997 on Century Media, Devin Townsend had recruited a full band. *City* is the album that made this band, and more importantly Devin Townsend, a household name in the metal world. It's certainly an interesting album, if nothing else. Strapping Young Lad blend industrial music elements with thrash and even some death/grind influences. There are songs on this album where Townsend is certainly tapping into something primal, attempting brutality sometimes for brutality's sake. Although it will never be mistaken for the heaviest album listed herein, it is certainly chock-full of raw aggression.

Recommended Track: "Detox"

606. Borknagar – The Archaic Course

Norway's Borknagar play a very melodic form of black metal that also combines clean vocals, folk elements, and lots of progressive influences. *The Archaic Course* was their third full length album and their second for Century Media Records. Released in 1998, it's the last album to feature the legendary Grim on drums, who unfortunately committed suicide via drug overdose. It's also the first album to feature new vocalist ICS Vortex. If you are a fan of the later works of bands like Emperor and Enslaved or enjoy the unpredictability of bands like Ulver and Arcturus then there's no reason to not be a Borknagar fan. This band has an extremely distinctive take on what black metal should sound like and this album has clearly stood the test of time.

Recommended Track: "Oceans Rise"

605. The Haunted – The Haunted

After the demise of At The Gates, three-fifths of the band went on to form The Haunted. Carrying the torch of thrash-infused, Swedish death metal, The Haunted debuted their self-titled album on Earache Records in 1998. It was a landmark album within the genre and one that garnered a ton of critical acclaim. The first thing you are going to notice about this album is that The Haunted do their best to make it as thrashing as possible. Although there are obvious melodic elements and it carries that distinct 'Swedish sound' this album has way too much of a punk aesthetic for it to truly be dubbed 'melodic.' Regardless of how you try to label it, from the metalcore scene to the retro-thrash scene there are a ton of bands that owe this album a debt of gratitude.

Recommended Track: "Hate Song"

604. Fear Factory – Soul of a New Machine

This was the official debut studio album by L.A.'s Fear Factory, released in 1992 on Roadrunner Records. This record is a pretty heavy slab of metal. Unfortunately, this would be by far the heaviest and most brutal album this band would put out. They would spend the following years industrializing their sound and attempting to make it more and more accessible to the mainstream music buying populace. This record though has as much in common with some of the earliest grind and death metal bands, such as Napalm Death and Terrorizer, than it ever would with anything that carried the industrial music label.

Recommended Track: "Suffer Age"

603. Mastodon - Leviathan

Leviathan was the second full length album released by Mastodon, this one coming to us in 2004 courtesy of Relapse Records. With their debut full-length Mastodon was already on their way to becoming one of the biggest names in the metal underground. But this was the record that would truly see them blow up. Several music publications, including Terrorizer Magazine, would bestow Album of the Year honors on this thing. By 2009 one website in particular called this album the "best metal album of the 21st Century". I think you get the point. This album was huge for this band and the scene they came lumbering out of. This is also an album that Neil Fallon of Clutch and Scott Kelly of Neurosis would make guest appearances on. Needless to say when you can get one of the dudes from Neurosis to show up on your album you must be doing something right.

Recommended Track: "Blood and Thunder"

602. Queensryche – Operation: Mindcrime

It would be hard to deny that Queensryche is an immensely influential band in the world of metal and beyond. You can't even begin to count the number of bands and individual musicians who have pegged this album in particular as an influence. Upon its release in 1988 it was as heavy as any other band that major labels were trying to push as "metal" and it came with an interesting concept behind it. (A recovering drug addict is recruited by a revolutionary group who want him to assassinate political leaders.) If nothing else, you should, at the very least, be aware that this was not only the album that brought them international acclaim but wound up in the vinyl collections of several of your favorite metal musicians.

Recommended Track: "Operation: Mindcrime"

601. Pantera – Far Beyond Driven

Pantera. This band is the New York Yankees of the metal world – they are either unconditionally loved (as 'one of the heaviest metal bands ever') or completely hated (mostly as the godfathers of nu-metal), and not very often will you find people that aren't firmly entrenched in either camp. The truth lies somewhere in between. Pantera was the "gateway band" for an entire generation of metalheads. A lot of people would not have discovered things like grindcore or death metal if they didn't first hear Pantera in their formative youth. One reason this album is in this book is because it reached #1 on the Billboard charts and proved to be an amazingly influential album on the current metal landscape upon its release in 1994. Love them or hate them it would be foolish to completely dismiss Pantera altogether.

Recommended Track: "I'm Broken"

600. Cattle Press – Hordes To Abolish The Divine

In the late '90s the hardcore scene started to go through a lot of experimentation. One of the best combinations was when bands got even heavier and dirtier by marrying their sound with doom and/or grindcore. Enter Brooklyn's Cattle Press. When you put on their *Hordes To Abolish The Devine* album all this splitting hairs and scene classification whatnot just fades away in a barrage of sludgy riffs, nasty growls, and an all-out aural assault similar to what many doom/crust/sludge bands are dishing out today. Cattle Press never got as big as they could or should have in part because this wound up being their only full-length album. But after they released this gem on Hydra Head Records in 1999 they did have quite the cult following, especially in the hardcore and crust circles.

Recommended Track: "The Gift"

599. Altamont – Civil War Fantasy

Formed as a side project by Dale Crover of the Melvins and the rhythm section of stoner rock band Acid King, California's Altamont is exactly what you would expect it to be - fuzzed out, low end, stoner rock of the highest order. Crover plays guitar and sings on this album like he's possessed by both Blue Cheer and Hendrix at the same time. This is easily one of the lost gems of the original 90s stoner rock movement. *Civil War Fantasy* was their second album, released in 1998 on Man's Ruin Records and it is seriously the type of album you put on at a biker rally and no one skips a beat. It's heavy, dirty rock n' roll the way the rock gods intended it to be (cow bell included).

Recommended Track: "Ezy Rider"

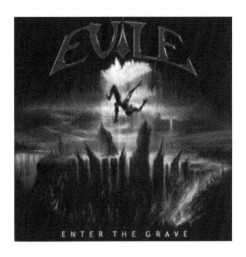

598. Evile – Enter The Grave

When the guy who produced three classic Metallica records (not to mention Morbid Angel's Coven and a truckload of other solid albums) is lined-up as the producer on your debut record you must be doing something right. That's exactly where England's Evile found themselves with their debut album *Enter The Grave* – sitting in Flemming Rasmussen's studio in Denmark. This album, originally released by Earache Records in 2007 has a definite Anthrax meets Testament influence running through it. These guys play it fast and heavy on nearly every track and there really isn't a weak song anywhere to be found. One of the things this band does really well is to capture that old school 'feel' that so many great original thrash records from the 80s had and so many of their contemporaries do not.

Recommended Track: "Schizophrenia"

597. Benümb – Soul of the Martyr

Sometimes the fine line between crust and grind gets obliterated in an explosion of blast beats, primal screams, Slayer-styled riffing and the occasional doom-inspired breakdown. This is exactly what happened when Benümb exploded onto the Bay Area hardcore/metal scene in the mid-'90s. Benümb was one of those bands that could unite scenes, bringing together all fans of heavy, politically charged, sonic venom. *Soul of the Martyr* was their first full-length album, released on Relapse Records in 1998. It consists mostly of new material but does include previously released songs from various other releases. Regardless of how you want to classify them Benümb were a band that simply attacked their music with ferocity. They were an absolute sonic force and I'd go on record as stating they are one of the most underrated grind bands of all-time.

Recommended Track: "Stuck Pig"

596. Gorerotted – Mutilated in Minutes

In 2000 the UK's Gorerotted released one of the most underrated gore-grind records of all-time. This album was released in North America in 2001 via Relapse and this band and this album should absolutely have appealed to every single person who owns a Cannibal Corpse record. Blast beats, insane riffing and dual screams (both the high-pitched and the guttural variety) are all over this record like flies on a rotting corpse. If you are a fan of the ultra-extreme then it's a really well constructed album. After three albums the band would regroup under the name The Rotted, release two more albums under the new name, and eventually split up.

Recommended Track: "Hacksore"

595. Lord Mantis - Pervertor

Pervertor is the second full length album by Lord Mantis, released on Candlelight Records in 2012. Lord Mantis play a blackened form of doom that mixes in elements of sludge as well. It's an album that fans of Celtic Frost, Electric Wizard and even Darkthrone should eat up. It's also an amazingly unsettling album at times. Personally, I've listened to metal music in all its various forms for more years than I should probably admit, and it's not often that an album upon first listen will raise the hairs on the back of my neck the way this one did. It's clearly a record made by some very depraved souls who have distinct apocalyptic visions that they'd like to share with you...

Recommended Track: "Perverter of the Will"

594. Will Haven – El Diablo

El Diablo was originally released in 1997 on Crisis Records, which was an imprint of hardcore heavyweight Revelation Records. To be perfectly honest with you this album is heavy and dark enough that if they weren't signed to a label that had historically been branded "hardcore only" Will Haven would probably be considered a noise rock band. These guys always had more in common with bands like New York's Unsane or Helmet, for example, than most of their label mates. Regardless, this is easily one of the better and more metallic 'hardcore' albums of the '90s.

Recommended Track: "I've Seen My Fate"

593. Bison B.C. – Quiet Earth

Canada's Bison B.C. absolutely reek of bong water and empty whiskey bottles, which when you play heavy doom, thrash, and crust inspired stoner rock that's a really good thing. They play it similar in vein of bands like Motörhead and High On Fire where the goal is to just beat you into submission. But, at the end of the day, they aren't afraid to mix it up either. *Quiet Earth* was their second full length album, but their debut for Metal Blade Records. Released in 2008, this album draws influences from a varied assortment of places along the metal landscape. There's the obvious stoner rock ties, the sludge, and early doom worship. But the vocals are done in deathly snarls that only add to the nastiness of it all. Bison B.C. are just simply heavier than you're average stoner rock band.

Recommended Track: "Wendigo, Pt. 1"

592. Wolf - Wolf

The metal landscape in 1999 was a vastly different one than today and the thought of a new band throwing on studded denim and rocking out like it was 1983 was still a bit foreign. So when Sweden's Wolf released their self-titled debut album on Prosthetic Records it was a pleasant surprise and helped set off a scene that is still growing over a decade later. Although this band borrows some from the thrash and speed metal genres it has more in common with all the great NWOBHM acts of the early '80s. Angel Witch, Witchfinder General, Saxon, and of course Priest and Maiden have their influential hands all over this album. In turn Wolf have done their best to take all of those influences and force feed them to an entirely new generation of unsuspecting metal fans. In all honesty there have been few bands over the last decade plus who have been able to capture the true essence of metal's earliest pioneers the way Wolf have on this album.

Recommended Track: "Moonlight"

591. Pilgrim – Misery Wizard

One would think that you could only do so much with the doom genre. There are only so many down-tuned notes you can play and only so slow you can play them, right? One listen to the debut full length from Rhode Island's Pilgrim would absolutely annihilate any such thoughts. First and foremost, it should be noted that the brand of doom that Pilgrim meddle with is actually a throwback to all the great doom from the late 70s and '80s. Candlemass, Saint Vitus and Cathedral fans are going to find a lot to love about this album, as are fans of the original masters such as Pentagram, Sir Lord Baltimore and of course Black Sabbath. *Misery Wizard* stands as one of the best albums released in 2012 and a must-own for doom fans.

Recommended Track: "Astaroth"

590. Damaged – Do Not Spit

It's Australia's Damaged who get the distinction as the first band to notch two albums in these pages. *Do Not Spit* was the bands debut album, originally released on Black Hole Records in 1993 (re-released in 2001 on Rotten Records). The first two things you should notice about this album are a) the somewhat unique vocals that sound like someone is gargling broken glass and b) the completely insane drumming. Really if you can nail those two things then you are more than halfway to creating some seriously face-melting grindcore. It's safe to say that Damaged were a completely underrated band and probably deserve much more recognition than they ever received when they were still active.

Recommended Track: "Nails"

589. Genocide SS – We Are Born of Hate

Sweden's Genocide SS (Superstars) play it crazy fast and angry as hell, just the way good crusty punk rock should be played. They mix in elements of grind and sleazy rock n' roll to form this kind of punk-and-roll hybrid that's become more and more popular over the years. *We Are Born Of Hate* was the band's first full length album, originally released in 1999 but reissued in the U.S. by Relapse in 2002. This album is a non-stop festival of madness. It never lets up. From beginning to end it's like a sonic dump truck doing 90 miles per hour through a nuclear reactor. It's a nasty and mean record. Sadly, founding member Mieszko Talarcyzk was a victim of the tsunami that wiped out parts of Southeast Asia in 2004. Shortly thereafter this band called it a day and unlike his primary band, Nasum, there has never been any plans to record or tour without him. This album will surely stand as a testimony to his talents in extreme music.

Recommended Track: "Under Attack"

588. Yob – The Illusion of Motion

Portland, Oregon's Yob take songs and just stretch and pull them to absolutely oppressive levels. Yob are the musical equivalent of trying to breathe with an elephant sitting on your chest. They are like trying to swim to the surface of the lake while consistently being dragged back under water in a bad dream. Yet they are also so psychedelic at certain points that they could be the soundtrack to your most tripped out dreams as well. Their brand of doom mixes sludge and psych rock in equal parts making it a pretty unique sound. *The Illusion of Motion* was their third full length album, but their first released for Metal Blade in 2004. Arguably, this was the album that put these guys on the map and made them a major player in the U.S. doom metal scene.

Recommended Track: "Exorcism of the Host"

587. A.C. – Morbid Florist

With every single album A.C. got goofier and goofier. Songs will sometimes degenerate into silly voices that often just sounded like fart noises or they would go out of their way to spend four minutes singing about someone's mustache (true story, look it up). But even though they supposedly started as a joke and their later albums would certainly attest to that, their debut album, *Morbid Florist*, is a great example of how extreme you could take the grindcore genre. Released in 1993 on Relapse Records, *Morbid Florist* was, and still is, one of the sickest grindcore records around. It only took this band 17 minutes to set the bar at a level that your average band still can not attain.

Recommended Track: "Radio Hit"

586. Arckanum – Fran Marder

Sweden's Arckanum has, for the most part, been the one-man project of Shamaatae, who at one point played in the band Grotesque (the band that essentially gave birth to At The Gates). *Fran Marder* was the debut album from Arckanum, released in 1995 on the now defunct Necropolis Records. It is not included here because it's one of the most polished examples of black metal. On the contrary, one of the things that makes black metal so special is the ability to craft raw, aggressive music and make it sound fantastic no matter how much production it really lacked. Arckanum also were one of the first black metal bands to truly embrace the folk/nature elements of the genre as opposed to just standing around screaming about Satan. Most of the lyrical content herein deals with Pan, old Norse mythology and runic magic, all sung in "Old Swedish."

Recommended Track: "Svinna"

585. Woods of Ypres – Woods IV: The Green Album

Woods of Ypres was criminally underrated and not on many people's radar prior to 2011. That's when Earache Records re-released their fourth album, *Woods IV: The Green Album*. It was also the year the band announced plans for their fifth record, which some early listens had projected to be one of metal's biggest hopes for 2012. Sadly, 2011 was also the year founder and front man David Gold was killed in a car accident thus effectively ending the band. For the uninitiated Woods of Ypres plays a hybrid style of doom, mixing in elements of funeral doom with blackened death metal. They combine clean and gruff vocals, piano, synths, and serene, often psychedelic interludes with crushingly heavy doom. This album in particular was a great example of how they combined influences from all over the heavy music spectrum to create a unique musical experience.

Recommended Track: "I Was Buried In Mount Pleasant Cemetery"

584. 3 Inches of Blood – Advance & Vanquish

In 2004, Canada's 3 Inches of Blood dropped their second full length album, and their first for Roadrunner. It was the album that would put them on the map, as well as at the forefront of the thrash revival which had already begun to explode all over the metal world like a burst pimple. It's a fantastic hybrid of speed and thrash metal, peppered with traditional metal influences. Killer riffs abound, and the dual vocal attack (that includes some of the best high notes you'll hear this side of Bobby Blitz) is potent. There are songs about bar fights, pirates (oh, hello Running Wild), and Orcs. You don't get much more metal than that combination.

Recommended Track: "Fear on the Bridge"

583. Weedeater – God Luck and Good Speed

Although sludge metal, for all intents and purposes, was a product of the rich and talented New Orleans scene in the late '80s/early '90s, the great state of North Carolina has done their absolute best to keep that hellfire raging like a mother. At the forefront of the N.C. scene is Weedeater, a band that riffs like Black Sabbath, rocks like Crowbar and crushes like Eyehategod, sometimes all in one song. I can imagine that if whiskey actually made a sound while it was distilling it would probably sound something like Weedeater. *God Luck and Good Speed* was the band's third full length album, but their first for the mighty Southern Lord Recordings, originally released in 2007.

Recommended Track: "Weed Monkey"

582. Usurper - Diabolosis

Usurper have always been categorized as a black metal band, but they are much more closely related to the first wave of black metal than they ever were to the second. This band has more in common with Celtic Frost and Bathory than they ever would with, say, Emperor. They always were a kind of throwback as well, donning bullet belts and patch-clad denim jackets long before those things became en vogue again in the metal scene. *Diabolosis* was the bands debut full-length album, released in 1995 on Head Not Found Records. Not only did this band aid in the formation of the U.S. black metal scene but I'd also argue they are a big reason that Chicago's metal scene is as vibrant as it is today. This band and album are truly underrated gems of the '90s metal scene.

Recommended Track: "Full Moon Harvest"

581. Viking – Man of Straw

One of the bands to leap up from the rich L.A. metal scene was Viking. *Man of Straw* was the band's second full length album, originally released in 1989. So why does a band playing a killer style of technical thrash, with distribution through Caroline, not have a bigger name in the metal scene today? Well, probably because this was also the band's last album they would release, until an independently released album in 2015. This album was probably best known for the killer cover of Pat Benatar's "Hell Is For Children" but really Viking was so much more than a cover song. While 1989 generally marks the beginning of the end of the greatest era in thrash metal, Viking were able to capture some of that remaining magic and deliver an absolutely shredding album.

Recommended Track: "Man of Straw"

580. The Black Dahlia Murder – Unhallowed

Unhallowed was the debut full-length album from The Black Dahlia Murder, released on Metal Blade Records in 2003. Their signing to Metal Blade came on the heels of some legendary live shows…it also came at a time when Metal Blade signed about a dozen "metalcore" bands and threw them at the wall to see which ones would stick. Thanks to one of the better debut albums you'll hear from that era, The Black Dahlia Murder 'stuck.' In reality, The Black Dahlia Murder sounded nothing like the other bands that Metal Blade was pushing at this time. They always sounded like a melodic death metal band, with very heavy thrash influences, more than anything else. This album compares favorably to a lot of the melodic Swedish death metal from whence they are clearly descended.

Recommended Track: "Contagion"

579. Cavity – Somewhere Between the Train Station...

Somewhere Between the Train Station and the Dumping Ground was Cavity's second official full length album, released in 1997 on Rhetoric Records. Technically their third release if you count the aforementioned *Drowning*, which was a compilation album. Cavity play a dirty, Deep South version of doom/sludge metal, which on this record they really took to another level. This is their first full length album where the production matched the talent level as well. Often compared to bands like EyeHateGod and Buzzov*en, this is the album you could put up against some of the other greats of the sludge metal scene and not ever bat an eyelash.

Recommended Track: "Shake 'Em On Down"

578. Paradox - Heresy

Everyone knows the amazing output of the German thrash metal scene in the '80s. A lot of German thrash was the straight ahead, punch you in the mouth variety. But there was a slew of bands coming out of Germany that also played a more melodic style of thrash that included elements of traditional heavy metal as well. One of those bands was Paradox, who released their second album, *Heresy*, on Roadracer Records in 1989. The guitar playing alone is worth the price of admission. Killer riffs, killer tone, everything you could ask for in a thrash record and more. This is also a concept album about the 13th Century Catholic Crusades. You don't get much more metal than people traveling hundreds of miles to off as many people as they can find.

Recommended Track: "Search For Perfection"

577. Haemorrhage – Anatomical Inferno

Spain's Haemorrhage has been around for a long time and today stands as one of the oldest, continually active gore-grind bands in the world. Their 1998 album, and third full-length, *Anatomical Inferno*, is an absolute classic of the gore-grind genre. Released on Morbid Records, it was their first album with widespread distribution here in the U.S. and across Europe. This was the album that got them from obscure to "cult." This band has done a lot to influence the current gore-grind scene and it really started with this album. However, there is no shortage of material for you to select from should you choose to partake in this band's maniacal ramblings. Since 1995 they have released an amazing 21 splits with other acts, along with multiple EPs and full-length albums.

Recommended Track: "A Cataleptic Rapture"

576. Crisis – The Hollowing

New York's Crisis always were and always will be one of the hardest bands to classify. They blurred the lines between hardcore, thrash, doom, post-metal, and stoner rock. They were one of the most unique bands to emerge out of the U.S. metal scene in the '90s. *The Hollowing* was their third album and second for Metal Blade Records, originally released in 1997. When you look back at this band's history this album will go down as their darkest, and frankly, most accomplished. The doom and sludge scenes certainly had an affect on this band over time and they do a fantastic job of incorporating those styles into the already hodgepodge-like collective of influences showcased on their first two albums.

Recommended Track: "Surviving The Siren"

575. Dekapitator – The Storm Before The Calm

Originally formed in the late 90s as a side project by two members of Exhumed, Dekapitator would release their debut album in 1999, long before the retro-thrash movement reached its current level of popularity. In fact you could even say Dekapitator was thrash when thrash wasn't cool. Presumably because of their various other projects, it would take eight years for this band to release a follow up album. But it was well worth the wait because *The Storm Before The Calm* pretty much melts every face that gets close to it. Honestly you could do the blind taste test with this record and think it was released 20 years earlier than it actually was. That's the true testament (metal pun intended) to how good this record sounds. *The Storm Before The Calm* was originally released in 2007 on Relapse Records.

Recommended Track: "Deathstrike Command"

574. Belphegor - Blutsabbath

Now categorized as a "blackened death metal" band, Belphegor started out playing some pretty fierce black metal as evidenced by their 1997 release *Blutsabbath*. This was the band's second full-length album, released on Last Episode Records out of Germany. This album wouldn't see a proper U.S. release until almost five years later but by then the reputation of Belphegor had begun to proceed them. Everything about this album is pure blasphemy - from the naughty cover art to the musical annihilation the listener faces immediately upon first listen. This is top notch, second wave black metal. The vocals are shredding, blast beats abound, and the riffing is some of the most inventive you'll hear on a black metal album at that time.

Recommended Track: "Blutsabbath"

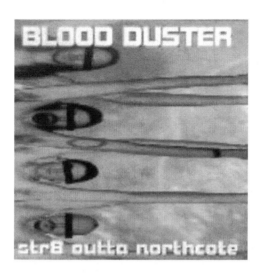

573. Blood Duster – Str8 Outta Northcote

Some genres of metal just don't belong together, right? I mean, take stoner rock and grindcore for example. There's no way you can take the slowed tempos, and dirty, Southern riffs of stoner rock and combine them with the blasting madness of grindcore, right? There's no way you can make that work, right? Well that's exactly what Australia's Blood Duster did. They took big, beefy, psychedelic riffs and combined them with bursts of grind and grind/death metal styled vocals to form a totally unique extreme music experience. *Str8 Outta Northcote* was the band's first full length album, released in 1998 through Relapse Records.

Recommended Track: "Chop Chop"

572. Skinless – Foreshadowing Our Demise

Skinless hail from upstate New York and that's obviously close enough to NYC to be heavily influenced by all the great death metal that lurched forth from the sewers of the Big Apple, most notably Suffocation. Get ready for the occasional bass drop and the addition of a little "groove" to your listening experience. But this band doesn't play death metal because the chicks dig it. They play it because they want to aurally assault you as fast and as often as possible. Mission accomplished. *Foreshadowing Our Demise* was the second full length album for Skinless, originally released in 2001. It was also their first album for Relapse Records. If you like your metal with a healthy dose of brutal then I will quote the opening sample: "Sit back. Slip on your absorbent undergarments. And let the mayhem begin…"

Recommended Track: "Foreshadowing Our Demise"

571. Zyklon – World Ov Worms

When members of Emperor started to branch out and form other bands rumors started to swirl. By the time of their initial demise in 2001 all eyes were firmly fixated on what each member was going to do moving forward. Enter Zyklon, which at the time was the newest project of both guitarist Samoth and drummer Trym. They released their debut album, *World Ov Worms*, in 2001 on Candlelight Records, and it immediately added another notch in the belt of the Scandinavian metal scene. This album is usually classified as "blackened death metal," and although there are definitely death metal elements, there is still a distinct Emperor influence, which needless to say is not a bad thing at all.

Recommended Track: "Hammer Revelation"

570. Ed Gein – Judas Goats & Dieseleaters

Ed Gein was a very politically-driven (and very angry) hardcore/screamo/grind band that first made a name for themselves with their debut, which attracted a lot of attention in the underground hardcore and metal scenes for it's ferocity. *Judas Goats & Dieseleaters* was the band's second full length album, originally released in 2005. After gaining some momentum with their debut, this album would be released on the label Black Market Activities which had a distribution deal with Metal Blade Records at the time (and was owned by the vocalist for The Red Chord). The change to a somewhat larger label with a much larger distribution deal certainly didn't lessen the blow from these guys, nor did better production. This album is arguably just as fierce and psychotic in its delivery as their debut.

Recommended Track: "Christianity as Foreign Policy"

569. Logical Nonsense – Expand The Hive

Despite the fact that they were not on a label known for constantly churning out metal acts, New Mexico's Logical Nonsense put out some of the fiercest hardcore/crust you will ever hear. I actually had the pleasure of seeing these guys live in NYC right after this album was released in 1997. I was one of about six kids who knew who this band was, but they got up on stage and proceeded to melt every damn face in the room. You see, this band isn't listed here because they wielded some massive influence on the metal world. No, they are listed here because they shred. They shred like a cheese grater going the wrong way across your face. If you like your hardcore fast and your crust brutal as hell then you may have just discovered your new favorite band.

Recommended Track: "Hypo-Christian"

568. Sacrifice – Forward to Termination

Simply put, Sacrifice were criminally underrated during their first incarnation in the '80s and early '90s. They were one of the best thrash bands that Canada offered up during this time period and their style has that proto-death metal sound that bands like Possessed made famous. *Forward to Termination* was the band's second full length album, originally released on Metal Blade here in the U.S. in 1987. This was their first proper release for Metal Blade, as their first album was originally released on Diabolic Force out of Canada and picked up by Metal Blade a year later. The songs on this record are a little slower in tempo at times than the first album but it really just adds to the pseudo-death metal elements found within. This is top level thrash released at a time when the genre was just starting to show signs of being watered down.

Recommended Track: "The Entity"

567. Aborted – Goremageddon...

Belgium's best metal export over the last decade or so has been Aborted and their brand of grindcore influenced death metal. You could realistically call these guys gore-grind, especially given their lyrical content. *Goremageddon* (as we will call it for short) was the third full length album by Aborted, originally released in 2003, and the second for Listenable Records. This album was licensed in the U.S. by Olympic Recordings. It's safe to argue that up to this point in their careers this was Aborted's best sounding album both from a production and songwriting standpoint. The production is crisp and the songs simply maul you from note one. If you want someplace to start with Aborted's back catalog it is highly recommend you start with this album.

Recommended Track: "Meticulous Invagination"

566. Bongzilla - Gateway

Wisconsin's Bongzilla play sludgy, riff-oriented, stoner rock meets doom metal. After two very good albums and a ton of splits and EPs, these guys really came into their own this release. In the process they established themselves as one of the better sludge/doom bands the U.S. scene was churning out at the time, not to mention one of the better live bands as well. *Gateway* was their second full length album for Relapse Records, originally released in 2002. If you are a fan of bands like Eyehategod, Electric Wizard, Goatsnake, Saint Vitus, etc. then Bongzilla will be right up your alley (whether you smoke copious amounts of pot or not).

Recommended Track: "Keefmaster"

565. Enthroned – Towards the Skullthrone Of Satan

Despite black metal being all the rage around Europe in the mid to late '90s, Belgium is not one of the first places that comes to mind when you think of corpse paint, gauntlets, and band photos taken in forest settings. However one of the underrated gems of the 90s European black metal scene was Belgium's Enthroned. This was a band that could write solid, atmospheric, second wave black metal with the best of them while still maintaining the grim and frost-bitten aesthetic that made the genre so appealing in the first place. *Towards The Skullthrone of Satan* was Enthroned's second album, originally released in 1997 through the U.K.'s Blackened Records.

Recommended Track: "Dusk of the Forgotten Darkness"

564. Daughters – Canada Songs

This one may in fact be the shortest album on the list. Clocking in at a whopping 11 minutes is the album *Canada Songs* from Rhode Island's Daughters. Back in the late '90s and early 2000s there were a bunch of bands that played this crazy mesh of hardcore and grindcore that was so technical they would eventually give birth to both "mathcore" and later on djent. This is one of those bands. *Canada Songs* is the debut full length from Daughters, released in 2003 on Robotic Empire Records. Daughters were as beloved in the punk scene as they ever were in the hardcore and metal scenes. But when you play music as wild, as rabid, and as completely insane as this record you sometimes just need to embrace your dark side. Hence, their inclusion in these pages.

Recommended Track: "And Then The C.H.U.D.S. Came"

563. Strapping Young Lad – Heavy As A Really Heavy Thing

Heavy as a Really Heavy Thing is the debut album from Strapping Young Lad, released on Century Media in 1995. This is the album that unleashed Devin Townsend and his songwriting on an unsuspecting metal fan base, and for good or bad the metal world has honestly never been the same since. Strapping Young Lad melds together influences as wide ranging as thrash, death metal, grindcore, industrial, and various forms of electronic music to create a fairly unique listening experience. This album actually tanked upon its release so don't believe anyone who bought this album "when it came out" because the first six months saw it sell less than 150 copies. Yet despite the early hiccups the influence that Devin Townsend now wields is, frankly, astonishing.

Recommended Track: "Goat"

562. Integrity – To Die For

Cleveland's Integrity is one of a small handful of hardcore bands who are simply too dark and too heavy not to be embraced by metal fans. They infuse elements of grind, death metal and even a little thrash from time to time. However the one thing that set Integrity apart from even other "metallic hardcore" bands is the sheer darkness this band brings down upon their listeners. *To Die For* was the band's seventh studio album, released on Deathwish Inc. in 2003. In the mid-'90s Integrity released three classic albums for Victory Records. When they reappeared after a brief hiatus, with *To Die For* in hand, this album reestablished them as one of the major players in the metal underground.

Recommended Track: "Dreams Bleed On"

561. Impaled – Death After Life

Oakland's Impaled made a pit stop with Century Media Records, who released the album *Death After Life* in 2005. *Death After Life* was the band's third full length album and is arguably both their best produced and most well written effort. A lot of people lump Impaled into the gore-grind genre simply based off their Carcass-like infatuation with medical themed lyrical content. (Their name is actually an acronym for: "**I**mmoral **M**edical **P**ractitioners **A**nd **L**icentious **E**vil-**D**oers".) However from a musical standpoint they incorporate death metal influences from both the U.S. and Europe as well as the occasional thrash influence. In other words these guys don't just rage for two and half minutes on every song. There is both breadth and depth that most gore-grind bands never achieve. Frankly, for the life of me, I can't figure out why this band, and this album don't hold the place of higher esteem they deserve in death metal circles.

Recommended Track: "Preservation of Death"

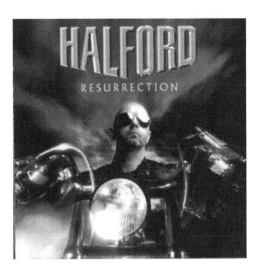

560. Halford – Resurrection

When you think of heavy metal music there are a small handful of figures who should be top of mind. One of those figures who stands tall and can really be considered one of the faces of heavy metal for the laymen is Rob Halford. Halford (the band) was an absolute return to form for Halford (the man). *Resurrection* was the band's debut album, released in 2000 on the Sanctuary imprint, Metal-Is Records. This album is really in these pages for two reasons. Because a) it brought Rob Halford back to the metal forefront with a potent NWOBHM-styled assault after languishing for a few years with a couple projects that didn't live up to the hype, and b) it helped quicken the rise of the neo-thrash scene that is so prominent today.

Recommended Track: "Resurrection"

559. Ulver – Shadows of the Sun

If you've never heard Norway's Ulver and decided on a whim to pick up a random album, you are probably going to hear music that you won't hear on any other Ulver record. That's the beauty of this band. Ulver started out as a folk-inspired black metal band and their first and third albums are fairly grim. However, like many European metal bands, the 2000s brought a lot of experimentation and drastic changes to their sound. Some of these bands have successfully transitioned from one style of music to another…other bands have not. Ulver is one of those bands that not only successfully bend genres to their will but they seem to do it on every single record. *Shadows of the Sun* was the seventh studio album from Ulver, released in 2007 on The End Records here in the U.S. Despite the fact that this record should be justifiably classified as "ambient" this record is still very dark and very atmospheric. (But this might also be the only record in this book that utilizes horns and a Theremin.)

Recommended Track: "What Happened?"

558. Daylight Dies – No Reply

No Reply was the debut album from North Carolina's Daylight Dies, released on Relapse Records in 2002. Daylight Dies plays an absolutely epic form of doom mixed with melodic death metal. You may remember how many great doom bands the UK was churning out at one point – My Dying Bride, Paradise Lost, Anathema, etc. – those bands took what the early doom pioneers created, built upon it, and birthed this amazingly unique form of doom they could call their own. A decade or so later there were few bands in the world that were doing a better job of picking up where those other bands left off and bravely carrying it into a scene that hasn't always embraced this style of music (meaning the U.S. metal scene in general). If you're a fan of amazingly textured and sometimes oppressive doom metal then I highly suggest you give this album a go.

Recommended Track: "Minutes Pass"

557. Pentagram – Last Rites

Originally formed back in 1971, Pentagram would remain a cult act for much of the decade and not see any proper album released until the '80s. *Last Rites* was officially Pentagram's seventh studio album, released in 2011 on Metal Blade Records. I say 'officially' because I don't know of any other band that has seen their material bootlegged and released 'unofficially' through the years more than this one. It was refreshing to see Pentagram find a home on a solid label that could finally give them the promotion they needed. It was their first studio album in seven years and it was also refreshing to hear just how damn good this record was. This was a total return to form for an act that has had way too many periods of inactivity. Rest assured this will go down as one of the better doom/stoner rock efforts of this decade.

Recommended Track: "Treat Me Right"

556. Bloodlet - Entheogen

Eclectic may have been Bloodlet's first full length release but really it was just a collection of early singles. Their first official full length album was *Entheogen*, released in 1996 on Victory Records. So the minute you see that this was released on Victory Records you automatically think 'hardcore' right? They were arguably the biggest and best hardcore label in the world at the time of this album's release. However, I hesitate to label Bloodlet as simply a 'hardcore' band. It is certainly no insult to be labeled one. However, their music, their lyrics, the fret-less bass they employed, the heavy, chunky riffs - everything about this band seethed this brooding darkness that endeared them to as many, if not more, metal fans as it did punk fans. Anyone looking for some good and swampy riffs could do a lot worse than this album.

Recommended Track: "The Triumph"

555. Cattle Decapitation – To Serve Man

To Serve Man was Cattle Decapitation's second full length album, released in 2002 on Metal Blade Records. This was their first album released on Metal Blade and therefore the first Cattle Decapitation album that a lot of kids in the scene even would hear. That alone makes it one of their most influential. Prior to this album Cattle Decapitation could easily be considered a gore-grind band. But this album saw them move towards a more traditional death metal approach, writing songs that had more in common with Cannibal Corpse than Carcass. Yet both of those bands remained highly influential on what this band was spewing forth. They incorporate pseudo-dual vocals (guttural growls vs. higher pitched screams, all from the same throat) and write some pretty sick riffs, similar in style to bands like Deicide and Suffocation.

Recommended Track: "To Serve Man"

554. Naglfar - Diabolical

Naglfar (named after a boat from Norse mythology that was made out of the toenails and fingernails of the dead...), much like fellow country men Dissection, were always lumped into the black metal category. While I take no umbrage with that, their death metal influences should not be completely overlooked. When you go back and listen to this album it's slightly mind-blowing that this band is not more often mentioned amongst that wave of bands who really started to push the boundaries of black metal and open the doors for a lot of other bands to experiment a bit. This band wrote fantastic atmospheric, blackened metal with great production that never came off sounding polished or over-produced. *Diabolical* was the band's second full length album, originally released on War Music in 1998. They were distributed by Relapse here in the U.S.

Recommended Track: "Horncrowned Majesty"

553. Sigh – Imaginary Sonicscape

Originally started as a pure black metal band (they were at one point signed to Euronymous' label) Japan's Sigh has spent the last two decades morphing and changing their sound into something that, only at times, resembles their black metal roots. They've gone out of their way to incorporate genres as varied as classical music, new age, jazz, psych rock, thrash, and pretty much everything in between. Imagine you had a friend who had the most eclectic music tastes and a huge music collection to prove it. That's kind of what Sigh reminds me of on every single record. This album in particular does an exceptional job of melding all of these bizarre elements into a metal melting pot. There is certainly enough talent and vision in this band to make sense of the hodgepodge of influences going on here. *Imaginary Sonicscape* was Sigh's fifth full length album and their first for Century Media, released in 2001.

Recommended Track: "Bring Back The Dead"

552. Vio-lence – Eternal Nightmare

It would be the world's biggest understatement to say that the original wave of thrash to emerge from the Bay Area was pretty epic. Testament, Exodus, Possessed, Forbidden, Death Angel, just to name a few. By the late '80s there was a slew of thrash bands cropping up all over the place trying to emulate bands like these. Many were awful, some, like San Francisco's Vio-lence were torch carriers. Vio-lence's most famous former member is Robb Flynn, founding member/guitarist/vocalist for one of the most popular metal bands in the world today – Machine Head. However, as you could probably surmise, we are a long way from Machine Head with this album. Vio-lence mixed in elements of thrash from their East Coast and European brethren on their debut album to form a pretty potent mix. Released in 1988 through Mechanic Records, this album actually cracked the Billboard 200, peaking at #154.

Recommended Track: "Kill On Command"

551. Wolves in the Throne Room – Celestial Lineage

To say that Washington's Wolves In The Throne Room play an atmospheric style of black metal is almost too simplistic. Few bands in the world today are able to create these lush textures and rich backing elements supported by traditional black metal the way this band has. However, even at their most grim moments, Wolves In The Throne Room has always been a band that has pushed the boundaries of what's "acceptable" in black metal. Sometimes it's as simple as taking traditional elements (i.e. keyboards, clean female vocals, etc.) and utilizing them in different ways then what most black meal bands would think to do with them. On this album alone it's not uncommon to hear the use of bells, harp, synthesizers, and field noises in an attempt to capture the essence and the eternal spirit of Nature itself. *Celestial Lineage* was the bands fourth album, released in 2011 on Southern Lord.

Recommended Track: "Thuja Magus Imperium"

550. Mortician – Hacked Up For Barbecue

Take all of your favorite horror movies, your favorite haunted houses, and the most brutal death metal you can think of and that pretty much sums up New York's Mortician. Often times lumped into the New York death metal scene, Mortician play a style more closely resembling gore-grind/grindcore than straight death metal. Their use of a drum machine turned up to about 6,000 BPM alone makes them a unique force in the death metal world. What also stands out with Mortician are the movie samples. This album alone features killer samples from such films as *The Texas Chainsaw Massacre, Suspiria, Maniac, Blood Sucking Freaks, When A Stranger Calls, The Fog* and *The Road Warrior,* just to name a few. It's almost as much fun to try and play "Guess what movie that sample came from" as it is to rock out to the seriously abrasive form of metal these guys peddle. *Hacked Up For Barbecue* was the bands first full length album, released in 1996 on Relapse Records.

Recommended Track: "Eaten Alive By Maggots"

549. Anaal Nathrakh – The Codex Necro

England's Anaal Nathrakh released their debut full length album, *The Codex Necro*, back in 2001 through Mordgrimm Records. To say this album is extreme is like saying a volcanic explosion is 'messy.' Although black metal for all intents and purposes, Anaal Nathrakh has been able to do black metal with a sort of grindcore twist and wound up producing some of the most ridiculously awesome and absolutely abrasive black metal that has ever been put to record. Their influence on the world of black metal can absolutely not be understated. The music of Anaal Nathrakh, especially what's on this album, is almost trance inducing. It's so fast-paced it's almost like white noise with the screams of a dying man over top of it. Yet they are able to pull it all together into a cohesive and brutal picture.

Recommended Track: "The Codex Necro"

548. Sacred Reich - Ignorance

While mainstream hair bands were singing love ballads and songs about drinking and screwing there was an underground scene that was pretty pissed off about the Reagan administration, our horrific foreign policy at the time, and the growing AIDS epidemic just to name a few. One of the bands in the thrash scene that pointed to social injustice was Arizona's Sacred Reich. They released their debut full length album, *Ignorance*, in 1987 on Metal Blade Records. Unfortunately a lot of the topics they covered then still exist today. Just look at the album cover and its somewhat frightening foreshadowing of horrible things to come. Sacred Reich had a lot to say, lyrically speaking. It also shows in their musical style as they played a hybrid thrash/speed metal mix. They had the occasional melodic moment but for the most part this album is heavy on speed/thrash power riffing with drums that come up just shy of full on blast beats at certain points.

Recommended Track: "Ignorance"

547. Bloodbath – Resurrection Through Carnage

Bloodbath arrived on the scene at the beginning of the last century boasting a pretty hefty lineup featuring Mikael Åkerfeldt (Opeth), Dan Swano (who is a living legend in the Swedish metal scene both in front of and behind the mixing board), and members of Katatonia and Diabolical Masquerade. The line-up has since changed quite a bit and they've gone from being a side project to a full time band. Their debut album, *Resurrection Through Carnage*, was released on Century Media in 2002 and this band was part of the next generation of purveyors of the "buzz saw" sound of death metal production that acts like Entombed, Grave, and Dismember perfected. Forget for a minute that this album contains some of the most recognizable Swedish metal musicians of all time and listen to this album as if it were just a bunch of dudes. I promise that doing so will not diminish this albums excellence one iota.

Recommended Track: "So You Die"

546. Crowbar – Odd Fellow's Rest

Odd Fellows Rest, was Crowbar's fifth full length album and marked a couple different turning points for the band. It was their first album for Mayhem Records after leaving long time label, Pavement Music. (The album would be re-released only a year later by Spitfire Records.) This album also holds a special place because it's the only Crowbar album to feature the holy sludge triumvirate of Sammy Pierre Duet (Acid Bath and currently Goatwhore) on guitar, Kirk Windstein (Crowbar founding father) on guitar and vocals, and Jimmy Bower (EyeHateGod) moving over to drums. You could make the argument that thanks to this all-star line-up that this may be Crowbar's most complete record. Crowbar sound exactly like their name – a big and possibly deadly piece of metal used to break stuff open. Their sound has always been the antithesis of what you would expect a Louisiana swamp to be – dirty, gritty and prone to danger.

Recommended Track: "And Suffer As One"

545. Absu - Tara

Upon their formation, Texas' Absu were (and still are) masters of the thrash-black metal hybrid. Although their sound has become more and more progressive, adding in elements of prog rock, folk metal, etc., they still know how to thrash with the best of them. However, their association with Osmose Productions (a predominantly black metal label out of France) and the various mythologies that surround their lyrics (Celtic and Sumerian mostly) gave them an air of black metal right from the start. In 2001 Absu released their fourth full-length album, *Tara*, on Osmose. *Tara* is still considered by many to be one of Absu's finest hours. On this record the band really started to take their experimentation to the next level. They had always dabbled in adding little elements like flute and synths, for example. But here the songwriting itself seemed to take on a more progressive tone in general.

Recommended Track: "Stone of Destiny"

544. Krisiun – Conquerors of Armageddon

Krisiun are a death metal band. There really is no middle ground here. They are a blasphemous, extreme, death metal band who write lyrics as evil as Deicide and riffs as sick as Morbid Angel. Actually Krisiun does indeed owe some of what they do to some of the early inventors/pioneers of the death metal genre, namely Possessed, Sodom and Kreator. They are immensely talented musicians and because so they are also one of the best live death metal bands you'll ever see, especially when you can catch them in a tiny club where the darkness and evil can just completely engulf you. In 2000, Krisiun released their third full length album and debut for Century Media, *Conquerors of Armageddon*. It could be argued that this was the album that took them from being a "kvlt" favorite to being a household name to death metal fans around the globe.

Recommended Track: "Conquerors of Armageddon"

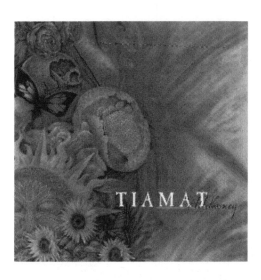

543. Tiamat - Wildhoney

Tiamat started off as a blackened death metal band, which anyone stumbling upon this band today might not be able to believe. They began to transition over a handful of exceptional albums, expanding their sound by adding various elements of prog rock, doom, and psych rock. In 1994, Tiamat released their fourth full length album, *Wildhoney*, on Century Media. This album was absolutely genre bending at the time (it still is really) and honestly you'd be hard pressed to find many bands in 1994 that were doing what Tiamat was doing sonically. They alternated between clean and gruff vocals, added well-placed synths and really created this dark, dreary atmosphere that fans of classic doom could latch onto. But possibly the best part about this album was the amazing way it was structured, as it comes off as almost one continuous 40+ minute song. It's a lush album in a lot of respects and has stood the test of time very well.

Recommended Track: "Whatever That Hurts"

542. Hate Eternal – Conquering The Throne

Hate Eternal was formed by Erik Rutan (guitar/vocals) who had previously done stints in the seminal thrash act Ripping Corpse and as the second/touring guitarist for Morbid Angel. So those two bands right there should give you a starting point when discussing Hate Eternal. It's easy to pinpoint Morbid Angel as an influence on pretty much any death metal band that came after them, but it takes a bit more ear to hear the thrash influence involved in this record. Several tracks have a distinct thrash flair to them in some of the riffs being laid down. But at the end of the day, let's not kid ourselves. At its most rotten core this album is a brutal, pummeling death metal assault. *Conquering The Throne* was Hate Eternal's debut album released in 1999 on Earache subdivision Wicked World.

Recommended Track: "Darkness By Oath"

541. Nile – Black Seeds of Vengeance

South Carolina's Nile took the concept thing to a whole new world when they decided that everything about their band - from the name to the lyrics to the bells and whistles they add to each song - would revolve around Ancient Egypt. Conceptual themes aside, if you're a fan of amazingly intricate, technical death metal then look no further than Nile. The layers upon layers of sound that this band puts on an album, yet retains all brutality, defies all death metal logic. *Black Seeds of Vengeance* was the band's second full-length album, originally released in 2000 on Relapse Records. It was, at the time, their most ambitious effort and absolutely stood out amongst all other death metal releases that year.

Recommended Track: "Black Seeds of Vengeance"

540. Kylesa – To Walk a Middle Course

Kylesa formed in Savannah, GA out of the ashes of a band called Damad. You could make the case that Damad were one of the godfathers of the Savannah metal scene and the whole "Southern sound" found in metal these days. Kylesa creates this beautiful yet chaotic combination of sludge, doom, stoner rock, crust punk, and psych rock. They employ three vocalists and right after this album they started to use two drummers. It really is one of the more unique bands and albums you'll find in these pages, and if you like any of the genres listed above, any at all, there's a good chance you are going to dig this band. *To Walk a Middle Course* was the band's second full length album, originally released in 2005 on Prosthetic Records.

Recommended Track: "Train of Thought"

539. Anacrusis – Suffering Hour

St. Louis' Anacrusis released their debut album, *Suffering Hour* in 1988 on a European label called Axis (soon changed to Active) Records, but would see U.S. distribution through Metal Blade. Anacrusis would make their name as a progressive thrash band and really perfect a sound that was quite unique in the thrash world. However their debut album was an aggressive ripper and their style at this time could best be described as Overkill meets Megadeth. The vocals on here are all over the place from a sort of talking/clean style to a normal sort of thrash growl to these high-pitched yelps that, frankly, are their best moments, vocally speaking. This band would make a name for themselves with a style shift from this sort of early thrash worship to the more progressive stuff. However there is a reason this album made a label like Metal Blade sit up and take notice.

Recommended Track: "Imprisoned"

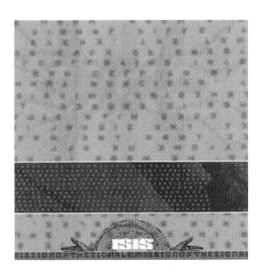

538. Isis - Celestial

Founded originally in Boston, Isis would eventually relocate to L.A. Where they are from is only important though when discussing all of the band member's previous efforts, which included some luminaries of the Boston metal/hardcore scene. Isis are one of a handful of bands who were the first wave of direct descendants of Neurosis, and to a slightly lesser extent, Godflesh. Their sound is predicated by the use of repetitive rhythms and this fantastic evolution of song structure on almost every track. They successfully mix in elements of ambient psych rock, doom and sludge. Their sound seamlessly fluctuates from super heavy riffs to moments of aural serenity. *Celestial* was the bands first full-length album, released by both Escape Artist Records (on CD) and Hydra Head (on vinyl) in 2000. This was really a transition album from the heavy sludgy stuff they had done on their first two EPs and the more progressive albums that would follow. Because of that this album my be the best example they have of their ability to merge styles and influences.

Recommended Track: "Celestial (The Tower)"

537. Annihilator – Alice In Hell

Canada has a pretty long and rich metal history, spawning some truly great bands over the years. *Alice In Hell* was Annihilator's debut album released in 1989 on Roadrunner Records. Roadrunner at the time was a powerhouse of a label, but these Canadians exceeded expectations as it became the label's highest selling debut at the time selling more than 250,000 copies. If there was ever a sentence that should be a testament to the popularity of metal at the time, that last one is it. Annihilator played a mostly mid-paced brand of thrash metal but did mix in elements of both speed and power metal. The vocals on this record could shatter glass at certain points, but that was part of their appeal. Few bands outside of King Diamond in 1989 were still trying to crack high notes like these.

Recommended Track: "Alison Hell"

536. Dimmu Borgir - Stormblast

Norway's Dimmu Borgir were popular enough at one point to hit the road as part of an Ozzfest here in the U.S. I can remember sitting there during their set, surrounded by old dudes who were waiting for Judas Priest and Slayer to come on and a bunch of young kids who wanted to see whatever metalcore/nu-metal bands were there and thinking 'Man, I am the only person here appreciating this right now.' *Stormblast* was their second full length album, released in 1996, originally on Cacophonous Records (later reissued by Century Media). It's marked by two main traits: 1) It's the last album where all the lyrics are in the band's native Norwegian and 2) the keyboards/synths first came to prominence on this album. There are tracks were the keys play as much of a role as the guitars giving them that symphonic black metal sound which would become their trademark.

Recommended Track: "Stormblast"

535. Brutality – When The Sky Turns Black

Florida has produced some of the most brutal and blasphemous death metal you will ever hear starting in the mid 80s. You can add this album to the list of Floridian classics. *When The Sky Turns Black* was the second full length album from Florida's Brutality, originally released on Nuclear Blast Records in 1994. I can remember this album getting a ton of play on college radio where I lived at the time because of their cover of Black Sabbath's "Electric Funeral". This choice of covers was genius because Brutality, like a lot of death metal bands at the time, were experimenting with the slower tempos and outright doom elements that made Sabbath who they were. To hear some growling vocals over the top of it just kind of makes sense in a weird sort of way. But forget the cover for a second. This album is chock full of killer, mid-tempo, American death metal.

Recommended Track: "When The Sky Turns Black"

534. Mayhem – Wolf's Lair Abyss

Mayhem. Just one mention of this band conjures up images of church burnings, suicides, murders and just about every other extreme thing you can throw into a band's history. With the death of founding member Euronymous in 1993, it seemed Mayhem was pretty much finished. That is, until drummer Hellhammer decided to get the gang back together and re-enlisted some former members, namely Necrobutcher on bass and Maniac on vocals. In 1997 the band released their first new material in over four years with the EP entitled *Wolf's Lair Abyss* on Misanthropy Records. Vocalist Maniac, minus some slightly misconceived clean vocal parts, gives a stellar performance and Hellhammer delivers what would appear to be 24 straight minutes of blast beats. It may never come close to topping their debut album, but this was a fine way for Mayhem to return to the metal scene.

Recommended Track: "Symbols of Bloodswords"

533. Katatonia – Brave Murder Day

Like so many of their death/doom colleagues from this time period Sweden's Katatonia would eventually morph their sound into something a little more accessible to the masses. However in the mid to late '90s they were one of the best in the business at creating truly epic and depressive doom metal. In 1996 they came off of an extended hiatus and released their second full length album, *Brave Murder Day* on Italian label Avantgarde Music. The album would later be picked up by Century Media here in the States and released on their short lived "Century Black" sub label. This one is still hard to believe, but this album was sent to the pressing plant without being mastered. But it takes away virtually nothing from the overall listening experience. The songs on this record are just so good that you are basically listening to an unfinished product and it still stands the test of time. In 2006 Peaceville Records would finally put out a mastered version.

Recommended Track: "Brave"

532. Coroner – No More Color

Coroner were a three piece band cobbled together by dudes who all served as roadies for Celtic Frost. So it's no wonder that some of their early material (especially the vocals) mirrored the intensity and delivery of Frost. They were faster and thrashier than Frost but even on this album you get tracks like "No Need To Be Human" that had that Frost feel to them. It was on this album though that they started to dabble in the progressive and avant-garde elements that would be so prevalent on their final two full lengths. *No More Color* was the band's third full length album originally released on Noise Records in 1989. This band would split up in the mid-'90s never having really achieved the worldwide success of some of their label mates (i.e. Helloween, Celtic Frost and Kreator). Going back and revisiting this record though, and seeing the influence they have today, it could be argued it was because the metal world simply wasn't ready for them yet.

Recommended Track: "Tunnel of Pain"

531. Hypocrisy – Osculum Obscenum

We are dipping a bit further back into the history of Hypocrsy for this one. Back before their alien obsession kicked into high gear and back to when they wrote some of the most brutal death metal in the world. *Osculum Obscenum* was their second full length album, released in 1993 on Nuclear Blast Records. The songwriting is solid and if you've ever seen this band play any of these songs live you would agree that there is some seriously aggressive and pummeling stuff happening on this album. It also happens to be the last release with their original vocalist, Masse Broberg, who would later take the stage name Emperor Magus Caligula and spend the next 15 years fronting Dark Funeral. Fans of classic, early death metal should hold this one in high esteem.

Recommended Track: "Osculum Obscenum"

530. Obsession – Scarred For Life

Those Metal Massacre comps that Metal Blade started producing in 1982 were key in the formation of a massive nationwide metal scene here in the U.S. That can't be understated. Those comps were a lot of kids first taste of bands such as Metallica, Slayer, Overkill, Trouble, Voivod, Armored Saint, etc. There were also a ton of other bands who came off those comps and put out quality metal albums for the remainder of the decade and beyond. One such band was Connecticut's Obsession. They released their first full length album, *Scarred For Life* in 1986 on Enigma and to this day it is criminally underrated. A lot of people think this band and this album were released on a "major" label, but Enigma was originally an independent that worked with a lot of killer underground acts. By 1986 they were distributed by Capitol/EMI but this album never got the massive marketing push that a true major label would have given it. Regardless, if you dig great, old school '80s heavy metal then this album is going to be right up your alley.

Recommended Track: "Losing My Mind"

529. Only Living Witness – Prone Mortal Form

Boston's Only Living Witness was one of those bands that had fans in every scene, but really didn't fit in any. They came rumbling out of the hardcore scene originally but both metal and non-metal fans dug these guys too. So how the hell would you classify this band? Honestly, you could look at Only Living Witness as the East Coast version of Kyuss. The riffs, the vocals, the thundering bass lines - it has early stoner rock written all over it. I think as we look back on all the bands that played such a huge roll in the formation of the stoner rock scene today that Only Living Witness plays a much greater role than a lot of people give them credit for. *Prone Mortal Form* was the band's debut album released in 1993 on Century Media Records. It was also the only album they would release while still an active band, as their second and final album was posthumously released three years later.

Recommended Track: "Prone Mortal Form"

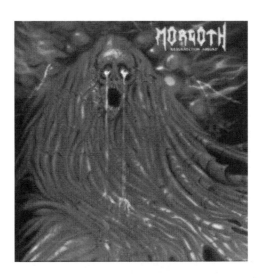

528. Morgoth – Resurrection Absurd

Germany's contributions to the metal world have been immense. One band that personified excellence in German death metal was Morgoth. This is another one of those bands that just never seems to get as much credit as they should. Part of that might be their relatively short lifespan. Part of it might be the disastrous direction they took their sound on what would be their final release (until a triumphant return in 2015). But all of that should be discounted when you are talking about their classic material. In 1989 Morgoth put out their first proper release, entitled *Resurrection Absurd* through Century Media Records. This was most fans' first taste of Morgoth and it would leave them hungering for more. Morgoth play a style of death metal that falls somewhere between the sludgy, thick riffs of Obituary and the more thrash influenced style of fellow European bands. Despite this album only being five tracks *Resurrection Absurd* is still one of the finer examples of early death metal coming out of Europe in the late '80s.

Recommended Track: "Travel"

527. GWAR – Scumdogs of the Universe

GWAR is one of those bands I feel like I shouldn't have to go into great detail to describe. I mean, if you don't know what GWAR are all about just go to YouTube and type in their name. The audio/visual display that comes up could certainly do them more justice than I could. But if you really need a description: They dress in ridiculous costumes and sing ridiculous songs in a thrash/punk/crossover style. Their stage show is really the money shot (pun grossly intended). Everything from decapitations to disembowelments to various flying bodily fluids, it really is a site to behold and at certain points the music is almost secondary. *Scumdogs of the Universe* was the band's second full-length album (and their first picked up by Metal Blade Records), released in 1990. This was the album that put them firmly in the consciousness of the metal world, thanks in part to the video for the song "Sick Of You". Regardless of what you think of GWAR you have to admire their uniqueness if nothing else.

Recommended Track: "The Years Without Light"

526. Skyclad – The Wayward Sons of Mother Earth

England's Skyclad formed out of a couple immensely influential bands, Sabbat and Satan. Skyclad's goal right from the start was to be a 'pagan metal' band both in sound and lyrics. They released their debut album, *The Wayward Sons of Mother Earth*, in 1991 on Noise Records. So how did they do with the whole pagan metal thing? Well from a lyrical standpoint, total success. From a musical standpoint there is a reason they are considered one of the first ever folk metal bands. The metal part of their sound is rooted in thrash, especially on this album, which might be the heaviest of their catalog. However, all throughout this album they drop random Celtic and Anglo-folk influences, whether it be a well-timed fiddle or simply riffing on ye olde folk tunes. Thinking back to 1991 even those slight touches of the traditional folk music was pretty unique. Compared to the folk metal bands of today this album is way more thrash based and has a greater metal to folk quotient. But again, there's no denying this band's influence on that scene.

.

Recommended Track: "Our Dying Island"

525. Broken Hope – Swamped In Gore

Broken Hope released their debut album, *Swamped In Gore* in 1991 on the Grindcore International label. This album though would lead to them getting signed to Metal Blade (who would eventually re-issue this record with new artwork shown above) Throughout the '90s they were putting out some of the heaviest death metal around. In 1991, death metal was still a fairly new genre to a lot of people. But in a fairly short timeframe death metal had evolved from the likes of Possessed and Death to bands like Broken Hope. That's a somewhat dramatic shift in style as bands continually tried to "out heavy" one another. If you like mid-paced death metal with super guttural vocals then this album is right up your alley and a great example of where the death metal scene was at the time. This was also apparently the first death metal album ever recorded digitally from start to finish.

.

Recommended Track: "Swamped In Gore"

524. Beowulf - Beowulf

Venice Beach, CA in the early 1980s. For a lot of people this is where they hedge their bets that the thrash/punk crossover scene first took shape. What we can all agree on is that Southern California was a hotbed for the crossover scene and some of the best bands of the genre did emerge from this part of the world. Now, of course, everyone is going to immediately think Suicidal Tendencies when you say the words 'California' and 'crossover'. Beowulf was one of many punk/thrash crossover bands that emerged out of the same Venice scene as S.T. In 1986 they released their self-titled debut album on Suicidal Records (which also happened to be the label of Mike Muir from S.T.). The band played a fantastic mix of punk rock and of course thrash but they threw in this crazy Motörhead vibe as well that distinguished them from a lot of their peers.

.

Recommended Track: "Americanizm"

523. Vicious Rumors – Soldiers of the Night

The Bay Area of California is best known in the annals of Metal as one of the first and most productive breeding grounds for thrash in the '80s. It's quite literally a who's-who of American metal. One band though that came rumbling out of the Bay Area at this time that doesn't get their just desserts is Vicious Rumors. And that is probably because they weren't a thrash band. It could be argued that over the course of time Vicious Rumors simply got lost in the shuffle a bit. That's a shame because their debut album, *Soldiers of the Night*, is a blueprint for the modern day power metal scene. Released on Shrapnel Records here in the U.S. in 1985, *Soldiers of the Night* would cement Vicious Rumors as the West Coast version of Manowar, complete with the occasional sing-a-long chorus and us vs. the world lyrical content. This is also the only album to feature guitar player Vinnie Moore who would later join Alice Cooper and UFO.

Recommended Track: "Ride (Into The Sun)"

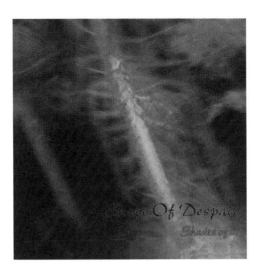

522. Shape of Despair – Shades Of...

By the time you are done with these pages you'll be able to surmise pretty easily the contribution that the country of Finland has made to metal music. One such act that has had a profound influence within their respective genre is death/doom act Shape of Despair. Combining ambient and depressive doom with the growling vocals of death metal, Shape of Despair was able to somehow make doom even more brutal without losing any of its core ambiance. Their debut album, *Shades Of...*, was originally released in 2000 on Spikefarm Records and is nothing short of a landmark in the death/doom field. While this album may be less experimental in nature than the ones they would release after it, there is simply no denying the influence this album has wielded over the last 15+ years.

Recommended Track: "...In The Mist"

521. Desultory - Bitterness

Desultory was, and should always be remembered as, one of the first wave of Swedish death metal bands playing right alongside the likes of Entombed and Dismember. Their first two full lengths are extremely solid editions to the death metal lexicon. Their second album, *Bitterness*, was originally released on Metal Blade in 1994, and frankly if you are looking for something that helped to start the melodic style of death metal that would begin to rule Sweden shortly after this album's release you could certainly do worse. *Bitterness* really is an essential album if you are doing a study on the history of Swedish death metal and honestly these guys are criminally underrated in my book. (Most likely because after this record they put out an album that was so out of left field, and then promptly broke up, reforming as an alt-rock/stoner rock band under a different name.)

Recommended Track: "Life Shatters"

520. Riot - Thundersteel

New York's Riot formed in the mid-'70s and from 1977-1983 put out five studio albums, all of which were varying degrees of hard rock. Their record label supposedly dropped them for having a name that too closely resembled Quiet Riot, who had just "broke" and they disbanded shortly there after. However guitarist and founding member, Mark Reale, reformed the band with an entirely new line-up and in 1988 released their sixth studio album, *Thundersteel*, on CBS Records. You want to talk about a style change for the better? This album would be the poster child for it. Reale recruited unknown vocalist, Tony Moore, who had some serious pipes, and he set about writing some seriously kick-ass thrash and speed infused power metal. You know why a band like Hammerfall covered these guys? Because there wouldn't be a Hammerfall without Riot and more specifically this album. Simply put this is a power metal masterpiece.

Recommended Track: "Thundersteel"

519. Cradle of Filth – Dusk and Her Embrace

Cradle of Filth are possibly England's most argument-inducing metal export of all-time. Love them or hate them this band has had a pretty large impact on the world of metal over the last 20 years. They originally started as a death metal band, quickly converted to black metal and then just as quickly modified their sound to fit the symphonic black metal vibe that was just starting to grow in popularity at the time. Truly, if you dig symphonic black metal or just symphonic variants of metal at all then you should be all over this band. Cradle of Filth originally started out on Cacophonous Records but after one full length and one contractual obligation EP, they jumped ship to Music For Nations. They then promptly released their second full length album, *Dusk...And Her Embrace*, in 1996. From this point forward, with various rather large labels behind them throughout their career, Cradle of Filth would become the poster children for super polished black metal.

Recommended Track: "Dusk and Her Embrace"

518. Hallows Eve – Tales of Terror

Hallows Eve are from Atlanta, GA and were one of the first handful of bands that Metal Blade ever signed. They gained some acclaim by appearing on the now (in)famous soundtrack to the film River's Edge and at one point they had members who were affiliated with Rigor Mortis. They play an in-your-face style of old school thrash that's high on intensity. Hallows Eve released their debut album, *Tales of Terror*, on Metal Blade (distributed through Combat) in 1985. One thing you can be sure of is this band is not for poseurs. Unfortunately Hallows Eve has not garnered the long-term acclaim and respect that some other early Metal Blade signings have received. But they have maintained a pretty strong cult following in the metal scene and this album in particular is often spoken of fondly when discussing the history of Metal Blade's roster.

Recommended Track: "Metal Merchants"

517. Flotsam and Jetsam – Doomsday For The Deceiver

This record is famous for two reasons. The first being because Jason Newsted, later of Metallica fame, played bass on this record and had a large hand in the songwriting process. Secondly this was the first album that Kerrang! Magazine out of the U.K. gave a 6 star (or "K") rating…out of a possible 5 stars/'Ks'. O.k., so they had a guy who would go on to be a Metallica member and the backing of an overzealous magazine that overlooked some of the greatest metal albums of all-time to give this album its highest rating ever. But was the album any good? The short answer is, yes. Yes it is. Flotsam and Jetsam emerged out of the Arizona desert playing full-on thrash metal. They released their debut album, *Doomsday for the Deceiver*, on Metal Blade in 1986. Thanks to some killer vocals and memorable riffs this album absolutely stands the test of time. Six out of five stars? You can decide that for yourself.

Recommended Track: "Hammerhead"

516. Wehrmacht – Shark Attack

Portland OR's Wehrmacht were a thrash/punk crossover act and they played their brand of crossover thrash so fast and pissed that a lot of people have lumped this band into the speed metal category as well. Honestly they've got elements of all three sub genres so you really can't go wrong calling them any of those. In 1987, after a ton of demos, Wehrmacht released their debut full-length album on New Renaissance Records. It's an album that never, ever lets up. From start to finish this album is just a swift kick to the sternum. Wehrmacht was one of those bands that both metal and punk kids could get into back in the day, although when you go back and listen to them now they sound much more on the metal side. Sure the songs are short and structured like punk songs but this band played them so fiercely that if they had used gruff vocals they might have gone down as one of the first ever grindcore bands.

Recommended Track: "Shark Attack"

515. Vader – The Ultimate Incantation

Poland's Vader released their debut album, *The Ultimate Incantation*, in 1992 on Earache Records. Little known fact about this album – they recorded it twice. The first time they went into Sunlight Studios in Sweden (the studio that helped birth the "Swedish sound" in early death metal) but the band didn't like the way it sounded, supposedly because they were forced to use a drum machine. So they scrapped it and re-recorded the whole damn thing at a studio in the UK. As it stands, buzzsaw guitars or not, this is still an immense death metal album. By the early 90s death metal had already started to see their ranks infiltrated by some second rate bands so, at the time, hearing this relatively unknown band from Poland tear it up was rather refreshing.

Recommended Track: "Final Massacre"

514. Overkill – Taking Over

In 1987, New Jersey's Overkill released their second full length album, *Taking Over*, on Megaforce Records, and for the first time in conjunction with Atlantic Records. Overkill would actually have an association with Atlantic until the mid-'90s, which was a lot longer than most metal bands. This album, although being the first to have major label backing, was not hugely successful. It charted on the Billboard 200 for all of one week. But what Overkill did do with this record was basically knock over the first major domino in creating a legacy as one of the most popular thrash metal bands to ever come off the East Coast of the U.S. Overkill has been an immensely influential thrash band through the years and a lot of it has to do with this album.

Recommended Track: "Deny The Cross"

513. Nevermore - Nevermore

This is Nevermore's debut album, originally released by Century Media Records in 1995. If you think back to 1995, what comes to mind? For millions of people I'm sure it's probably "grunge" music. So even though this album was heavier than anything else Seattle was producing then (although, not for nothing early Soundgarden was pretty heavy) you could still see that it potentially had some crossover appeal to the mainstream. However, the riffs would be deemed a little too gritty and chunky and Warrel Dane's vocals especially were just a little 'too metal' for them to really break it big. But that didn't stop them from becoming one of the most popular US metal bands the '90s would produce and this is the album that started it all.

Recommended Track: "What Tomorrow Knows"

512. Warlock - Hellbound

Germany's Warlock started out in the early '80s and were led by front woman Doro Pesch. Now, no offense to the rest of the band because the songs are excellent examples of traditional metal, but this band did what they did because Doro was out front leading the charge. *Hellbound* was the band's second full length album, originally released in 1985. This was also the first album the band would do on a major label as it was released by Vertigo in Europe and through Mercury Records here in the US. Their first album was just as solid from a songwriting standpoint but had virtually nothing for distribution. Therefore, this was really the first taste of Warlock that a lot of people, especially in the US, would have and it wouldn't be their last. Because of that this album still remains a highly influential gem from a halcyon era.

Recommended Track: "Hellbound"

511. Sabbat - Dreamweaver

These days Sabbat is just as famous for being the band that Grammy Award winning producer Andy Sneap played guitar in. But what they should be remembered for is their brand of blackened thrash. I say "blackened thrash" because when you look back on this band with metal hindsight you can clearly see some Venom and Celtic Frost influences in there. That's not to say that Sabbat should be considered one of the forefathers of black metal. On the contrary, they are as thrash as thrash gets. But putting them up against other thrash bands from this era only points out their unique take on the genre. The full name of this album was *Dreamweaver (Reflections of Our Yesterdays)* and was the band's second full length album released in 1989 on Noise Records. It's a concept record based on a book about an Anglo-Saxon sorcerer and reflects the bands love of Celtic and Anglo-Saxon mythology, as well as various pagan themes.

Recommended Track: "The Clerical Conspiracy"

510. Sentenced – North From Here

At their core, Finland's Sentenced were a melodic death metal band, not completely unlike some of their Swedish counterparts. But unlike a lot of the bands in Sweden, Sentenced was not afraid to mix it up, especially over time. *North From Here* was the band's second full-length album, released in 1993 originally on Spinefarm Records (later reissued by Century Media in the U.S.). This album is a fantastic blend of death metal mixed with black metal, thrash and various progressive elements. Not afraid to throw in the occasional keyboard and certainly not afraid to change the pace as far as time signatures, this album was a unique piece of music upon its release. Very few bands that fell under that broad umbrella of death metal were changing the death metal paradigm like this 20+ years ago. Frankly, their influence on both the death metal scene and the Finnish metal scene in general is far reaching.

Recommended Track: "Northern Lights"

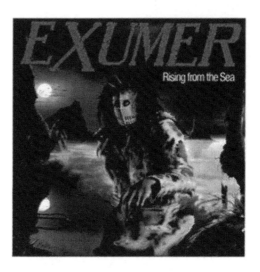

509. Exumer – Rising From The Sea

The number of seminal bands from various genres that Germany has produced is staggering. Just like in other parts of the metal world though there are bands that often get overlooked simply because of the sheer amount of talent within a particular scene. One such band that often gets overlooked when discussing German thrash is Exumer. Perhaps one reason this band is often overlooked is because of their relatively short lifespan in their earliest incarnation. Regardless of their short stay in the metal consciousness, Exumer was still able to produce some quality German thrash metal back in the late '80s. *Rising From The Sea* was the band's second and final studio album, until a somewhat recent reunion that has since produced two more albums. This album was released in 1987 on Disaster Records.

Recommended Track: "Shadows of the Past"

508. Penance – The Road Less Travelled

Penance was formed in Pittsburgh, PA, a city that, at the time, had their reasons for producing music of this ilk. Penance play traditional doom in the style of bands such as Candlemass, Saint Vitus and Trouble. They play it slow and steady with mostly clean vocals over top of sick riffs and Black Sabbath aesthetics. In 1992 they released their debut album, *The Road Less Travelled*, on Rise Above. Penance was actually one of the first doom bands Rise Above would work with and they released this album long before the label worked with the likes of Electric Wizard, Orange Goblin, Sleep or any other bands that would go on to gain more worldwide success. At the end of the day, Penance is one of those bands that waved the flag for doom metal when few other bands were doing it as vigorously.

Recommended Track: "The Unseen"

507. Disembowelment – Transcendence into the Peripheral

Some bands just defy description, going out of their way to bend and meld genres to their will, and forming a sound that is truly all their own. A perfect example of a band that didn't play by the scene rules was Australia's Disembowelment (or dISEMBOWELMENT as it was often spelled). This band was just a crazy collage of sounds. Over the years they've been labeled a death/doom band. While they certainly have several characteristics of the death/doom genre and borrow freely from traditional death and doom metal, they really do go beyond the description itself. Toss in everything from grindcore to ambient/shoegaze to even early elements of black metal and what you come up with is a band that, on paper, seems like they should be all over the place but simply are not. Picture if Neurosis, Napalm Death, Swans, and Morbid Angel all made a love child together. It would probably be this band. In 1993 they released their lone full-length album, *Transcendence into the Peripheral*, on Relapse Records.

Recommended Track: "The Spirits of the Tall Hills"

506. Edge of Sanity – Nothing But Death Remains

Before Opeth started to experiment, before they started to mix and match genres and were allowing their brand of death metal to become more and more prog influenced there was Edge of Sanity. Now, I'm not saying that, from a songwriting perspective, these bands should be considered peers. No, what I am saying though is when you talk about trendsetting metal bands, especially of the Swedish variety, Edge of Sanity needs a bigger voice in the discussion. Edge of Sanity released their debut full-length album, *Nothing But Death Remains*, in 1991 on Black Mark Productions. Make no mistake, this is a death metal album and a fine one at that. While band mastermind, Dan Swano, might go down as one of the greatest experimentalists (and producers) in metal history he first contributed to some killer death metal in the form of vocalist and lyricist on this album.

Recommended Track: "Maze of Existence"

505. Darkthrone – The Cult Is Alive

The Cult Is Alive was Darkthrone's eleventh studio album, released in 2006 on Peaceville Records. Sonically, to say this was a bit of a departure from previous efforts, is both an understatement and an exaggeration. Norway's Darkthrone are one of the earliest and best of the famed second wave of black metal arising in the early '90s. Although they helped foster and create the "black metal sound" they never really strayed too far from what bands like Bathory and Celtic Frost had done before them. By the time this album hit the streets everyone was still expecting that "black metal sound" they had perfected and instead what we all got was a proverbial gut punch of old school metal…in the vain of Bathory and Celtic Frost. So while most fans were pleasantly shocked at the direction the band decided to go on this record, what Darkthrone was really doing was paying homage to their roots in a slightly different way, and it totally worked.

Recommended Track: "Too Old Too Cold"

504. In Flames – The Jester Race

The Jester Race was the second full length album from In Flames, originally released in 1996 on Nuclear Blast Records. Since 1996 there have been literally hundreds of bands trying to copy this band's formula and this album has proven to be immensely important for both the scene which it influenced and the band themselves. This was their first album on Nuclear Blast and therefore their first album that had a large, worldwide distribution, especially here in the U.S. Although this band was never as heavy as some of their contemporaries (i.e. Amon Amarth) they would go on to be one of the most popular of the Gothenburg bands. Take that for what it's worth. Whether you like their current output or not (which has changed quite drastically over time) and whether you like the bands they've influenced, you can't deny this album's place in recent metal history.

Recommended Track: "Graveland"

503. Entombed – Wolverine Blues

Wolverine Blues was Entombed's third full-length album, released in 1993 on Earache Records. Their first two albums were seminal death metal albums of the highest order. Entombed was one of a small handful of bands who basically perfected the 'buzzsaw' Swedish death metal sound. On this album though they started to incorporate more elements of rock, traditional metal, and even metallic American hardcore. (Don't believe me? Listen to the track "Contempt." Remove the guitar solo and it sounds like something a band like Earth Crisis or Bloodlet would have produced at this time.) This new sound they helped pioneer at this point in their career would later be dubbed 'death n' roll' and Entombed would spend a lot of time following that career path. This album was co-released through Columbia records, also marking the band's foray into more mainstream success thanks to massive distribution and a mellower sound.

Recommended Track: "Wolverine Blues"

502. Pantera – Vulgar Display of Power

Well, here it is. The album that almost single-handedly created Nu Metal and helped influence the musical careers of literally hundreds of bands, most of which are…just…terrible. Honestly, it's a shame that we may wind up remembering this album as such because it's a decent record with some very solid tracks. To briefly rehash this band's history: They started out as a hair/speed metal band, put out a bunch of albums no one paid attention to, gradually started to shift their sound on *Cowboys From Hell* and then by the time this album was released in 1992 on Atco (owned by Warner) they had suddenly helped give birth to this sound we would come to know as "groove metal." They were right there with Guns N' Roses and post-1988 Metallica as mainstream America's poster boys for what was considered "metal." Whether you consider that a good thing or not is on your own terms, but you can never deny this album's place in the history of metal music.

Recommended Track: "By Demons Be Driven"

501. W.A.S.P. – W.A.S.P.

In the early '80s, as a child, what really turned me on to metal was the 700 Club. True story. These zealous religious groups used to produce pseudo-documentaries about the evils of heavy metal. There was something so dangerous about the music that it fascinated and instantly hooked me from a pretty young age. One of the bands they constantly picked on was W.A.S.P. Whether it was the sexual content of songs like "Animal (F*ck Like A Beast)" or the 'Satanism' of songs like "Sleeping (In the Fire)" they were always in the cross hairs of someone with a Jesus-based agenda. Neither of these songs are as heavy as 99% of what is held within these pages, but W.A.S.P deserves their own dirty, perverted spot, and here it is.

Recommended Track: "Animal (F*ck Like A Beast)"

500. Ides of Gemini - Constantinople

Ides of Gemini released their first full-length album, *Constantinople*, in 2012 on Neurot Recordings. The fact that this album was released on the label founded by members of Neurosis should immediately tip you off to the fact that this is going to be something unique in style and substance. The overall sound is sparse yet powerful. It has this vibe of ancient darkness behind it, as if upon each listen you're perpetually stumbling upon some long lost ritual that you aren't supposed to witness. The first thing that strikes you is Sera Timms and her otherworldly vocals. Her voice soars over songs and immediately stands out as one of the most dynamic and downright perfect elements of each track. Fans of such occult rock outfits as The Devil's Blood and Blood Ceremony will immediately fall in love with this album.

Recommended Track: "The Vessel and the Stake"

499. Flesh Parade – Kill Whitey

Kill Whitey was the first full-length album by New Orleans' Flesh Parade, released on Relapse Records in 1998. This album contains two demos released in 1993 and 1994 and the Kill Whitey 7" which was also released in 1998. When I say it is abrasive, unrelenting grindcore, that's probably an understatement. Although they do have the occasional death metal styled breakdown, for the most part this album is 12 tracks (and roughly only 16 minutes) of face smashing grind. This album also has, in my opinion, one of the best grindcore vocalists in the world. Jason Pilgrim must gargle with broken glass and sand before he performs because this guy's screams are, frankly, sick as hell. I'm not going to lie. Even for a lot of metalheads this album may be an acquired taste, but if it's a taste you've acquired then welcome to the club.

Recommended Track: "Backstabber"

498. Abattoir – Vicious Attack

Quick fun fact about this band: Los Angeles' Abattoir was the opener for the first two shows Megadeth ever played. Abattoir played a fantastic hybrid of speed, thrash and early power metal. This album is more about the speed metal than their next album would be, and it's a galloping ride of an album that never really lets up (including their killer cover of Motörhead's "Ace of Spades" – giving it a speed metal make-over). So why are we not talking about this album and this band more? Well, Abattoir had troubles galore keeping a solid line-up in place and wound up releasing only two full length albums before pretty much vanishing for good. But *Vicious Attack* still stands as a highly underrated album. It was originally released in 1985 on the legendary Combat Records.

Recommended Track: "Screams From The Grave"

497. Taake - Taake

When metal historians look back on the last fifteen or so years of black metal one of the bands they'll most likely be talking about is Norway's Taake. Now, why they are talking about this band is a whole different ballgame. They may be talking about the grim, brutal and completely blasphemous black metal these guys deal in...or they may be talking about all the controversy that surrounded this band. In 2008 they released their self-titled, fourth full-length album on Dark Essence Records. This album not only received a lot more press but was arguably the catalyst for them becoming one of the more "kvlt" bands in the black metal scene. Part of that is because up to this point this was arguably their best album both from a songwriting and a production standpoint. However this album also followed roughly two years of controversy which is just a Google search away for your reading pleasure. At the end of the day though, controversies or not, this is a fantastic black metal album.

Recommended Track: "Doedskvad I"

496. Grief - Torso

Somewhere on the playground of music, hardcore and various forms of metal, including grindcore and doom, all got together and shared the sandbox. They eventually grew up, married, and helped give birth to a large portion of today's metal scene. Boston's Grief was directly born out of this union. They played this amazing hybrid of all the styles listed above. It was this unique mixed bag of sounds, especially in the '90s when they were most prevalent. Their songs ranged from crust blasts to these drawn out, epic doom masterpieces. The vocals however maintained the crust/punk/hardcore tenacity so picture a band like say His Hero Is Gone covering a band like Sleep and you've pretty much summed up Grief. *Torso* was the band's fourth full-length album, released in 1998 on Pessimiser Records .

Recommended Track: "Amorphous"

495. Goatwhore – Carving Out The Eyes Of God

Formed by former Acid Bath and Crowbar guitarist Sammy Duet, along with Soilent Green vocalist Ben Falgoust, Goatwhore is a pretty drastic departure from the bands those two were/are involved in, and for the most part from the rest of the New Orleans scene as well. Goatwhore play an old-school hybrid of blackened trash. Although they certainly have their death metal-like moments, especially on the first two albums, they have evolved over time to more resemble that awesome first wave of early black metal, especially Celtic Frost and Bathory. That's not to say that there aren't second wave influences as well. You still have the occasional tremolo picking and plenty of blast beats abound but you'll never confuse this band with Mayhem or early Darkthrone. *Carving Out The Eyes of God* was their fourth full-length album, originally released in 2009 on Metal Blade Records.

Recommended Track: "Apocalyptic Havoc"

494. Ozzy Osbourne – The Ultimate Sin

What can be said about the legendary Ozzy Osbourne that hasn't already been written a thousand times over? In 1986, Osbourne released his fourth studio album, *The Ultimate Sin*, on CBS/Epic Records. The album followed one of many stints in rehab and, frankly, marked the beginning of the end as far as his solo albums being essential to own. However, thanks to a handful of very solid hard rock/metal anthems, *The Ultimate Sin* was the album that would cement Osbourne as an international superstar, and for a lot of kids my age would be the album that first turned them into fans. I mean, you can't have a record go double platinum and be your highest charting record up until that point and not make new fans, right?

Recommended Track: "Lightning Strikes"

493. Cattle Decapitation – Human Jerky

One band that mastered the art of goregrind early in their career was San Diego's Cattle Decapitation. *Human Jerky* was the band's second EP, originally released by Satan's Pimp Records in 1999. It's 18 songs in just over 12 minutes, so I think you'll get the point real quick as to where this band was coming from. They would eventually evolve over time to resemble a death metal act more than a grindcore band, but on this album it's about as grind as it gets. Obviously the one other factor that always separated this band from other bands of their ilk was the lyrical content. Instead of writing about zombies and mass murderers they were writing songs about the terrors of factory farming. (Don't laugh. Those PETA videos are the real deal.) *Human Jerky* was a catalyst album for this band as it was the first album to open a lot of eyes, and the album that would eventually get them signed to Metal Blade.

Recommended Track: "Cloned For Carrion"

492. Logical Nonsense – Soul Pollution

Soul Pollution, was originally released by New Mexico's Logical Nonsense in 1995 on Tee Pee Records. Alternative Tentacles would reissue this record when their A.T. debut would hit the streets in 1998. (The artwork included here is the A.T. artwork.) This might be their second full length and there was a split with Grimple floating around but this was the album that put them on the scene map. This was the album that got them signed to A.T. and made a lot of kids outside their local scene take notice. Logical Nonsense played a hybrid of crust and hardcore with some serious metal influences. It's music that just seethes anger and disillusionment the way good crust, hardcore and metal should. My only disappointment with this band is they didn't stick around long enough to reap some of the benefits of their own influence.

Recommended Track: "Hatework"

491. Dark Funeral – The Secrets Of The Black Arts

Dark Funeral emerged from the Swedish scene, releasing their debut album, *The Secrets of the Black Arts*, on No Fashion Records in 1996. By 1996 black metal had already gained quite the worldwide following. Bands like Darkthrone, Emperor, Satyricon, etc. were relatively huge. But this album stacks up well against any other black metal album released that year, and it's worth owning if you are even the slightest connoisseur of the blasphemous. One interesting side note about this album is they recorded it twice. The entire album. Twice. They originally recorded it with Dan Swano behind the board but were so displeased with the results that they decided not to release it at all. Instead they re-recorded the album with Peter Tagtgren behind the board. Later reissues of the album would include the previously unreleased version.

Recommended Track: "The Secrets of the Black Arts"

490. GWAR – Hell-o!

Hell-o! was GWAR's debut album released in 1988 on a little label called Shimmy Disc. They would quickly be snatched up by Metal Blade though, who would reissue the album in CD format. If for no other reason this album makes this list because it launched the careers of a bunch of dudes from Virginia who had a goofy idea, some punk-infused metal songs, and ran with it – leaving a trail of fake blood and entrails a billion miles long behind them. This album more than any other showcases their punk rock roots. In fact this album has more in common with groups like Butthole Surfers, The Mentors, and The Cramps than with the world of metal in 1988. But there was a hardcore edge to them and signing with one of the biggest metal labels in the world would prove beneficial as they were quickly embraced by most of the metal community. The rest, as they say, is history.

Recommended Track: "Americanized"

489. Fu Manchu – King of the Road

Although most stoner rock bands are too heavy to be classified as anything other than metal you occasionally come across a band that really could/should have that crossover potential to commercial radio. One such band is California's Fu Manchu. Fu Manchu has been kicking ass and taking names for a long time. These guys are one of the original wave of stoner rock bands to crop up in Southern California in the early '90s. In 1999 they released their sixth studio album, *King of the Road* on Mammoth Records. This is still one of their best albums even though they've continued to release quality material. There isn't a bad track on this record and even a track like "Boogie Van", which has somewhat goofy lyrics, has such a killer riff running through it that you can't help but rock out. If you dig killer, riff-heavy rock then Fu Manchu and this album are for you.

Recommended Track: "King of the Road"

488. Buzzov*en - ...At A Loss

The members of Buzzov*en would go on to play in and/or form Weedeater, Bongzilla, and Sourvein just to name a few. To say their influence on the sludge genre is far reaching is an absolute understatement, especially seeing as they were one of a small handful of American bands from the deep South who pretty much invented sludge metal to begin with. ...At A Loss was the band's third, and for a long time, final full-length album. It was released in 1998 on Off The Records. Prior to this album they were signed to Roadrunner for a red hot second, releasing one album for them four years earlier. After this album they would start to lose members to other projects and a full-length that was recorded in 2001 wouldn't see daylight until a decade later. It really is a shame that this band didn't stick around long enough to reap some of the benefits of their immense influence.

Recommended Track: "Kakkila"

487. Rotting Christ - Theogonia

Greece's Rotting Christ has always been a band that was classified as 'black metal' but in reality I don't think they ever really fell completely into that realm the way some of their contemporaries did. Their sound was always just a little far left of field to be pigeon-holed into any one genre. They released their ninth studio album, *Theogonia* in 2007 on Season of Mist. After their first two albums, in the mid to late '90s, the band started to add Gothic and rock elements galore. While the end result of this shift in musical direction was mixed at best they thankfully managed to stay relevant in the metal world, culminating in a return to blackened form with this record. What makes this record stand out though is not just the heaviness of it but the successful addition of certain folk metal and world music elements. No one will ever fault Rotting Christ for putting out the same record twice, and this album is just another example of their unique take on black metal.

Recommended Track: "Keravnos Kyvernitos"

486. Starkweather - Croatoan

Philadelphia's Starkweather were a band, who despite not releasing any new material for roughly a decade just continued to grow in stature. That continued with the release of their first new full length album in 2005. *Croatoan* simultaneously ended a ten year hiatus between albums and turned an entirely new generation of hardcore and metal kids on to this band. Originally released on vinyl only in 2005, Candlelight Records would release a CD version in 2006. Starkweather spent the 1990s turning out some of the best metallic hardcore around and at the same time turning themselves into an extremely influential band. On this album there are mellow, doom-like interludes that include clean-sung vocals over top of guitars lacking any semblance of distortion. Then there is the other side of the coin where Starkweather get dark...real dark. It's not out of the question to liken what this band was doing on this record to some of the more progressive doom and black metal projects at that time.

Recommended Track: "Slither"

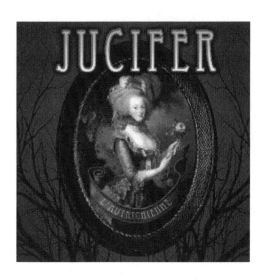

485. Jucifer – L'Autrichienne

Released on Relapse Records in 2008, *L'Autrichenne*, was Jucifer's fourth album. It's an absolutely amazing 70 minute frolic through various genres as the band tells the story of Marie Antoinette. That's right, a concept album about one of the most well-known and misunderstood figures in European history. The album starts with a song so catchy and accessible that hard rock radio stations could have been all over it. But then they take a left turn into a track that can only be described as grindcore, and so the journey begins. Outside of rock n' roll and grindcore they successfully mix in elements of doom/sludge, indie rock, post-rock, death metal and ambient/psych rock. It is literally like 21 different bands got together and recorded a comp album. It's such a bizarre and fun ride, plus Amber Valentine gives one of the best vocal performances you'll ever hear as she hops from style to style, never missing a note and sounding absolutely perfect the whole way.

Recommended Track: "Blackpowder"

484. Krieg – Blue Miasma

When metal historians look back at the annals of US black metal they are going to find a handful of bands that will have positioned themselves as the true leaders within the genre. For my money's worth one of those bands will absolutely be Krieg. Krieg has had a long, and sometimes complicated history, but one thing they have never left in doubt is the ability to piece together an album's worth of pure, sonic depression. *Blue Miasma* was Krieg's fifth full-length album, originally released in 2006. This album takes the fury of previous efforts and mixes in more melodic/doom-laden passages. The opening instrumental track alone is a wholly depressive experience and a certain harbinger for things to come. While there is plenty of tremolo-picking and blasting to go around, it's the overall oppressive atmosphere that this record puts forth which makes it a benchmark of USBM.

Recommended Track: "Under An Uncaring Moon"

483. Old Man Gloom – Meditations In B

Originally started as a side project of sorts by Isis mastermind and Hydra Head Records founder Aaron Turner, Old Man Gloom would very quickly take on a life of their own. They released their debut album, *Meditations In B*, in 1999 on Tortuga Recordings. Over the years they've gotten the 'super group' moniker as they've featured members of other Boston bands, such as Converge, Cave-In, and Doomriders. Old Man Gloom play a sort of bastardized version of doom that combines elements of crust, hardcore, post-hardcore and even some grind for good measure. They are a riff-first type of band, meaning a lot of their songs hinge around these driving, pummeling riffs with tortured screams and various electronic elements layered over top. They also have several instrumental/experimental tracks on here, complete with the obligatory crazy samples and some trance inducing electronics.

Recommended Track: "Sonic Wave of Bees"

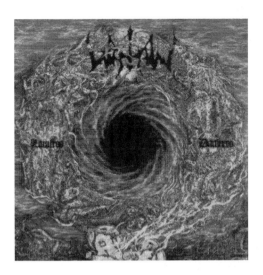

482. Watain – Lawless Darkness

Lawless Darkness was the fourth album from Swedish black metal horde Watain. It was originally released in 2010 on Season Of Mist. One could easily argue that this is their most accomplished and acclaimed work to date, certainly one of at least. Eschewing the total lo-fi sound for a more progressive and, dare I say, epic one, Watain delivered one of the best black metal albums of this decade thus far. It's a complete and total homage to the likes of Emperor and Dissection but without being any type of rip-off. This album is pure atmosphere and the way the entire thing is structured is absolutely exceptional. When they talk about worshiping the Dark One, I fully believe that each song is created as a gift to Lucifer himself. It's as complete a black metal album as you are going to hear any time soon.

Recommended Track: "Kiss of Death"

481. Cult of Luna – The Beyond

Cult of Luna is one of Sweden's more unique metal exports from the last decade. Originally coming together through the Swedish hardcore scene the music early in their career reflected that. But it was on their second full length album, *The Beyond*, that they started to heavily experiment with the post-metal, shoegaze, and atmospheric doom combination that they would become known for. *The Beyond* was released in 2003 on Earache Records and was the first album of new material that Earache would release. Therefore for the vast majority of fans this was their first taste of Cult of Luna. Being this is the album that sent them on the amazing musical path they tread today it very well may be the most important album they've done, at least in terms of historical context.

Recommended Track: "Receiver"

480. Skepticism - Stormcrowfleet

Long, slow, and oppressively heavy songs are the order of the day here, complete with well-placed organs, vocals from the bowels of Hell, and Sabbath-like riffs dragged out note by note. *Stormcrowfleet* was the debut album by Finland's Skepticism, released in 1995 on Red Stream, and it stands today as one of the benchmarks of the genre. Funeral doom has grown exponentially in both popularity and the number of bands playing this style, however in 1995 Skepticism was a pretty unique band playing a style of music that even some of the most hardcore metalheads had trouble wrapping their arms around. I mean, it's not like you can 'rock out' to funeral doom. Yet the style of music Skepticism played on here was so elegant and atmospheric that it's hard not to be swallowed up by this band. Let yourself be engulfed by the music.

Recommended Track: "The Rising of the Flame"

479. The Locust – Plague Soundscapes

Plague Soundscapes was the second full length album from San Diego's The Locust, released in 2003 on ANTI-Records. What an absolute sonic hodgepodge it is. The entire album, all 23 tracks, clocks in at roughly 21 minutes. But what this band does with roughly fifty-second songs is more than what a lot of bands can pull off in three or four minutes. It's pretty jaw-dropping at certain points. Grindcore and punk are thrown into a blender with noise rock, post-rock, and just about every other extreme form of music. Then they hit the 'High" button and just allow it to spew this sonic concoction all over the place. Don't expect them to clean up after themselves either. Easily one of the more unique albums you'll find on this list.

Recommended Track: "Listen, The Mighty Ear Is Here"

478. Mindrot - Dawning

California's Mindrot had been kicking around for quite some time when Relapse Records finally picked them up. They had released three demos and various 7" records, but their proper debut, full-length album, *Dawning*, wasn't released until 1995. At the risk of sounding hyperbolic this album was absolutely trend-setting. Sure the gothic-inspired, atmospheric doom thing had been around for quite some time. But I'm not sure if any band (or at least any American band) had mastered the art of atmospheric doom the way Mindrot had. They blend the gruff and clean vocals in a way that's not pretentious at all, and the music itself is downright mesmerizing at certain points with sweeping, all-encompassing riffs. Plus, like a lot of great doom albums, it's meant to be listened to in one continuous listen, front-to-back. There's something to be said when a band can tell a seemingly continuous story through the music alone for 40+ minutes.

Recommended Track: "Anguish"

477. The Red Chord - Clients

For The Red Chord they always seemed to ride a fine line between death metal and hardcore. Yet neither fully applies to their sound. Listen to the track "Fixation on Plastics" and you can't deny that it's a death metal song. However, this band emerged out of the very rich Massachusetts hardcore scene and with the breakdowns/spoken word passages you get in a song like "Black Santa" it's hard to deny their hardcore roots. *Clients* was the band's second full-length album, but first for Metal Blade, released in 2005. Their debut album was the one that helped grow their fan base and get them signed to Metal Blade. But it was this album that would sell a ton and lead to an eventual spot on an Ozzfest. Regardless of what you want to call it, this album has a huge, pummeling sound with an awesome lyrical concept/theme.

Recommended Track: "Fixation On Plastics"

476. Regurgitate – Effortless Regurgitation...The Torture Sessions

You are warned: This is extreme metal with the emphasis on the 'extreme' part. Sweden's Regurgitate spent the 1990s in virtual obscurity, only really known to the select fans who somehow stumbled upon them. But in 1999 that all changed. That was the year Relapse Records released the compilation album *Effortless Regurgitation...The Torture Sessions*. First of all the album has 63 tracks to it. 63! So you know right off the bat there is a lot of grinding goodness on here. The album is comprised of their 1994 album, *Effortless Regurgitation of Bright Red Blood*, their *Concrete Human Torture* demo, and a bunch of tracks from various splits and 7"s. As a general rule I'm not a huge fan of comp albums unless it's one that culls together material that would otherwise be unavailable. This would be the case here. Therefore this album is absolutely key in introducing one of the better goregrind bands in the world to a worldwide audience.

Recommended Track: "Fleshfeast"

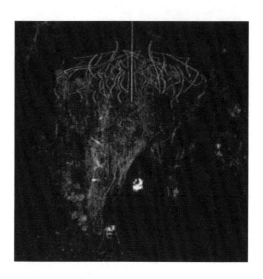

475. Wolves In The Throne Room – Two Hunters

There are those that hesitate to call Washington's Wolves In The Thrown Room a black metal band because of all the experimentation that goes on with their albums. Hogwash. There is zero doubt that this is a black metal band first and foremost, and one that helped mold the USBM scene into the force that it is today. However the fact that they dabble in doom, ambient, various forms of folk music, etc. can not be understated. There is as much of a Neurosis influence on this band as there is Emperor. *Two Hunters* was their second full length album, released in 2007 on Southern Lord. This album was seminal for many reasons, not the least of which was that this was the album where they really started to experiment and expand their sound. It's an absolute gem of a record and a triumph of the American black metal scene.

Recommended Track: "Vastness and Sorrow"

474. Kiss It Goodbye – She Loves Me, She Loves Me Not

Kiss It Goodbye formed out of the ashes of two of the most influential hardcore bands of all-time – Deadguy and Rorschach. Originally from New Jersey the band relocated to Seattle and produced their debut full-length album, *She Loves Me, She Loves Me Not* in 1997 for Revelation Records. Sadly this band would be gone about a year later, having only recorded one more EP. If you are familiar at all with Deadguy and/or Rorschach then you'll be ahead of the game in picking up what this band is putting down. They are similar in style to both bands, yet are heavier and darker than either of them as well. Their brand of discordant, relentless hardcore felt so despondent, so utterly hopeless. Plus, for my money, Tim Singer was easily one of the best vocalists in the history of hardcore and his throat-shredding, maniacal performance on this album is worth the price of admission alone.

Recommended Track: "Helvetica"

473. Realm – Endless War

Milwaukee's Realm played an awesome hybrid of speed and power metal, especially on their first album. I'm not sure if anyone has ever coined the term "progressive speed metal" but if they did they were probably talking about this band. Realm's debut full length album *Endless War* was released in 1988 on R/C Records. One can wonder if this album had been released maybe two or three years earlier if we wouldn't be talking about these guys in the same breathe as some of their contemporaries, like Anthrax for example. Sadly these guys would put out only one more album for Roadracer after this one. From what's been written, when their contract ended they went looking for another label/deal and nothing came from it. This was 1992 and unfortunately the metal landscape was changing drastically by then. They wound up disbanding, and a third full length album they recorded remains unreleased to this day.

Recommended Track: "Endless War"

472. Diabolical Masquerade - Nightwork

At one point Katatonia member Anders Nystrom (a.k.a. Blakkheim) must have realized that he had a whole world of dark ideas brewing. Because in the mid-90s he formed a one-man, symphonic black metal project called Diabolical Masquerade. The sound would progress from album to album growing more and more avant-garde in nature, incorporating odd time-signature changes, a virtual symphony's worth of orchestration and a penchant for intriguing story-telling in each song. What makes it even more impressive is with the exception of recruiting producer and metal legend Dan Swano to fill in on a few instruments here and there, this is almost completely a one-man show. I know we tend to think of one-man black metal bands at this time as lo-fi stuff recorded in someone's bedroom. This is anything but that. In 1998, Diabolical Masquerade released their third, and most accomplished, album, *Nightwork*, on Avantgarde Music.

Recommended Track: "The Ghoultimate Omen"

471. Krisiun – Apocalyptic Revelation

Brazil's Krisiun play death metal the best way possible. Take early thrash metal albums from bands like Slayer, Sodom, Kreater and Possessed - all the great proto-death metal - and combine it with the delivery of bands like Deicide and Morbid Angel. What you are left with is a pretty decent summary of the Krisiun sound. It's fast, it's pissed, it's unrelenting, and frankly it's the sheer definition of brutal. But unlike some bands that just try to be brutal for the sake of it, Krisiun are also extremely technically proficient. *Apocalyptic Revelation* was the band's second full-length album, originally released in 1998 on GUN Records out of Germany. This is the album that would lead them to a record deal with Century Media and eventually allowed them to claim their rightful place as one of the better and most renowned death metal bands in the world.

Recommended Track: "Kings of Killing"

470. Morgion - Solinari

The fact some acts get lost to the metal history books is just criminal. One band that simply never received the acclaim they were due was Morgion. Mixing atmospheric and epic doom with death metal, California's Morgion was an absolute beast of a band. Their sound was all-encompassing. (And yet they weren't just a studio band. I had the pleasure of seeing them live multiple times and they brought down the skies and rained doom upon every venue, leaving it trembling in their wake.) *Solinari* was the band's second album, released on Relapse in 1999. More than any of their other releases this one feels the most complete. Songs blend and flow into each other telling this really compelling musical narrative, while just laying waste to everything in its path. If you are a doom fan at all, specifically the more ambient style favored by many European bands, then this is a record you need to hear or revisit immediately.

Recommended Track: "Canticle"

469. Pig Destroyer – Phantom Limb

Pig Destroyer play a type of grindcore that mixes in elements of everything from death metal to hardcore. Compared to some other grindcore bands it can come off as a somewhat polished sound. However when you talk perspective, calling Pig Destroyer "polished" is a misnomer from the word go. But there is something to be said about the pristine production that accompanies Pig Destroyer albums, including this one. Yet the sick barrage of deranged lyrics, crazy blast beats, monster riffs and psychotic samples make you forget how clean it all sounds. *Phantom Limb* was the band's fourth studio album, released in 2007 on Relapse. It's an absolute must-have for any and all grindcore fans – really all metal fans in general. At this point in their careers Pig Destroyer on a bad day is still better than about 90% of all other grindcore bands. That's got to be something close to scientific fact by now.

Recommended Track: "Jupiter's Eye"

468. Nifelheim - Nifelheim

Sweden's Nifelheim are one of those second wave black
metal bands that did everything they could to rekindle the
magic of the earliest days of the genre. Call them rip-offs,
call them cheesy, call them whatever you want...they don't
give a f*ck. And really why should they? Isn't black metal
all about not giving a f*ck? In all seriousness though
Nifelheim was one of the more extreme black metal bands
to emerge in that gloried second wave in the mid-'90s
playing a stellar thrash-infused mania. This, their debut
album, was released through Necropolis Records in
1995. From the absolute throat-slitting songs to the
insanely creepy/campy album cover, Nifelheim was pretty
blatant in their desire to burn poseurs at the stake. This is
an album that was trying to be as nasty and gritty as
possible and completely succeeded.

Recommended Track: "Black Curse"

467. Gun - Gun

In 1968 a relatively unknown band emerged out of the U.K. by the name of Gun. They would release two albums, have nominal success with one Top 10 hit and then vanish forever. But their impact is immense, probably more than anyone realizes. Their self-titled debut album hit the streets a full year before the first Zeppelin record and two years before the first Sabbath record. That's important, especially seeing as they come from the same tiny island nation. 1968 saw it's share of tripped out, acid rock bands but few had the "evil" artwork, lyrics and sounds this band had. They are truly one of the unknown godfathers of the modern stoner rock movement for sure. The horns and occasional strings on this record may throw some people off. They may listen to this and want to know how the hell it fits with metal today. But the fact that bands as wide ranging as Judas Priest to Japanese doom act Church of Misery have covered these guys must mean something.

Recommended Track: "Race With The Devil"

466. Enslaved - Ruun

Norway's Enslaved started out in the early '90s as one of the darlings of the storied second wave of black metal. Their split with Emperor is the stuff of legends and their early releases reflected all the power and glory of those halcyon days of the black metal scene. Almost as quickly as they appeared on the scene though they began to change the scene from within. Their music would start to morph into this sort of post-black metal/Viking metal/prog metal hybrid that truly sounded unlike anything else at the time. *Ruun* is the band's ninth studio album, released in 2006 via Candlelight Records. This album took that progressive black metal sound they had started to perfect and really stretched it to new and exciting places. It's like black metal meets Iron Maiden meets Pink Floyd and is an excellent example of this band's ability to write compelling songs rooted in black metal, but experimenting with multiple genres at the same time.

Recommended Track: "Path To Vanir"

465. Mortician – Zombie Apocalypse

When you talk about goregrind and brutal death metal one band should always come to mind. That would be New York's Mortician. There are very few bands in the world who've had success playing the kind of super extreme death metal that these guys churn out. Drum machines turned up to a million beats per minute? Check. Vocal growls so oppressively low they almost sound like a bass guitar? Check. Copious amounts of killer horror movie samples on pretty much every song? Check. You put those three things together and you pretty much sum up Mortician. Now that's not to trivialize what these guys do. They are the end result of pushing death metal to its absolute limit and in turn have influenced a ton of goregrind and death metal bands the world over. *Zombie Apocalypse* was the bands fourth official release, (three of which were EPs, including this one) originally released on Relapse Records in 1998.

Recommended Track: "Zombie Apocalypse"

464. The Gathering – Nighttime Birds

Regardless of style, one of the best musical imports from the Netherlands has been The Gathering. The Gathering have had three very distinct phases to their career. Phase I saw them start off as a doom-inspired pseudo-death metal band. Phase II started with the addition of Anneke van Giersbergen on vocals and saw them begin to transition to this doom metal/shoegaze hybrid. If metal is your first love this is probably their high water mark for you as it includes some of their most progressive albums while still maintaining some modicum of heaviness. Phase III saw them move pretty much completely away from metal altogether and really embrace the more ambient, alt rock, radio friendly passages from previous albums. *Nighttime Birds* was the band's fourth full length album, released in 1997 on Century Media Records. This album falls smack in the middle of that Phase II period. There are still some heavy, dark moments on this album but it is also one of the most beautiful and serene albums you'll find on this list.

Recommended Track: "The Earth Is My Witness"

463. Sigh – Infidel Art

Around the same time some Scandinavians were running around killing each other and burning down churches Japan's Sigh was on the other side of the world producing some pretty progressive and unique black metal. The first thing you should always remember when dealing with any band from Japan, no matter what genre, is that they are never going to sound exactly like what you've come to expect. I don't know if it's the cultural influences or the fact that they are isolated on this island nation out in the Pacific, but there's something a little 'off' in a good way when you talk Japanese bands. Sigh is no different. The total left turns found on this album would also become the norm for them down the road…and there are a lot of left turns on this album. *Infidel Art* was the band's second full-length, released in 1995 on Cacophonous Records.

Recommended Track: "Izuna"

462. Sepultura - Schizophrenia

If you don't know Brazil's Sepultura by now you are probably reading the wrong book. From their humble beginnings in Brazil to eventually having videos plastered all over MTV, Sepultura was easily one of the most recognizable names in extreme music. *Schizophrenia* was the band's second full-length album, originally released in 1987. Roughly three years after its initial release it would get a proper U.S. release through Roadrunner Records. One could argue that this album is decidedly more thrash-oriented than the previous album, or any album to come after it. It's a raw, nasty thrash record that honestly held very little clues to the almost constant shifting in styles this band would undertake from album to album. While it suffers from less than stellar production, it's the production that helps give it the right atmosphere for these songs to germinate properly. Not to mention that killer riffs abound here for anyone willing to partake.

Recommended Track: "To The Wall"

461. Grief – Come To Grief

When you look at the long, strange history of doom metal, it's safe to say that Boston's Grief were, and still are, criminally underrated. Their brand of crust covered doom metal was not the most popular style of metal when they were putting out albums. Yet they managed to put out some highly influential pieces of music that both the crust and doom scenes owe a ton to. *Come To Grief* was the band's third release (second full-length) put out in 1994 on Century Media. This was their one and only album with C.M. as they would spend a big chunk of their career in the Theologian/Pessimiser camp. If you think back to the metal landscape in 1994 and see what bands had grabbed the attention of the metal majority you can easily see how this band was underappreciated. Simply put, it's because they were way ahead of their time. If you're a fan of that Eyehategod/Iron Monkey style of sludgy, nasty doom then this album is going to be right up your alley.

Recommended Track: "I Hate You"

460. Macabre – Sinister Slaughter

Macabre have always played this sort of thrash and death metal hybrid with a very heavy focus on serial killers and mass murderers. But they took it to the next level on their second full-length album, 1993's *Sinister Slaughter*, released on Nuclear Blast Records. There are songs about all the usual culprits – Richard Ramirez, Ted Bundy, John Wayne Gacy, Jeffrey Dahmer, The Zodiac Killer, etc. There isn't a song on this record though that doesn't degenerate into some sort of goofiness, whether it be the lyrics, the vocals or the actual music itself. Picture a heavier GWAR minus the ridiculous get-ups. It's a pretty entertaining album and even though the lyrical material is about some of the most brutal and bloodthirsty sons of bitches in the world Macabre is somehow able to deliver the content in a way that could actually have you smiling at certain points. It's pretty genius if you think about it.

Recommended Track: "Nightstalker"

459. Phobia – Means of Existence

Phobia are equal parts crust and grind. The crust kids love their politics and the grind fans their delivery. The beauty of Phobia though is that they have also toured with hardcore and death metal bands and fit right at home on those tours as well. Their sound is rooted in the killer SoCal punk scene but they were so much heavier than any other bands coming out of that scene at the time. They've been around for a long time and in true crust/grind fashion they've put their name on about 25 various splits, EPs, and full-lengths over the last 20 or so years. There's no shortage of material for you to check out. But I suggest you start with this one. *Means of Existence* was Phobia's first full-length album, released in 1998 on Slap-A-Ham Records. It's a non-stop assault. From the first creepy sample to the last blast beat, this thing is an absolute beast of a record. Not only will this record get your head banging but it will make you want to rage against the oppressive powers that be (like good crust should).

Recommended Track: "Rape Theft Murder"

458. Rage – Reign of Fear

Reign of Fear is technically the debt album from Germany's Rage, originally released on Noise Records in 1986. 'Technically' because the same line-up had recorded a full-length album and an EP under the name Avenger, but due to a naming conflict they changed to Rage and the rest, as they say, is history. History has unfortunately not been as kind to this band as some of their contemporaries, despite the fact these guys never really stopped recording. (They've recorded an amazing 21 albums over the last 25+ years.) Rage play a killer hybrid of melodic thrash and early power metal. It's not the most technically proficient album you'll hear but what it lacks in technicality it makes up for in being able to get your head banging. There are plenty of fist-pumping anthems on this album and it stands as one of the better German releases from a year that saw several exceptional ones.

Recommended Track: "Deceiver"

457. Baroness – Blue Record

I think almost everyone who comes to these pages has probably at least heard of Baroness by now. They've quickly grown into one of the most critically acclaimed bands in the metal world. Their brand of Southern metal is one that's heavy enough for fans of the more brutal stuff, and also accessible enough that they've gained a ton of fans over the last few records who wouldn't normally have picked up an album this heavy. Between the catchy melodies, the clean vocals and the ability to write memorable riffs, these guys are able to blend multiple genres into a fairly unique sound. *"Blue Record"* was the band's second full-length album, released on Relapse Records in 2009. It's an album that's had a ton of accolades dumped on it. Decibel Magazine called it the best record of 2009 and LA Weekly named it the "20th Greatest Metal Album of All Time." Debatable rankings aside, this is a really killer album, and has proved in the short time it's been out to be immensely influential.

Recommended Track: "The Sweetest Curse"

456. Dead Horse – Peaceful Death and Pretty Flowers

Some bands just simply defy logical description and challenge anyone who listens to pigeonhole them into one specific genre. Such is the case with Texas' Dead Horse, a band that so seamlessly combined genres as varied as thrash, pseudo-death metal, doom, and stoner rock. This band were geniuses in terms of bending the entire metal spectrum to their will. They were literally all over the map, sometimes within the confines of an individual song. They could rip out a thrash song or switch it up and write songs that clearly had an influence on the "Southern metal" movement. Dead Horse were true experimentalists who were looking to expand the boundaries of what you could do with metal. *Peaceful Death and Pretty Flowers* was the band's second full-length album, released in 1991 jointly on Big Chief Records and Metal Blade. The album was also re-released by Relapse Records in 1999.

Recommended Track: "Peaceful Death"

455. Twisted Sister – Stay Hungry

If there was one album everyone knows from Twisted Sister it would be this one. *Stay Hungry* was the band's third full length album, released in 1984 on Atlantic Records. It also has sold over three million copies. But the early '80s, as we know, were a great time for bands that straddled that metal/hard rock line. Bands like Twisted Sister, who were heavy enough for the hardcore metalheads to dig, yet accessible enough for chicks with big hair to request them at the school dance, were an instant home run for major labels back in the day. Surely when you hear the two big singles on this album – "We're Not Gonna Take It" and "I Wanna Rock" – there are going to be people questioning the inclusion of this album at all. But when you hear tracks like "Burn In Hell", "The Beast" and "Horror Teria" you realize that this was a heavy metal band at heart. Forget the good-timing, hard rock singles. These guys had their dark moments, and really added some killer material to the lexicon of traditional metal.

Recommended Track: "Burn In Hell"

454. Ulver – Nattens Madrigal

To say that Norway's Ulver is an experimental band is like saying the Pope is Catholic. It's a brutally obvious understatement. Their debut album was lush, atmospheric black metal. Their second album was completely acoustic, including strings and cello accompaniment and sung exclusively in this choir-like manner. Their third album, *Nattens Madrigal*, is a lo-fi, face-melting, non-stop black metal explosion. Simply put, this is as close as Ulver ever came, or ever will come, to being mentioned in the same breath as bands like Mayhem and Darkthrone. *Nattens Madrigal* was originally released in 1997 on Century Media. It was the first and only album they originally released through Century Media. There was also a long-standing rumor surrounding this album (since refuted by the band) that in order to achieve the raw and primal sound they recorded it on an eight-track cassette recorder and then used the bulk of the advance that the label gave them to buy fancy clothes, drugs, etc. Refuted or not, it just adds to this album's lore.

Recommended Track: "Hymne II: Wolf and The Devil"

453. Benediction – Transcend The Rubicon

Partially famous for being the band that gave current Napalm Death singer, Barney Greenway, his start Benediction has always been a bit overshadowed by some of the other U.K. bands that were making killer records at the time this one was released. But Benediction, as far as mid-paced, '90s death metal goes, was pretty damn good in their own right. *Transcend The Rubicon* was the band's third full-length album, released in 1993 on Nuclear Blast Records. It has a style very similar to what a lot of the Swedish bands were doing and it's no wonder they toured constantly with the likes of Dismember (who were label mates at the time). They also have a somewhat progressive sound that plays well if you're a fan of bands like Nocturnus, Pestilence or Athiest, for example (although they aren't nearly as experimental as any of those bands). Plus tracks like "I Bow To None" are prime examples of that galloping death metal style that can still get pits moving.

Recommended Track: "I Bow To None"

452. Indestroy - Indestroy

Here today, gone tomorrow. Sometimes bands have 'what it takes' yet just implode like a black hole. Take for example '80s thrash/speed outfit Indestroy. They were originally from Maryland but relocated to the Bay Area at some point in their relatively brief time together. They put out two records on New Renaissance Records. Their self-titled effort was their debut full-length, originally released in 1987. It would be an obvious understatement to say that this band and this album are completely underrated. Indestroy specialized in blistering speed/thrash metal that was not unlike early Megadeth. Unfortunately, both this band and album are considered underrated because after their next release they promptly broke up. It's hard to stay in the collective metal conscious when leaving behind such a brief history with an equally brief discography. With that said, don't allow their small output to blind you to this amazing record.

Recommended Track: "U.S.S.A."

451. Katatonia – Dance of December Souls

Sweden's Katatonia would eventually and gradually massage their sound over time into this sort of lush and ethereal post-metal/alt-rock vibe. However, at their inception they were one of the pioneers of merging death and doom sounds. *Dance of December Souls* was the band's debut album, originally released in 1993 on No Fashion Records. This album, along with albums from bands such as My Dying Bride and Paradise Lost, among others, would take the epic song structures of doom metal and combine them with death metal styled vocals and the occasional death metal breakdown to form this really unique sound. The overall aesthetics of this album though are strictly rooted in doom metal (specifically the European brand of doom) and even incorporates some slight black metal influences as well. If you're a fan of heavy, atmospheric, dark music than this album is going to be right in your wheelhouse.

Recommended Track: "In Silence Enshrined"

450. Pungent Stench – For God Your Soul…For Me Your Flesh

For Austria's Pungent Stench there is just one way to describe their sound on this album: death metal. In fact early on they were about as death metal as they came. But as they evolved so did their desire to branch out, mixing in some seriously random genres that you just didn't ever hear other death metal bands experimenting with. Their lyrical content also, at times, makes that of bands like GWAR and Macabre look downright childish. These were some seriously depraved dudes when it came to taking some very taboo (mostly sexual subjects) and toying with them. *For God Your Soul…For Me Your Flesh* was the band's debut full-length album, originally released on Nuclear Blast Records in 1990. Forget for a second that this album is a loosely themed, tongue-in-cheek album about cannibalism and just take in all that sonic brutality. Upon its release this was an absolute beast of a death metal album and it has stood the test of time very well.

Recommended Track: "Just Let Me Rot"

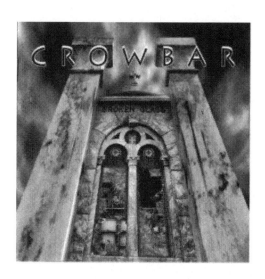

449. Crowbar – Broken Glass

When they initially crawled forth from the swamps of Louisiana, Crowbar were a solid band with solid material. But it wasn't until their fourth studio album, *Broken Glass*, that they started to really take it to the next level. The production on this album is exceptional and the songwriting itself is top notch. It should also be noted that this is the first Crowbar album that Eyehategod guitarist, Jimmy Bower, shows up on drums. *Broken Glass*, as mentioned, was the bands fourth studio album, released in 1996 on Pavement Music. The style of songs on here are exactly what you would expect from a Crowbar record – down-tuned, brooding, sludgy metal with blasts of hardcore-inspired breakdowns. This album started a string of albums that were some of the best material they would ever release.

Recommended Track: "Conquering"

448. Desultory – Into Eternity

Drastic and unforeseen shifts in musical direction aside, Sweden's Desultory should be remembered for being one of the great contributors to the history of Swedish death metal, and this album is one reason why. *Into Eternity* was the first full length album by Desultory, released in 1993 on Metal Blade Records. Apart from being their first album for one of the biggest metal labels in the world it was also an absolutely key addition to the foundation of Swedish death metal and its rise to supremacy. It was not only extremely important to the melodic/Gothenburg sound but it also borrowed from the more brutal American scene as well. This combination of styles would give Desultory a somewhat progressive, yet heavy-handed, style that dozens of bands were attempting to copy afterwards. Total shame that when we think of the great bands who helped put Swedish death metal on the map that we don't think of Desultory and this album more often.

Recommended Track: "Into Eternity"

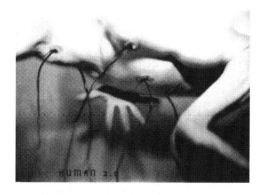

447. Nasum – Human 2.0

The Indian Ocean tsunami of 2004 essentially ended this band as vocalist/guitarist/co-founder Mieszko Talarczyk was killed while vacationing in Thailand. It's a shame because they had already established themselves as head and shoulders above all other grind contenders. Their brand of grindcore was the best of both worlds for fans. Not only was it some of the heaviest, most abrasive, and most powerful music you'll hear, it was also some of the cleanest sounding grindcore to blow up your speakers. Nasum found that happy medium between "kvlt" and "polished" so that it not only sounded brutal but the sound quality was top notch as well. *Human 2.0* was the band's second album, released in 2000 on Relapse Records. This album took what they did on their debut and expanded on it. The entire album feels bigger and heavier than the previous album, which, knowing how important that record wound up being is saying a lot

Recommended Track: "Shadows"

446. Nasty Savage – Nasty Savage

The list of bands (both classic and obscure) that Metal Blade worked with in the early to mid-80s is pretty damn impressive. One of those fairly obscure bands though that deserves a little more attention is Florida's Nasty Savage. They were known back in the day for their crazy stage antics (and there's actually some interesting live footage online if you care to search for it). But in reality they were so much more than a gimmick band. Nasty Savage played an awesome hybrid of thrash and power metal. Most of their songs fell into that mid-tempo school of thrash that borrowed greatly from traditional metal sources. Their debut, self-titled album was released in 1985. It may not be the most technically proficient album you're going to see on this list, yet this band was highly instrumental in the formation of a Florida metal scene that would become downright dominant over the course of the next decade after this album's release.

Recommended Track: "Metal Knights"

445. Moonspell - Wolfheart

Wolfheart was originally released in 1995 on Century Media Records and to this day still stands as the heaviest and darkest album that Portugal's Moonspell has gifted us. Moonspell was never a band that blew you away with blast beats and grind. Their brand of heavy was always about darkness and atmosphere and by the time this album came out what little bits of black metal they had on their debut EP were all but gone. The vocals alternate between Type O Negative styled clean vocals and legible growls. They also sang about things like vampires and werewolves so the Goth world latched onto this album as well. (The release of this album was honestly perfect timing, with vampires infiltrating every aspect of pop culture.) All discussion about vampires aside, if you like gothic-styled metal than this album should be right up your alley. It's quite lush and beautiful in certain parts, yet mysterious and brooding in others. Just the way a great gothic novel or film should be as well.

Recommended Track: "Vampiria"

444. Nile – Amongst the Catacombs of Nephren-Ka

If you are looking for violently technical death metal with pristine production and amazing musicianship then you really need to look no further than South Carolina's Nile. This band has spent roughly 20 years creating some of the most technically proficient death metal around. I would be remiss if in talking about Nile I didn't at least touch on their somewhat obsessive fascination with all things Ancient Egypt. Band name, album artwork, album titles, song titles, and lyrics all revolve around the history, mythology, religion, art, etc. of Ancient Egypt. Their music reflects all of this as well. Whether it's the actual howls in a song like "The Howling of the Jinn" or the bombastic opening of "Ramses, Bringer of War" these guys know how to properly capture the mood. *Amongst The Catacombs of Nephren-Ka* was the band's debut album, released in 1998 on Relapse Records. This is the album that put this band on the metal map and entered them into the discussion of best death metal band in the world.

Recommended Track: "The Howling of the Jinn"

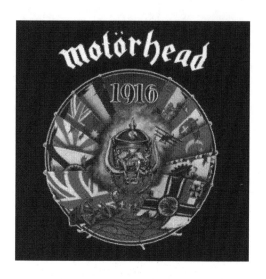

443. Motörhead - 1916

This is Motörhead's ninth studio album, originally released in 1991 on WTG/Epic. Sometimes I think because this band just does whatever the hell they want that people forget they were often on a major label. What other band can get away with writing a song like "Angel City" or "I'm So Bad (Baby I Don't Care)" with those lyrics ("I make love to mountain lions…") and still expect to be on said major label the next day. Well, who the hell is going to fire Lemmy?! Although the preceding three albums had some highlights this might be the best overall album they did since Iron Fist, which was released almost a decade prior. Even songs you would expect to be throwaways are absolute rippers. Yet, at the same time this is a fairly accessible record by Motörhead standards. In fact, I'm still shocked 20+ years later that this album didn't have a bigger presence on commercial radio at the time. It was however nominated for a Grammy, which is frankly, shocking and amazing. (It lost to Metallica's "Black" album, so there's that.)

Recommended Track: "I'm So Bad (Baby I Don't Care)"

442. Suffocation – Pierced From Within

New York's Suffocation were all about laying down the sick riffs and simultaneously pummeling their listeners into submission. They coupled crazy guitar work with a rhythm section that is straight up bowel movement-inducing at times. Possibly no other album showcases their talents the way *Pierced From Within* did. *Pierced From Within* was the band's third full-length album, released on Roadrunner Records in 1995. By 1995 metal was supposedly "dead" according to the mainstream press. Unfortunately I think Roadrunner started to believe some of those headlines and this would be the last album Suffocation would release for them as they continued to purge most of the heavier acts off their roster. But it wasn't before Suffocation delivered one of the better death metal albums of the decade and one of the best albums of their storied discography.

Recommended Track: "Pierced From Within"

441. Anathema – The Silent Enigma

Every band that drastically changes their sound over time has that 'transition' record if you will; the album where the roots of their old sound successfully mingle with the seeds of their new direction. For England's Anathema that transition album was *The Silent Enigma*. Released in 1995 on Peaceville Records, *The Silent Enigma* was the band's second full-length album. It's immensely important in the history of the band because it's the first album guitarist Vincent Cavanagh handled vocal duties, which was part of what gave this band an entirely new dimension from their debut. This album can still be considered a doom album. The darkness and misery on these songs is palpable for sure and Cavanagh does as much growling on this record as he does clean singing. But there are elements of this record, shades of what was to come if you will, that absolutely pointed to this band becoming one of the best alt/space/shoegaze rock bands in the world.

Recommended Track: "Shroud of Frost"

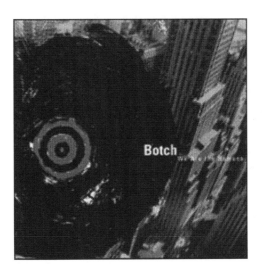

440. Botch – We Are The Romans

I personally believe there are only a few hardcore bands that came on the scene and absolutely changed the game so to speak. In fact I could probably count about ten total. The rest, although might be great at what they do, never broke new ground or really influenced large numbers of people outside of the hardcore scene. Washington's Botch did both and did it well. They are one of the true masters of discordant sound, complete with virtuoso riffing, and their legacy is still alive and well today over a decade after breaking up. *We Are The Romans* was the band's second and final full-length album (not counting a bunch of comp albums), released in 1999 on Hydra Head Records. These guys would be done as a band only three years later. It's a shame really because they are absolutely one of those bands who would have been fascinating to follow how their sound progressed over time.

Recommended Track: "Mondrian Was a Liar"

439. Dark Tranquillity - Skydancer

Skydancer was debut album from Sweden's Dark Tranquillity, originally released on Spinefarm Records in 1993. It would later be reissued multiple times (and often included the 1995 EP, *Of Chaos And Eternal Night*). It's an understatement to say that Dark Tranquillity were serious ground breakers in the world of death metal. Death metal wasn't supposed to have this much melody or atmosphere. Death metal wasn't supposed to include the occasional clean vocals or even clean female vocals. Death metal wasn't supposed to include the occasional acoustic guitar interlude. But Dark Tranquillity did all of those things and more. They helped set up a blueprint by which European death metal bands (and metal bands in general) have been copying ever since. This album is a great snapshot of melodic Swedish death metal at it's best and has stood the test of time to still sound fresh over 20 years after its release.

Recommended Track: "Crimson Winds"

438. Helstar – Burning Star

Burning Star is the debut album from Texas' Helstar, released in 1984 on Combat Records. First of all when you start off as label mates of Megadeth, Exodus, Venom, and Possessed you are going to be overshadowed, no matter how good you are. But the truth of it is that this album was solid enough to at least stay competitive with the releases of those bands and had more to do with the formation of the current power metal scene than any of those bands could realistically claim. Although never officially breaking up, Helstar would battle line-up changes, as well as label changes, throughout their career. They would also relocate to an already crowded metal scene in California at one point. Unfortunately all of this probably added to their inability to garner the acclaim that their early material deserves, especially this album. When we look back at the early formation of the current power metal scene this album should absolutely be included in the discussion of seminal and influential releases.

Recommended Track: "The Shadows of Iga"

437. Nuclear Assault – Handle With Care

Nuclear Assault was formed by bassist Dan Lilker after he parted ways with Anthrax. Lilker losing his position with them was, frankly, a boon for the rest of us. Nuclear Assault was heavier and angrier than his previous band and this album is 'Exhibit A' as to why. *Handle With Care* was the band's third full-length album, released in 1989 on In-Effect Records (the sister label of Relativity Records). It charted as high as #126 on the Billboard 200 and was, in affect, the high watermark for this band's career. But if you've been reading along this far you should have gleaned that record sales are not the most important thing at play. What I do care a lot about is the quality of the product and the influence it had on the scene in general and in both cases this album passes the test with flying colors. *Handle With Care* is easily one of the better thrash albums from the late 80s and a must own for thrash fans.

Recommended Track: "Critical Mass"

436. Arcturus – Aspera Hiems Symfonia

Aspera Hiems Symfonia was the debut album from Norway's Arcturus, released in 1995 on Ancient Lore Creations (an imprint label of Misanthropy Records). In the U.S. the album would be licensed to Century Media who would release it on their Century Black imprint. With the album after this, Arcturus would start to really experiment and all but drop the black metal aesthetics that permeated this album. But to be honest no one was truly surprised by this. As heavy as this album could be it was laden with bizarre, carnival-like keyboards, crazy time signature changes not found in the black metal world at the time, and quite frankly some sections that were downright silly sounding in comparison to some of the creepiness they could dish out. There was this strange dichotomy between the bizarre and the brutal that gave Arcturus a sound all their own and influenced a lot of the progressive metal that came after it both within and outside the black metal scene.

Recommended Track: "Wintry Grey"

435. Gorguts - Obscura

Canada's Gorguts started their careers on Roadrunner playing some seriously brutal death metal. Their second album saw a slight shift towards a more progressive and dissonant approach to the genre. However they were dropped from the label shortly thereafter. They went into this sort of hibernation but emerged on the other end with the album that would define their careers. *Obscura* was released in 1998 on Olympic Recordings and is the type of album that you either love or hate. It's obviously a death metal record at its core but it's so unique that you also had a lot of death metal purists whining at the time of its release about the insanity that takes place on this record. It's so fragmented and schizophrenic that I wouldn't be surprised if it still goes over some people's heads. Needless to say this album was a major game-changer not only in death metal circles but in extreme music in general.

Recommended Track: "Earthly Love"

434. Coroner – Punishment For Decadence

Although their sound would progress with the times and Switzerland's Coroner would become the "Rush of thrash metal," their early material was as volatile as thrash would get. *Punishment For Decadence* was the band's second album, released in 1988 on Noise Records. You could argue this is Coroner's 'lost record'. Their later, more prog-influenced material got plenty of love (or vitriol depending on who you talk to). Their debut album gets plenty of love, as well as, their *No More Color* album. But this album had arguably better production than the debut and you could also argue a better group of songs than most of their other offerings. This was the album that gave us a taste of their prog leanings and a vision of what was yet to come, yet still retained the raw, killer shredding that made them so beloved within thrash circles. A highly underrated album from an equally underrated band.

Recommended Track: "Skeleton On Your Shoulder"

433. Darkthrone – Ravishing Grimness

Ravishing Grimness was the seventh studio album in the long and storied career of Norway's Darkthrone. Released originally in 1999 on Moonfog Productions it's an album that has grown better with time. This was the album where the Darkthrone sound first started to shift away from the second wave black metal that made them household names. Almost completely gone were the constant blast beats and (purposely) tin can production. This album was cleaner, easier on the ears, and maintained, for the most part, a steady galloping pace. Some purists balked. They still balk today at this band. This is as good a black metal album as you'll hear from this time period and was an exceptional change of pace that would lead the band down the road of successful experimentation and further classic albums.

Recommended Track: "The Beast"

432. Dead Horse – Horsecore: An Unrelated Story That's Time Consuming

Dead Horse only released two full length albums in their original incarnation but they both wound up on this list. The little band from Texas had a Texas-sized influence on the thrash world and a lot of other scenes. So much so that Relapse thought enough of their work to re-issue both albums in 1999. *Horsecore* (as we will call it for short) was the band's debut full-length, released in 1989. It's a thrash record for sure but includes distinct punk rock influences, as well as, the Dead Horse sense of humor that somewhat defined their career. I'm not saying these guys were tongue-in-cheek ridiculous like GWAR, but they knew how to take serious subjects and make catchy songs out of them. There really isn't any good way to describe this band without making them sound like a generic thrash band which they were the absolute antithesis of.

Recommended Track: "Flowers For The Dead"

431. Dimmu Borgir – Enthrone Darkness Triumphant

Black metal in general has always been a divisive genre, with people constantly arguing over what's "true" or "kvlt" and what isn't. There are very few bands within the black metal world that have been at the front line of that divisiveness the way Norway's Dimmu Borgir has. *Enthrone Darkness Triumphant* was the band's third full-length album, released in 1997 on Nuclear Blast Records. This was the album that 'broke' this band – the album that took them out of the basements of black metal and into the arenas of accessibility. While their brand of super polished, symphonic black metal was a misnomer for those looking to keep the genre in the proverbial wintry forests of Scandinavia, the fact that this album became a gateway record for so many new fans to discover black metal should alone count for its inclusion here. Yet the fact also remains that as far as symphonic black metal is concerned, this album is absolutely top-notch in its execution.

Recommended Track: "The Night Masquerade"

430. Master's Hammer - Ritual

Born in the former Czechoslovakia in the late 80s Master's Hammer should be credited as one of the earliest second wave black metal bands. They were a band that truly bridged the gap between the first wave bands like Bathory and Venom and their Norwegian counterparts like Emperor and Darkthrone. Yet when you read up on the history of black metal these guys are only mentioned by a select few. Why? Well, one guess is that they were from the now Czech Republic and not Norway or Sweden (or even England). It is safe to say if this album came snowballing out of the Norse lands we'd be talking a lot more about this band and this album. *Ritual* was their debut, originally released in 1991 on Monitor Records (and later re-issued by Osmose Productions). It's a dark and triumphant record and one that Fenriz of Darkthrone called the "first Norwegian black metal album, even though they are from Czechoslovakia." High praise indeed.

Recommended Track: "Ritual"

429. Paradise Lost – Draconian Times

Paradise Lost started out as one of the Unholy Trinity of British death/doom/Gothic metal, alongside My Dying Bride and Anathema. *Draconian Times* was the band's "transition" album, the album that bridges the gap between dark and depressing British doom and a much more polished sound. But if you're a fan of the Gothic side of metal or really any band that falls into the ridiculously broad "Gothic" term, then this album will be right up your darkened alley. *Draconian Times* was originally released in 1995 on Music For Nations in Europe and Relativity in North America. Despite the fact this album features cleaner vocals than on any other Paradise Lost album up to this point, and the music itself is way more accessible, the overall gloominess that Paradise Lost perfected from day one is still ever-present. This is, simply put, a masterpiece of the Gothic metal genre and proof that you don't need to be oppressively heavy to bring down a shroud of darkness.

Recommended Track: "Forever Failure"

428. Sentenced – Shadows of the Past

Shadows of the Past is the debut full length album from Finland's Sentenced, released in 1991 on Thrash Records (it would later be re-issued twice by Century Media after the band signed with them). To say that this is purely death metal would be a bit of a misnomer. There is actually some pretty fantastic thrash worship going on here at certain points, and the progressive elements that this band would hang their collective hat on with future releases was first conceived here. But, with all of that said, this is still some seriously heavy European-styled death metal. It's very similar to what their Swedish brethren were producing at the time, and easily their heaviest album. Clearly this band's influence upon the metal world rests mostly with their later releases. But the importance of this record on the blossoming Finnish metal scene absolutely can not be understated.

Recommended Track: "When The Moment Of Death Arrives"

427. Pentagram – Pentagram (Relentless)

Basically a perpetual club band who never got passed the demo stage of their career for the entire decade of the 70s, Pentagram would finally release a full-length album in the mid 80s but even then the history of it is shrouded in confusion. In 1982 the band (calling themselves Death Row) would record a demo version of this album. It wouldn't see a proper release until 1985 under the Pentagram banner and with a different mix. In 1993 Peaceville Records would re-issue this album with a new track listing, the original 1982 mix, and a new album title, *Relentless*. Most people now know this album as "Relentless" because it wasn't until the Peaceville reissue that the average metal fan finally heard it. This album still, to this day, stands as one of the heaviest albums this outfit ever recorded. It's chock full of some seriously sick riffs, Bobby Liebling's classic and unmistakable vocals, and the most doom this side of a Black Sabbath record.

Recommended Track: "20 Buck Spin"

426. Grave – Into The Grave

When you talk about death metal one of the places on this fair Earth of ours that you should immediately think of is Sweden. And when you think of Swedish death metal there should be a handful of bands that immediately come to mind. Grave was never the most technical band in the world. They aren't going to wow you with guitar histrionics. But they are as heavy as a dozen rhinos and they were among one of the first Swedish bands to really take the Swedish death metal sound to the masses with their debut album. This album was originally released in 1991 on Century Media Records. It's got any early semblance of that buzz saw guitar sound and some great hooks that will have you headbanging in no time. Grave has been pretty consistent throughout their career, offering up some quality releases for quite some time. But as far as metal debuts go this is a pretty solid addition to a growing list of classics and remains highly influential, within the death metal scene especially.

Recommended Track: "For Your God"

425. Running Wild – Branded and Exiled

In metal's earliest days Germany was especially potent when it came to thrash, speed and traditional metal. One such band that incorporated all three styles at one point was Running Wild. Most people now know these guys as "the pirate band" because…well, they've spent the last 20+ years writing pirate-themed albums. But before they became 'that band that sings about pirates' they were actually a pretty heavy thrash/traditional metal act that wrote about some pretty dark stuff (including Mordor for all you Lord of the Rings fans out there). In fact this was the last album they did before they went all Jolly Roger. (Which I say in complete good nature. Yar.) *Branded and Exiled* was the second full-length album, originally released in 1985 on Noise Records. It's a fantastic example of mid-tempo, German thrash metal, complete with sweeping solos and grunted vocals.

Recommended Track: "Gods of Iron"

424. Manowar – Battle Hymns

Few bands have the cult following and have made a name for themselves in the metal world the way New York's Manowar has. *Battle Hymns* was the band's debut album, originally released in 1982 on Liberty Records. (Liberty Records had been around forever and at one point in the 1950s worked with the likes of Henry Mancini and Eddie Cochran.) In 1982 there was still a lot of crossover between the hard rock world and this still fairly new metal thing that was going on. You had Priest and Maiden and even bands like Venom, but this Manowar album is the perfect example of that hard rock/metal hybrid that was still very prevalent at the time. You could go so far as to argue that if they weren't singing about being metal and Eric Adams wasn't hitting the high notes then this might not be considered a metal record at all. Classifications be damned though because this is the album that launched the careers of one of the biggest metal bands in the world.

Recommended Track: "Death Tone"

423. Death Angel – Act III

Death Angel were one of the many talented thrash bands to emerge out of Northern California, especially the Bay Area. *Act III* was the band's third full-length album, originally released in 1990 on Geffen Records. Compared to their debut album, this one sounds slick and maybe a touch over-produced. It doesn't detract from what is a full album of excellent second generation thrash metal. Death Angel would go through a lot of ups and downs with this record. Not the least of which was a bus accident while on tour that left their drummer in critical condition. To add insult to injury, rumors have swirled that their label wanted them to replace their drummer in order to keep touring and when they refused were subsequently dropped, only to break up soon after. Regardless of any tribulations surrounding this release it still stands as one of the best thrash records to emerge out of the early '90s and helped cement their legacy.

Recommended Track: "Seemingly Endless Time"

422. Unleashed – Across The Open Sea

Across The Open Sea was the third full length album by Sweden's Unleashed, released in 1993 on Century Media Records. This album, actually gets a slightly bad rap on a certain level because the production quality is considered sub par by some. (The album was originally produced by the band themselves. Century Media would eventually re-master and re-release it over a decade later.) However look at it from the flip side of the coin. The raw production adds to the mood of this record and gives it a certain level of bitter and depressive darkness it may not have had with slick production techniques. Regardless of what you think of the production, the riffs on this album are absolutely killer and their Norse-themed lyrics were trendsetting at the time. A classic piece of metal and a great snapshot of the amazing Swedish death metal scene in the early '90s.

Recommended Track: "The One Insane"

421. Necrophagia – Season of the Dead

When people talk about the pioneers of death metal one band name that gets left off the list way more than it should is Ohio's Necrophagia. They were not only pioneers of death metal but of horror-themed metal in general. Their debut album, *Season of the Dead*, was originally released in 1987 on New Renaissance Records. Unfortunately, right after this album was released, the band would break up and be lost to the annals of metal for over a decade. In that time there was a second, posthumously released album in 1990 but by then these guys were an afterthought. They would become one of those "cvlt" acts that few people remembered and for those that did very few actually owned this record. That would all change when Phil Anselmo would play guitar on their comeback album in 1998 (under a pseudonym) and that same year this album would be re-issued by Red Stream, opening this band up to an entirely new fan base, which they were more than deserving of.

Recommended Track: "Insane For Blood"

420. Onslaught – The Force

England's Onslaught actually started out as a crusty hardcore/punk band (and those influences can still be heard on their first album) before shifting their sound to a straight ahead thrash attack. One wouldn't consider Onslaught a "crossover" band, but their history is something to keep in mind when you listen to their earlier material. *The Force* was Onslaught's second full length album, released in 1986 on the Under One Flag label. (With distribution through Combat Records as well.) The guitars and some of the songwriting itself reminds me a lot of classic Megadeth, and these guys were not afraid to write songs about and use imagery of a "Satanic" nature. This album is pure, thrashing aggression and when we talk about the unheralded classics of the genre, those albums that simply deserve more praise than they get, this one should easily be included.

Recommended Track: "Fight With The Beast"

419. Exciter – Long Live The Loud

One of the first Canadian bands to really make a mark on the metal world was Exciter. Exploding forth with their vicious brand of metal, these guys are considered by many to be one of the pioneering bands of the speed metal genre. There are good reasons for that and this album is one of them. *Long Live The Loud* was their third full-length album, originally released in 1985 on Music For Nations (and licensed through Combat Records in the States). I've read reviews where people have felt that this album was more accessible and "mainstream" than their first two releases. If by accessible they mean adding more thrash elements (and even some Motörhead worship) then I guess it's totally accessible. In reality though this album is for headbangers and headbangers alone. It's 40+ minutes of pretty much non-stop thrashing, speed metal goodness.

Recommended Track: "Sudden Impact"

418. Satan – Court In The Act

Court In The Act was Satan's debut record, originally released on Neat Records in 1983. Right after this album's release they would change the band name to Blind Fury and release an album for Roadrunner under that moniker. That would normally not be the end of the world, except they changed their name back to Satan and released another EP and full length under that name. Five years after their debut album they would change the band name for an unprecedented third time and release three albums over a ten year period as Pariah. By then "Satan" was almost lost to the history books as an entirely new generation of metal fans would lose touch with the band as they were known under their original name. Fast forward a couple decades though and despite all the name changes this album is thankfully, and rightfully, still looked at as a benchmark album of the original NWOBHM movement.

Recommended Track: "Break Free"

417. O.L.D. – Old Lady Drivers

Sometimes a band forms as a parody and winds up being so much more than the goofiness of their lyrics. Take New Jersey's O.L.D. (Old Lady Drivers) for example. They originally formed as sort of a goof on thrash and the new death metal genre. But instead of being some joke band no one took seriously they inadvertently became grindcore pioneers, experimenting with everything from industrial music to full on techno at the tail end of their careers. *Old Lady Drivers* was the band's debut album, released in 1988 on Earache Records. Minus the occasional song that has zero seriousness behind it, this album is a shredding, grind affair. The vocals were almost black metal in their delivery and when this band got going at 100 miles per hour they were pretty damn brutal. If you can get past lyrics about things like people shooting gunk out of their tracheotomies you'll be rewarded with a gem of early grindcore experimentation.

Recommended Track: "Total Hag"

416. Samael – Blood Ritual

Blood Ritual was the second album from Swiss outfit Samael, and their debut for Century Media, originally released in 1992. Being their debut for Century Media means this was the first Samael album most people here in the States familiarized themselves with. The spirit of this album is securely rooted in black metal, yet the music itself plays out in this mid-tempo death-dirge more reminiscent of what a lot of US death metal acts were doing at this time. These guys, along with Dissection, absolutely belong in the discussion of bands that not only were the firsts to successfully merge the black and death metal genres but were links in the bridge between the first and second wave of black metal as well. It's an album that fans of acts as varied as Celtic Frost, Obituary, and of course, Dissection should be all over. It also belongs on a short list of albums that continued to pioneer black metal in Europe.

Recommended Track: "After The Sepulture"

415. Raven – All For One

All For One is the third full-length album from England's Raven, originally released in 1983 on Megaforce Records here in the U.S. (and on their original label, Neat Records, in the UK). This is the last album they did before jumping off to a major label. In the interim these guys not only wrote killer traditional metal, but were one of the bigger metal bands in the world for a red hot second. Here's some bar stool trivia for you: Who was the band Metallica opened for on their first ever full U.S. tour? Yup. Raven. That tour would help directly propel Metallica to the super stardom they enjoy today. But it was Raven's tour and this was the album they were touring off of at that time. So where does it stand against the first Metallica album? (Which was released on the same label, in the same year.) For a short while anyway, it was more highly regarded and much more influential. They aren't the only band to eventually be dwarfed by Metallica, and this album has aged amazingly well.

Recommended Track: "Hung, Drawn And Quartered"

414. Overkill – Feel The Fire

East Coast thrash over the years has taken a back seat to its West Coast brother. But one East Coast thrash band that has held their own, both in album sales and influence, is New Jersey's Overkill. *Feel The Fire* is the band's debut full-length album, released in 1985 on Megaforce Records. It's a dirty, gritty, raw album that sent this band down the path to becoming one of the most influential thrash bands of all time. You can't deny the sheer volume of fans and artists that consider this band and this album completely essential. While later albums would see more critical acclaim (and more album sales) this album maintains a sort of overall darkness that later releases would start to yield. A truly epic piece of American thrash metal.

Recommended Track: "There's No Tomorrow"

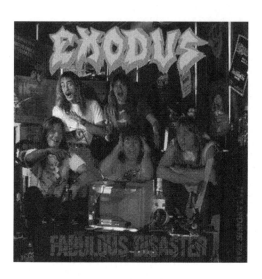

413. Exodus – Fabulous Disaster

Dave Mustaine of Megadeth was quoted in an interview as saying that he felt the "Big 4" of thrash metal could be extended to five and would include Exodus. Pretty hefty praise. Regardless of their proverbial ranking there's no denying that in the mid to late-80s Exodus were one of the best bands to come out of the Bay Area thrash scene. *Fabulous Disaster* was the band's third full-length album, originally released on Combat and distributed by Relativity Records here in the States. This is the first album that would have the help of wider distribution and simultaneously be the last album they would record for Combat as they would sign with Capitol Records after this album. Maybe it's because of the wider distribution, maybe it's because it's just a damn good record, but whatever the reason this is still one of their best selling albums. That's got to mean something because the first three Exodus efforts are absolute thrash classics.

Recommended Track: "Fabulous Disaster"

412. Sanctuary – Into The Mirror Black

If you are familiar with Nevermore then you have an idea already of what Seattle's Sanctuary is all about. Sanctuary, partly because of when they were making music, has more thrash influences than Nevermore but the nods to prog rock and traditional metal are beyond apparent. Maybe it was because Warrel Dane had such a ridiculously recognizable voice, maybe it was just the progressive elements of their music, whatever it was I personally considered these guys the "Rush of thrash metal." *Into The Mirror Black* was the band's second and (until recently) final album. It was released through Epic Records in early 1990. This album obviously alludes to what we would hear out of Nevermore (although guitarist Jeff Loomis wouldn't join the band until after the album hit the streets) and if you're a fan of both the traditional metal of the early '80s and prog rock then this album should be in your collection.

Recommended Track: "Future Tense"

411. Anvil – Metal On Metal

So we are all familiar with the story of Anvil by now right? We've all seen the documentary about the band which came out a few years ago? If not, allow me to give you the Reader's Digest version: Anvil was an up-and-coming power/thrash metal band in the early '80s, who according to people like Lars Ulrich, should have been the biggest metal band in the world. They got involved with a crappy manager who screwed them out of the record deal they were already in and then they "vanished" into thin air, never to be heard from again…except they didn't actually vanish. They signed to Metal Blade and put out two more albums for one of the largest indie metal labels in the world. *Metal on Metal* was their second full-length album, originally released in 1982 on Attic Records. One thing the documentary did get right is that during this time period Anvil was absolutely at the top of their game and arguably one of the best power/thrash metal bands in the world, and this album should be used as Exhibit A.

Recommended Track: "Heat Sink"

410. Corrosion of Conformity - Blind

C.O.C. started as a crossover hardcore/punk/thrash band in the early 80s and their first two full-lengths are still lauded as crossover classics. But after a six year hiatus, which saw them change up their line-up and their sound, they came back in 1991 to release *Blind*. This would be their first and only album for Relativity Records before they would jump ship to Columbia and further polish their sound. This is a solid stoner rock album, going back to a time before stoner rock bands became dime-a-dozen. To be honest, after the hiatus between the previous album and this one coupled with the different line-up you could theoretically look at this as a completely different outfit. Listen to almost any track and you get the juxtaposition of this album. It's heavy enough to still be considered "metal" but you could have totally seen these guys opening for someone like Alice In Chains or Soundgarden at this point in their career.

Recommended Track: "Vote With A Bullet"

409. Fates Warning – Night on Bröcken

Night on Bröcken was originally released in 1984 on Metal Blade Records and still to this day stands as possibly the heaviest album you'll hear from Fates Warning. That's not to say that you're going to find some crazy speed or thrash metal on this beast. The thrash elements are there but this falls more into the traditional or power metal realm (if for no other reason than the virtuoso vocal performance of John Arch). Fates Warning has gone on the be immensely influential, not only in the world of metal but in the world of prog rock as well. When you say "progressive metal" there's a pretty good chance that this band will be one of the first off most people's lips. But this album is probably your only chance to hear them play a style of metal where the progressive elements were only being hinted at as opposed to being the main focus.

Recommended Track: "Buried Alive"

408. Nocturnus – The Key

Nocturnus played a brand of technical, yet brutal, U.S. death metal very similar at its core to other Florida death metal bands such as Deicide and Morbid Angel. They had unique lyrical concepts based around the combination of the occult and science fiction. (This album was actually a concept record about a cyborg who goes back to the year 0 and destroys Christianity.) But where this band really set themselves apart from their contemporaries was in the use of progressive elements, specifically in the use of keyboards. Death metal and keyboards? In 1990 this was absolutely unheard of. *The Key* was the debut album for Nocturnus, released on Earache Records. This album is brutal as hell, and as guitar driven as any other death metal record. However, keyboards were used to create an ethereal and atmospheric vibe throughout the entire album. There simply were no other death metal bands in the world doing what they were doing at that time and for that reason alone it's a must own album.

Recommended Track: "Lake of Fire"

407. D.R.I. – Thrash Zone

Dirty Rotten Imbeciles started out in Houston in the early 80s but relocated pretty quickly to San Francisco, which happened to be the epicenter of American thrash metal at the time. So really it should come as no surprise that they would start out as a hardcore punk band, only to 'crossover' to a more metallic, thrash sound. Along with Suicidal Tendencies, Cryptic Slaughter and a small handful of other influential acts, D.R.I. would bridge the gap between punk and metal, simultaneously helping to give birth to skate punk or "thrashcore." D.R.I. could share a stage with literally anyone and no one would bat an eyelash. *Thrash Zone* was the band's fifth album, released in 1989 on Metal Blade here in the U.S. This album continues the "metal" part of their recording career. Despite the fact that a lot of thrash bands were starting to fade by 1989 and the genre was becoming a bit watered down, D.R.I. was still putting out quality, top-notch thrash.

Recommended Track: "Abduction"

406. OZ – Fire In The Brain

Formed in the late 1970s in Finland, OZ would eventually relocate to Sweden in order to seek a wider audience. In their wake they left an influence that was felt across both countries and would aid in both metal scenes exploding. These guys played a NWOBHM style that not only endeared themselves to metalheads in their homeland but got them radio play and some decent album sales in the rest of Europe, as well as Japan and the U.S. (thanks to strong distribution from Combat). No, they weren't selling records the way Iron Maiden or Judas Priest were, but they were one of the first Swedish/Finnish metal bands to help put these countries on the map. *Fire In The Brain* was originally released in 1983 on the aforementioned Combat Records. This is their second album and, frankly, is light years ahead of their first. If you're a fan of the traditional/early power metal of the early 80s this album should absolutely be in your collection.

Recommended Track: "Black Candles"

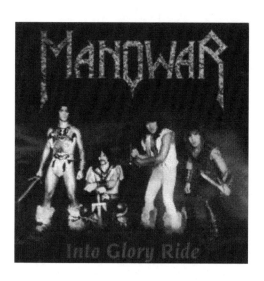

405. Manowar – Into Glory Ride

Into Glory Ride was the 2nd full length album from Manowar, originally released in 1983. It was also their debut for Megaforce Records here in the States. So why does this album rank about 20 spots higher than the debut? Well, for a couple reasons. First of all this album was more popular upon its release and the album that really started to cement them as a household name in the metal world. At least part of that being their union with Megaforce and Music For Nations, whom they were signed to in Europe. Secondly, this is the album where they started to experiment and dabble in the whole Norse/Viking motif they would keep coming back to. Hence the album cover, complete with swords, fuzzy booties and bear skin undies. Lastly, the songs on this album are simply stronger. The tracks on here have a variance of structure and maturity in songwriting that they lacked on the first album.

Recommended Track: "Gloves of Metal"

404. Carnage – Dark Recollections

Before Swedish death metal suddenly had to include "melodic" in front of it Sweden was churning out some of the most brutal and technically proficient death metal in the world. One of the bands that carried the flag of the original "Swedish sound' was Carnage. So it's not going to be often that a band puts out only one album and that sole output shows up on this list. Then again when your band includes 3/4 of Dismember at one point and Michael Amott (Carcass, Arch Enemy, Spiritual Beggars) is one of your founding members then there's a good chance that one album is going to be pretty stellar. *Dark Recollections* was originally released in 1990 on Necrosis Records. It would be picked up and released on cassette that same year by Earache as well. Despite the small recorded output this band and this album remain vitally important to the history of Swedish death metal.

Recommended Track: "Infestation of Evil"

403. Helloween – Keeper of the Seven Keys Part 1

One band that will always be synonymous with both Germany and power metal is Helloween. Power metal continues to have pockets of rabid fans around the world and possibly no other band did as much to help formulate and further the genre in its earliest days as much as this one. From the soaring vocals to the blazing technicality of the guitar work, this was a statement record for both the band and the power metal genre at large. *Keeper of the Seven Keys Part 1* (for those not familiar, there was in fact a Part 2) was originally released in 1987 on Noise Records. It's the album that broke them and made them a household name in 80s metal, and to this day stands as a crown jewel in their back catalogue.

Recommended Track: "Halloween"

402. Mastodon - Remission

Grammy Awards aside Mastodon's influence has been felt far and wide across the metal landscape. All of those awesome stoner/sludge bands from Georgia we've been seeing pop up for the last decade? They might have always been there but their "discovery" by labels was a direct result of said labels looking for the next Mastodon. Any geographic area that has bands has a "scene." But how do scenes in places like Sweden or Brazil or Japan…or Georgia…wind up on our collective radars? It often happens when one or two bands "make it" and the rest of the music world goes digging like miners in the California Gold Rush. *Remission* was the band's debut album, originally released on Relapse Records in 2002. It stands to this day as their overall heaviest album, and tracks like "March of the Fire Ants" still instantaneously start pits at shows. All of their success, all of their influence on the metal world, it all starts with this release.

Recommended Track: "March of the Fire Ants"

401. Meshuggah – Destroy Erase Improve

Destroy Erase Improve was the second full-length album from Sweden's Meshuggah, released in 1995 on Nuclear Blast Records. I'm not trying to be hyperbolic when I tell you that this album changed the metal game. On their first album Meshuggah was essentially a Swedish death metal band that threw in elements of thrash and some prog stuff, especially in the solos they were laying down. But this album was unlike anything anyone had ever heard at the time. Again, the Swedish death metal, the bits of thrash and the pieces prog rock were all there, but now add in some jazz fusion and crazy time signature changes and Meshuggah literally created something completely different from what anyone else was doing. Bands like Dillinger Escape Plan that throw around nasty tempo changes or drop some jazz-inspired riff into the middle of a song? All that djent stuff floating around? That's just a smattering of bands that probably wouldn't exist today if it wasn't for this record.

Recommended Track: "Transfixion"

400. The Mystick Krewe of Clearlight – The Mystick Crewe of Clearlight

Clearlight was a side project of members from such New Orleans legends as Eyehategod, Down and Crowbar. They play a raucous, funky brand of stoner rock that dabbles in everything from sludge to acid rock to prog rock. It's equal parts heavy and trippy with an amazing amount of sick, sick riffs. To be honest with you, this is far from being the heaviest record on this list. In fact I'll go out on a limb here and state that this album has just as much Allman Brothers and Jimi Hendrix influence as it does anything from the metal world. But Clearlight is comprised of those awesome musicians and this debut, self-titled album was released by stoner rock label Tee Pee Records in 2000. Sadly this is also the only full-length album they ever produced leaving us with a giant 'what if' to live with.

Recommended Track: "Swamp Jam"

399. Goatlord – Reflections of the Solstice

When I first launched this project as a website it was two years before former Goatlord guitarist, Joe Frankulin, committed a heinous murder-suicide that included taking the lives of a neighbor and her 8-year old son. The question eventually arose in my mind as to whether I would continue to include this album in future publications. There is no easy answer to this question. But the focus of this book has been, and always will be, the music itself. There have been some very shady characters in metal history and Frankulin ranks towards the top of that dubious list. Ultimately this album is still here because in 1991 (23 years before Frankulin's ultimate selfish act) this album broke ground as one of the first U.S. albums that you could slap the black metal tag on. Does the influence of this album lesson the impact of future actions of a former member? Of course not. Conversely those actions also don't erase the impact the music found here had on the extreme metal world.

Recommended Track: "The Fog"

398. Ihsahn – The Adversary

Ihsahn will forever be known, alongside Samoth, as one of the two most important pieces for arguably the most important second wave black metal band. His guitar work, vocals and songwriting are second to none. It should really come as no surprise that his solo work, of which he composes and plays everything except the drums, is very reminiscent of his work with Emperor. But if you are looking for an Emperor album here you will be sadly mistaken. *The Adversary* was his debut solo album, released in 2006 on his own label and licensed through Candlelight Records for worldwide distribution. While some tracks are certainly very Emperor-like and, quite frankly, probably would have wound up on the next Emperor record if there was one, even these tracks seem to digress in ways that Emperor tracks never did. The inclusion of experimental, post and prog rock elements on this album make it hard for anyone to ever call it a black metal record per se yet much of what you hear on this album is still rooted in the symphonic style of black metal.

Recommended Track: "Citizen"

397. Cephalic Carnage – Lucid Interval

Colorado's masters of "Rocky Mountain Hydrogrind" and smokers of more weed than you could ever possibly imagine, Cephalic Carnage, are truly a unique animal. They're a grindcore band for all intents and purposes. Vocals that alternate between guttural and screamed, sickening blast beats, and extreme technical proficiency on the guitars abound. But this band is also one of the few grind bands in the world that constantly experiments and does so with almost complete success. Whether it's poking fun at other metal genres or it's adding in some bizarre sonic disruptions and seizure-inducing time signature changes, this band is almost instantly recognizable to grind fans. (Plus any band that uses samples from Twin Peaks: Fire Walk With Me is alright in my book.) *Lucid Interval* was the band's third full length album and second for Relapse Records, originally released in 2002. While this album shows a little more depth than the previous two, it's still as brutally heavy.

Recommended Track: "Redundant"

396. Black Label Society – Sonic Brew

Zakk Wylde's first non-Ozzy project was a band called Pride & Glory that played this interesting hybrid of Black Sabbath meets Mountain meets Lynyrd Skynyrd. It was bluesy, jam based stuff that wasn't bad at all. After a brief stint playing under his own name he decided to found Black Label Society. This was their debut album, released here in the States in 1999 on Spitfire Records. People who tuned into B.L.S. after this record and went back to rediscover this one might have been a little surprised by what they were hearing. This is possibly the least "heavy" album of their careers. There are still plenty of Zakk Wylde, attention-worthy riffs. But if you know the trajectory of his post-Ozzy career this album will make more sense for you as it's a direct evolution from the work he was doing with Pride & Glory. Still if you like good guitar-driven, stoner rock you should probably get on this album post haste.

Recommended Track: "Born To Lose"

395. Testament – The Formation of Damnation

The Formation of Damnation was the ninth studio album from thrash titans Testament, originally released in 2008 on Nuclear Blast Records. It serves as a "comeback" record in a couple different ways. First of all it was their first studio album in nine years due to line-up changes (including the return of guitarist Alex Skolnick and bassist Greg Christian who had last recorded with the band in 1992 and 1994 respectively), as well as health issues that plagued front man Chuck Billy. Regardless of why it took so long I'd argue it was totally worth the wait as this was quite possibly the best overall record they had done since 1990s *Souls of Black*. While I completely dig albums like *Low* and *Demonic*, there are some truly great tracks on those records, it was this album that returned them to their thrash roots. It was like a wonderful sonic homecoming.

Recommended Track: "The Persecuted Won't Forget"

394. Opeth - Heritage

Heritage is the tenth studio album from Sweden's Opeth, originally released in 2011 on Roadrunner Records. Opeth spent a huge chunk of their careers creating amazingly lush albums that combined melodic Swedish death metal with prog rock. All of their albums prior to this one, with the exception of *Damnation*, followed this sort of formula. You know the story: as the years progressed so did their sound. The prog rock elements became more profound, albeit never drawing away from the intensity of the death metal passages. The vocals always alternated seamlessly from death growls to one of the best clean voices you'll ever hear in a metal band. Then this record happened. There are zero traces of the Swedish death metal that so many metal kids waited patiently for on albums and at live shows. This album is so prog and retro space rock that if it was released in say 1971 we'd be calling it one of the best "proto-metal" albums ever released. In a way it wasn't unlike stoner rock and doom bands putting out records that call on the spirits of the late '60s and early '70s.

Recommended Track: "The Devil's Orchard"

393. Acrid – Eighty-Sixed

Acrid were a straightedge band from Ontario, Canada. They put out one EP and this, their only full-length album, originally released in 1997. They then vanished. One of the guitar players would go on to become the front man of emo-hardcore outfit Grade. But don't expect anything emo about this record. Acrid were brutal as all get out. The Canadian hardcore scene in the '90s was phenomenal. Pound for pound one of the best scenes in the world at the time, especially the scene that revolved around Toronto and the rest of Ontario. Acrid was a direct product of this scene. So while they played shows almost exclusively with hardcore and punk bands they were for all intents and purposes a metal band. Hardcore bands don't blast beat. Hardcore bands don't write music dark enough to draw from black metal and doom influences. But these guys did. Acrid were one of a small handful of bands who successfully took the metal and hardcore scenes in Canada and merged them into one musical explosion.

Recommended Track: "Slow Death"

RED FANG
MURDER THE MOUNTAINS

392. Red Fang – Murder The Mountains

Red Fang hail from Portland, OR. Portland has a tremendous music scene, not just for metal or punk either. There are a ton of amazing bands in a lot of varied genres emerging from that city and frankly Red Fang do their best to draw from just about all of them. Obviously they are rooted in metal, playing a brand of stoner rock that varies from the truly heavy to the more ethereal rock of bands like Queens of the Stone Age. At the end of the day though these guys will put some hair on your chest and your chin. They alternate between these sort of growled and very smooth, clean vocals. All of which is layered over the top of some seriously meaty riffs that would rival any other stoner rock band in a riff war. *Murder The Mountains* was Red Fang's second full length album and debut for Relapse Records, released in 2011.

Recommended Track: "Wires"

391. Marduk – Serpent Sermon

If you don't know Sweden's Marduk, then frankly you don't know black metal. Their first EP was released all the way back in 1991, so these guys were on the ground floor of the rise of black metal in worldwide popularity. We have two eras of Marduk that I've dubbed B.M. and A.M. – or Before Mortuus and After Mortuus. I'm not sure what demon possesses this guy when they put a microphone in front of him, but he's one of the sickest and truly evil sounding vocalists in all of black metal. No offense to the three vocalists they had prior, but this guy adds an entirely new dimension to this band that's keeping them at the top of the black metal heap even 20+ years after their formation. *Serpent Sermon* is the band's 12th full-length, studio album and was released on Century Media Records. It's a record filled with eclectic sounds, creepy song intros and raw, unrelenting black metal. It is honestly not for the weak of constitution.

Recommended Track: "Souls For Belial"

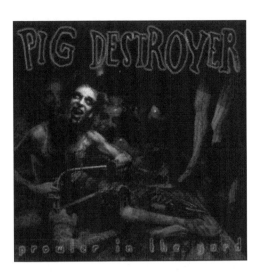

390. Pig Destroyer – Prowler in the Yard

Virginia's Pig Destroyer play a technically proficient brand of grind that borrows as much from the hardcore and punk scenes as it does the world of metal. They also write some of the most disturbing lyrics you'll ever read because they aren't necessarily "gore soaked." They take you just enough to the edge to creep you out and then leave you hanging there. And that's where this album hits all the right buttons. It is, for all intents and purposes, a concept record. A very depraved concept record and the tone is immediately set with the opening spoken word track done with a bizarre voice effect and telling a story of "art" battling lust and hatred for people's attention. It's a pretty poignant opener as the rest of the album is all sorts of hatred wrapped up in blast beats. *Prowler In The Yard* was the band's second full length album. It was also the first full album of new material they released for Relapse Records and was originally released in 2001. If there was a defining moment for this band in their rise to grindcore fame it could be the release of this album.

Recommended Track: "Piss Angel"

389. Goatwhore – The Eclipse of Ages Into Black

Made up of guys who are in very un-black metal bands (i.e. Soilent Green, Down, and Crowbar) and lumbering out of the swamps of New Orleans (which despite it's wonderfully haunted and voodoo heavy past is still not the first place you'd think of when it comes to black metal) came a band that paid great homage to the masters of the first wave such as Venom, Celtic Frost and Bathory. Born out of what seems like a highly unlikely set up, Goatwhore played a blistering brand of blackened metal that few U.S. bands were still attempting when they first burst on the scene. Goatwhore's debut album, *The Eclipse of Ages into Black*, was released in 2000 on Rotten Records. If you dig that type of galloping black metal that was first made famous in the first wave I suggest you give this album a go.

Recommended Track: "Nocturnal Holocaust"

388. Exhumed - Slaughtercult

California's Exhumed are kind of hard to label. I know that all of these sub-genres like death metal, grindcore and goregrind are all kissing cousins (and in reality very little separates them at times) but Exhumed have spent their entire careers hopping back and forth and seamlessly melding all of these genres with a strict old school thrash aesthetic. Point of fact about this particular album – there was zero use of the double bass. A staple of death metal for decades was left off completely and most people are none the wiser because of how fast and pissed (and brutal) this album really can be. This is the second full length album from Exhumed, originally released in 2000, and the second one they would release under the Relapse banner. For as much as the first full length would put these guys on the map, this was the album that really cemented them as one of the best death metal bands in the world at this time.

Recommended Track: "Decrepit Crescendo"

387. Watain – Sworn To The Dark

If I were to ask you today who were the bands at the top of the black metal heap; who were the bands that should be recognized as really carrying the torch of true black metal you would, or at least should, at some point mention Sweden's Watain. To not do so would be borderline criminal. *Sworn To The Dark* was Watain's third full length album, originally released by Season of Mist in 2007. Frankly, it was also, up to this point in their career, their best album in terms of both production and songwriting. Watain have always been able to write these amazingly catchy songs (as catchy as throat-slashing black metal can be) and it was on this album they really started to spread their wings a bit. This is not to say that this band wanted to reinvent the black metal wheel. On the contrary, they liked to play it dark and evil the way black metal should be played. But they weren't afraid to write that hook that's going to get stuck in your head for awhile either.

Recommended Track: "Legions of the Black Light"

386. Belphegor – Goatreich-Fleshcult

Austria's Belphegor started out as a straight black metal band, so along with the blood-soaked, anti-Christian imagery their own past gets them continually lumped into the black metal conversation. But by the time this album came out eight years later the traces of raw, primal, second wave black metal had all but disappeared. It was replaced by a death/black metal hybrid that in reality resembles Morbid Angel and Deicide more than it does Darkthrone or Mayhem. So what we have is a band with two very distinct periods to their career from a songwriting standpoint. This may be the best album from that second phase (but thankfully their book is still being written). *Goatreich-Fleshcult* was originally released in 2005 on Napalm Records. It's the perfect example of a band making a smooth transition from one style of metal to another without losing any of their intensity or integrity.

Recommended Track: "Bleeding Salvation"

385. The Red Chord – Fused Together in Revolving Doors

The Red Chord came lumbering out of the greater Boston area (and a Boston hardcore scene that has always been one of the strongest in the U.S.) playing a brutally heavy mixture of latter day hardcore meets death metal. There were never any pretenses with this band. They wanted to smash your face in with blast beats, monster riffs and stop-on-a-dime time signature changes from day one. These guys may not have "looked metal" but they sure as hell played metal. They always had more in common with bands like Suffocation and Immolation than they ever did bands like Snapcase or Strife. *Fused Together in Revolving Doors* was the band's debut album, originally released in 2002 on Robotic Empire. This was not only the album that unleashed this band on an unsuspecting metal world, but it would also directly lead them to being picked up by Metal Blade Records.

Recommended Track: "Nihilist"

384. Six Feet Under - Haunted

Haunted was the debut album by death metal super group Six Feet Under, originally released in 1995 on Metal Blade Records. Despite some missteps they stand currently as one of the top selling U.S. death metal bands of all-time. Forget for a moment that there may be bands playing a more technically proficient brand of death metal. In 1995, when death metal was supposedly "dying" Six Feet Under was one of the bands that helped invigorate the scene, at least in the greater public eye and the press. That's saying something because we aren't talking about an extremely popular form of music on a national scale to begin with. While record sales alone don't paint the complete picture of a band's legacy, there's no denying the influence this album has had over the last 15 or so years. It's as straight-forward and unapologetic a death metal album as you'll find in these pages, and helped spawn a whole new generation of death metal fans.

Recommended Track: "Lycanthropy"

383. Baroness – Red Album

The album that kicked it all off in a big way for Georgia's Baroness was their 2007 debut for Relapse Records. Simply called "Red Album," this album instantaneously made them media darlings with a bunch of metal magazines and web outlets, placing it firmly towards the top of several year-end lists. These guys have naturally progressed to a more serene vibe three albums later, but this album is chock full of prog-influenced stoner rock, complete with insane instrumental passages and the prerequisite maximum riffage. They somehow successfully found a way to merge all of the great stoner rock and doom influences they wear so proudly with this sort of avant-garde approach to delivering it. It's equal measures catchy and pummeling. I highly recommend that if you are a fan of anyone from King Crimson to Kyuss that you get on this album immediately.

Recommended Track: "The Birthing"

382. Electric Wizard – Black Masses

Black Masses was the seventh full-length album from England's doom masters, Electric Wizard, originally released on Rise Above Records in 2010. There are several parts to this album that render the title an accurate prediction. The whole thing in general has that typical, Electric Funeral ambiance and darkness around it. Tracks like "The Nightchild" could absolutely be the soundtrack to some sort of black mass. But at the same time this isn't some sort of Mickey Mouse b.s. where the band feigns evil just for shock value. One can honestly picture band mastermind, Jus Osborn, smoking copious amounts of pot and worshiping whatever dark forces he chooses. That's pretty much the name of the game here. Sex, drugs, and rock n' roll done in some of the most evil of ways possible. If you call yourself a doom fan at all, and I mean even in the slightest bit of the term 'fan', then you need to immediately check this record out.

Recommended Track: "Black Mass"

381. Suicidal Tendencies – Join The Army

On their debut album, California's Suicidal Tendencies, established themselves as one of the godfathers of the original thrash/punk crossover sound. Their live shows were legendary and the vitriol and angst on that first album were palpable. Eventually, just like fellow crossover heroes D.R.I., they would start to migrate to a more "metal" sound. *Join The Army* was the band's second album, originally released in 1987 on Caroline Records. This album was released four years after their debut due to a ton of issues within the band. When they returned from what was essentially their first hiatus they returned with a metallic aesthetic. They also returned to a larger fan base as this album would get all the way to #100 on the Billboard 200 chart. They would eventually sign to Epic Records and despite several more hiatuses would continue to establish themselves as thrash legends. This album is arguably what first put them there.

Recommended Track: "War Inside My Head"

380. Impaled Nazarene – Absence of War Does Not Mean Peace

Finland's Impaled Nazarene play a brutally nasty mix of black metal with grind and old school thrash elements. They started out exclusively as a black metal project, complete with corpse paint, but by the mid-'90s had altered both their look and sound. Nowadays, Impaled Nazarene is so fist-pumping, rock-kicking, headbanging, church-burning delicious that it's hard to think of them as just a black metal band. They really are one of those bands that has mastered the art of merging all their influences into a fairly unique style of metal. They are also one of those bands that has a way of attracting controversy. Whether it was the supposed tiff they were having with the Norwegian scene at one point, or their overt Satanic and/or sexual lyrics, these guys have a knack for pissing people off. Which in a way makes sense, because this is some pretty pissed off music. *Absence of War Does Not Mean Peace* is the band's seventh full length album, released on Osmose in 2001.

Recommended Track: "The Lost Art of Goat Sacrificing"

379. Spirit Caravan – Jug Fulla Sun

After the demise of The Obsessed it was said that Scott "Wino" Weinrich was planning on giving up music altogether. He was apparently coaxed into another band from his local Maryland scene and they would go on to become Spirit Caravan. They only released two full lengths and one EP together (not counting the three 7" records they also released) but in such a short time and with so little music this band helped to redefine an entire genre. The stoner rock scene today would look vastly different if Wino had been allowed to slip into potential obscurity back in the '90s. *Jug Fulla Sun* is the band's debut album, originally released in 1999 on Tolatta Records (a label run by a member of Fugazi). It's a record filled with absolutely flawless stoner rock, complete with some of Wino's best guitar playing. While not the most famous or critically-acclaimed project of Wino's storied career, this album has stood the test of time as one of the 90s best stoner rock albums.

Recommended Track: "Healing Tongue"

378. Buzzov*en - Sore

There is something to be said for starting your album with a two-plus minute sample of a woman screaming for mercy, followed by seven-plus minutes of punk fury meets Sabbath riffs meets throat-shredding vocals. But that's how this album kicks off and frankly it's all downhill (or really up) from there. Buzzov*en was a band that could create pure sonic debauchery with the best of them. There are so many bad trips and hangovers on this record you can almost smell the puke. But that was the beauty of Buzzov*en. *Sore* was the band's second album, released in 1994 on Roadrunner. Prior to and after this record the band would kind of languish on smaller labels incapable of providing the kind of distribution or support they deserved. (Not counting the two comp albums that have come out on Alternative Tentacles and Relapse over the last decade.) So for a lot of fans this was the record that introduced them to the sordid world of Buzzov*en and remains buried like a dirty needle in the hearts of sludge fans.

Recommended Track: "Unwilling To Explain"

377. Bruce Dickinson – Accident of Birth

As much as I personally love (LOVE) the first two Iron Maiden records, Bruce Dickinson is the voice that launched that band on a trajectory to being one of the greatest bands to ever record music, across any genre, ever. His solo work during his time in Maiden and specifically during his hiatus from the band was hit or miss, but a sure fire hit was his *Accident of Birth* album. *Accident of Birth* was originally released in 1997 on CMC International in the U.S. This album is special for two reasons. First and foremost, it features the guitar playing of fellow Iron Maiden alum Adrian Smith. (I had the distinct pleasure of seeing the tour that followed this record and I'm telling you right now to see two-fifths of the classic Maiden line-up on a club stage was mesmerizing, especially when they "covered" three Maiden songs during their set.) This album is also special because it's not only the best thing Bruce did on his own but it's arguably a better record than anything Maiden did without him after his departure. A true, traditional metal classic from start to finish.

Recommended Track: "Road To Hell"

376. Rotten Sound - Cycles

Cycles was the fifth full length album (not counting comp albums) from Finland's Rotten Sound, originally released in 2008 on Spinefarm Records. This album is the middle child in what I've recently dubbed the Holy Trinity of Rotten Sound, (*Exit* and *Cursed* being the other two). Rotten Sound play a fairly "clean" brand of grind. That is to say, their best albums don't sound like they were recorded within a shoebox or inside of a tin can. They also play a brand of grind that pulls very generously from the crust and powerviolence scenes, which despite the great production, gives them a really nasty sound. The whole experience is not unlike witnessing a rabid dog tearing apart some small woodland creature it's managed to capture. In the long and storied metal history of their native Finland, Rotten Sound may be the heaviest and meanest sounding act the country has ever exported, and this album is Exhibit A to that end.

Recommended Track: "Blind"

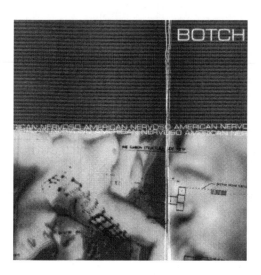

375. Botch – American Nervoso

When you talk about hardcore, metalcore, or more specifically "mathcore", one band that should certainly be discussed as one of the best of the genre is Seattle's Botch. They weren't around for long and despite what seems like a ton of EPs, splits and compilation records they only released two full-length albums. *American Nervoso* was the band's debut full-length, originally released in 1998 on Hydra Head Records. Prior to this album they had done multiple smaller releases, and the year before this album came out there was a comp album that brought together their first two EPs. But frankly, those are sub-par recordings compared to this material. If you are a fan of the frantic stop-and-go of the mathcore sound, complete with out of left field songwriting, then this album should be right up your alley.

Recommended Track: "Thank God For Worker Bees"

374. Toxik – World Circus

Thrash and speed metal have been kissing cousins for a long, long time. When the two came together in blackened wedded bliss you got some of the best metal albums of the 80s. One band that did a hell of a job taking the best of both worlds and successfully merging them is New York's Toxik. Two full length albums and a huge tour opening for the newly-solo King Diamond is all we have left to remind us of Toxik. This album in particular is worth reminiscing over. *World Circus* was the band's debut album, originally released on Roadrunner Records in 1987. It's also the only album to feature Mike Sanders and his crazy falsetto vocals. But the real reason to punch your ticket to this show is the guitar playing of Josh Christian. Christian is one of the most underrated players to emerge from that second wave of late '80s thrash and conversely Toxik are one of the most underrated thrash/speed metal bands to come crawling out of New York's tri-state area.

Recommended Track: "World Circus"

373. Coalesce - OX

There has never been, nor will there ever be, a band in the hardcore scene as unique and as brutal as Coalesce. This band were truly ground breakers and trail blazers at a time when the scene itself was beginning to grow stale. Unfortunately there are few bands that broke up and got back together as many times as Coalesce has done since as early as 1996 or so. But regardless of their seemingly constant internal strife they have managed to put out four full-length albums, this one being the fourth (and to date the last one). *OX* was originally released in 2009 on Relapse Records. It marked the first studio album in literally a decade because, among other reasons, they kept breaking up. This is also an album that sees the band at their most innovative, experimenting with everything from clean vocals to random expressions of the Blues. But in the end it always comes back to just being heavy as sin and rocking the hell out.

Recommended Track: "The Comedian In Question"

372. Arch Enemy – Black Earth

Nowadays Sweden's Arch Enemy are one of the most well-known metal bands in the world. But before their initial deal with Century Media and the high profile changes in vocalist, this band was considered little more than a side project of former Carcass guitarist Michael Amott, a potential footnote in the history of Swedish death metal. This album would make sure that didn't happen. *Black Earth*, although truly under the banner of "melodic Swedish death metal," still stands as the band's heaviest effort. This album has as much in common with bands like Grave and Dismember as it does In Flames or Soilwork. When you listen to a track like "Idolatress" for example the galloping death metal meets sludgy riffs of later Carcass is on full display in the most glorious of ways. *Black Earth* was originally released in 1996 on Wrong Again Records.

Recommended Track: "Idolatress"

371. Immortal – At The Heart Of Winter

At The Heart Of Winter was the fifth studio album from Norway's Immortal, originally released in 1999 on Osmose. Critically speaking, it was possibly their best received album, and there's good reason for that. This was the first album where they really started to experiment with their sound, specifically adding elements of old school thrash and allowing songs to go on these interesting journeys. (Not a single song under six minutes in length on this album.) Immortal had the ability to take something that seemed so simple and make it so brutally heavy and oppressive that you get lost in it over the course of the song. It really does feel as if they are sonically encasing you in ice and just leaving you buried in some glacial mountain somewhere. Even on their worst day ever Immortal is still one of the greatest and most important second wave black metal bands of all time. This album is one of several examples why.

Recommended Track: "At the Heart of Winter"

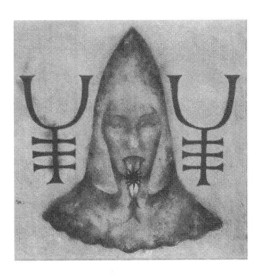

370. Integrity – Seasons In The Size Of Days

Cleveland's Integrity were one of the hardcore bands who had a handful of albums that were simply too "metal" to leave off the list. Their early material may be straight out of the hardcore punk handbook but albums like this one seethed metal and saw their music run through this 'evil filter' and into territory that most hardcore bands never dared to tread. (i.e. samples of cult leader Jim Jones, squealing pig noises, lyrical material that tackled a wide array of dark/occult subject matter, etc.) Not to mention this album was heavy as all hell with riffs that at certain points crossed into both thrash and doom/sludge territories. *Seasons In The Size Of Days* was the fourth full-length album for Integrity, originally released by Victory Records in 1997.

Recommended Track: "Sarin"

369. Benediction – The Grand Leveller

The Grand Leveller was the second full length album from England's Benediction, and the first one without Barney Greenway (Napalm Death) on vocals. It was originally released by Nuclear Blast Records in 1991. An important take-away from this album is its release date. One thing you can say about this band is they got in pretty early on death metal's ground floor and 25+ years later this record still sounds great. The album waxes and wanes from galloping rhythms to doomy, dirge-like passages. It's a pretty solid representation for both where the death metal scene stood in 1991 and where it was eventually headed as it evolved over the years.

Recommended Track: "The Grand Leveller"

368. Acme – To Reduce The Choir To One Soloist

Germany is known for contributing some of the greats to a lot of different scenes – thrash, speed metal, death metal, even black metal. One style they aren't as well known for (but probably should be) is hardcore. Yet in 1996 prominent hardcore label, Edison Recordings, unleashed a monster record from a German hardcore band called Acme. The hardcore scene here in the States would never be the same. This is a compilation album made up of about four years worth of comp tracks, seven inches, etc., and came out the year after Acme split up. They were from the Bremen area of Germany (which in the '90s was the epicenter of German hardcore). As far as metalcore goes, this band would probably have gotten way more credit for helping to perfect the union of 90s hardcore with other extreme forms of metal if they had existed long enough to even see one proper release. But the fact remains that every kid here in the States who got their hands on this record were instantly affected.

Recommended Track: "Blind"

367. Opeth – Ghost Reveries

This is Opeth's eighth studio album, and their debut for Roadrunner after their European label, Music For Nations, shuttered their doors. The album was originally released in 2005. It is a loose concept record that features Opeth's trademark death metal meets prog rock sound. But like all previous efforts, even though it's unmistakably the "Opeth sound" it's also an amazingly unique album. Maybe it's because of the varied musical concepts that Opeth was toying with or maybe it's all the references to ghosts in the lyrics, but this album, has a haunting, almost goth-like quality to it. When you listen to this album you can imagine some woebegone, lost soul living alone in this 19th Century mansion, constantly haunted by the dead. Like so much of the Gothic literature that follows the same course, it's a creepy yet beautiful album for sure.

Recommended Track: "Ghost of Perdition"

366. Solitude Aeturnus – Beyond The Crimson Horizon

When you are talking about doom metal, especially the epic, soaring variety you probably don't think of Texas. Let's be honest, no one does. But what most people don't realize is that one of the most accomplished and criminally underrated U.S. doom metal bands hailed from The Lone Star State. Playing a brand of doom that would rival their British counterparts for metal fan's tears and suicide notes was Solitude Aeturnus. *Beyond The Crimson Horizon* is the band's second album, originally released by Roadrunner Records in 1992. It would also be the last album they released for Roadrunner. Roughly 25 years after its release this still stands as one of the better U.S. doom albums of the 90s. Fans of more well known acts like Candlemass and Trouble would be wise to make every attempt to own this album.

Recommended Track: "Seeds of the Desolate"

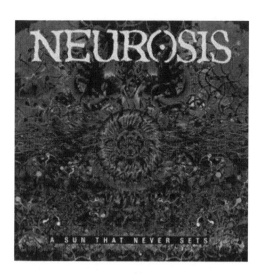

365. Neurosis – A Sun That Never Sets

Neurosis came storming out of the East Bay hardcore scene playing a pretty virulent brand of crust punk. Their first two albums hint at experimentation but they are throat-punchers more than anything else. By their third album the experimentation starts to rule out the crust elements and by their fourth album the full-blown "Neurosis sound" was underway. Doom metal mixed with dark ambient, neo-folk, and post-industrial elements might be the best way to describe this band, but even that doesn't do it all justice. *A Sun That Never Sets* was the band's seventh album, originally released by Relapse in 2001. It's the first album they showcase clean vocals and the album where neo-folk elements become prominent, giving this record an absence of overall heaviness others before it possessed with an iron fist. That's not to say this thing is radio friendly or that it isn't a dark and at times disturbing album. On the contrary, it was simply another step in their progression and opened the door for some of the styles that clash so well on the albums released after it.

Recommended Track: "From The Hill"

364. Sabbat – History of a Time to Come

UK's Sabbat played a very unique style of thrash. Their vocals were almost black metal in their delivery, and Andy Sneap, before becoming a world-renowned producer, was a pretty creative guitar player in the way he structured these songs. Sabbat also sang songs about Paganism, British history, and various forms of mysticism, which added to their uniqueness. I'm not saying these guys re-wrote the thrash manual, but they had a sound all their own and it was miles ahead of the vast majority of the thrash scene of the late '80s. *History of a Time to Come* was their debut album released by Noise Records in 1988. It is arguably their heaviest album and some of the folk metal elements that would start to creep into later releases didn't exist yet outside of the lyrical content, thus giving this album a nasty edge unseen on future albums.

Recommended Track: "A Cautionary Tale"

363. Burzum - Burzum

I'm not going to recount all the sordid details of the life and times of Varg Vikernes, but here's the Cliff's Notes for anyone who doesn't have them: Vikernes started Burzum in the early '90s. They were one of the first true Norwegian black metal bands. He also took part in the burnings of several historical churches in Norway, murdered his former Mayhem band mate, Euronymous, and his personal politics have always been controversial at best, racist at worst. It would have been extremely easy for me to just leave Burzum off this list completely. But we are talking about albums that are essential in a lot of ways and one of them was in the development of the current heavy metal landscape. As you listen to this album there are elements here of ambient black metal that hundreds of bands would take and make their own. Whether or not you think Vikernes is a nasty human being, from a strictly musical sense his influence counts for something. This is Burzum's self-titled debut album, originally released in 1992 on Deathlike Silence Productions.

Recommended Track: "A Lost Forgotten Sad Spirit"

362. Cryptopsy – Blasphemy Made Flesh

Rolling out of the Quebec metal scene in the early '90s, Cryptopsy played this unabashedly technical brand of death metal that would eventually lead them to full on "experimental" status by the end of the decade. But the first two albums are arguably their best and part of the reasoning is that their vocalist at the time, Lord Worm, was one of the better death metal vocalists around. His gurgling, squealing style of vocals was instantly recognizable and somewhat unique amongst the growlers of the day. *Blasphemy Made Flesh* was their debut album, originally released in 1994 on Invasion Records. After the collapse of Invasion it would be reissued by Displeased Records in 1997. The album would be reissued yet again by Century Media in 2001 (with different artwork not shown here). This album is so eclectic in it's technicality that it honestly, at times, sounds like the sonic equivalent of some split personality disorder.

Recommended Track: "Open Face Surgery"

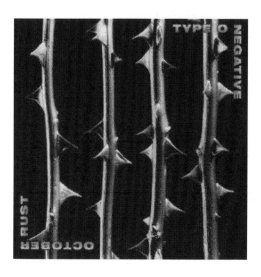

361. Type O Negative – October Rust

When you're talking about Gothic metal probably the first band that gets the Goth girls' corsets in a bunch is Type O Negative. If you don't know who Type O Negative is then you clearly were too young or not paying attention in the '90s because these guys had one album certified Platinum (Bloody Kisses) and this one certified Gold here in the States. You aren't going to find many bands on this list with a Platinum record to their credit, especially not one who seemed to care so little about those types of accolades based on their musical style and lyrical content. *October Rust* was the band's fourth full length album released in 1996 on Roadrunner Records. Where previous records were filled with dingy, Sabbath styled riffs mixed with thrash and punk outbursts, this album was by far their most accessible to non-metal fans. But it also contains some of their best songwriting. There was a definite shift in direction on this album that makes it a very unique one within their back catalogue, in the best way possible.

Recommended Track: "Love You To Death"

360. Today Is The Day – Temple of the Morning Star

Originally hailing from Nashville, and later relocated to Massachusetts, Today Is The Day could most likely first be described as a noisecore band. If nothing else it explains their original alignment with Amphetamine Reptile Records. But while they may be rooted in noisecore, their sound, especially by the time this record came out, was always heavier and more experimental than the average band of their ilk. They tended to pull from influences like grindcore and prog rock, to everything in between, giving their sound an unmistakable uniqueness. It's not uncommon, rather kind of the norm, for a Today Is The Day record to be extremely psychotic and unnerving. This album especially is filled with so much rage and depression it's downright fascinating. *Temple of the Morning Star* was the band's fourth full length album, and their first for Relapse Records.

Recommended Track: "Mankind"

359. Suffocation – Effigy of the Forgotten

Effigy of the Forgotten was the first full-length album released by New York's Suffocation, originally in 1991 on Roadrunner Records. This album is comprised of mostly re-recorded tracks that had appeared on various demos and their original EP for Relapse. It basically culls together the blueprint for what this band would come to represent for years to come – unrelenting, karate chop to the throat, death metal. Although they maybe didn't sell as many records as some of their American contemporaries (i.e. Morbid Angel and Obituary) nor do they have the same cut following as others (i.e. Deicide and Cannibal Corpse) there is no denying that this band and this album helped put American death metal on the map for good. If you like your death metal brutal with a couple extra "U's" thrown in there for affect, I highly suggest you dive into this album without delay.

Recommended Track: "Seeds of Suffering"

358. Converge – Petitioning The Empty Sky

Before Boston's Converge started to make a concerted shift away from their punk and metal roots they were one of the heaviest and fiercest hardcore bands in the world; and truly pioneers who helped forge the metalcore and hardcore scenes that we know today. *Petitioning the Empty Sky* was the second album released by Converge and there is some discussion as to whether this is even a full-length or should be considered an EP. Originally released as a 4-song EP by Ferret Records in 1996 it would later be reissued in 1998 by Equal Vision Records to include some live material, but also a couple more studio tracks as well. However you want to classify it, this is a rabid animal of a record, with a distinct thrash influences at times. It's easily one of the best albums in the Converge pantheon, but also one of the best, and most influential, hardcore releases of the 90s.

Recommended Track: "The Saddest Day"

357. Tiamat - Clouds

Prior to their shift to a more accessible, Gothic rock sound, Sweden's Tiamat wrote some very unique and progressive metal. This album was the first where a lot of those progressive elements started to show up in full force. Truth be told, when you strip away all the extraneous accoutrements, this album still manages to contain some of their dirtiest, most doom-inspired riffs and there are multiple tracks on here which give a nod to their doom/death/black metal roots. *Clouds* was the band's third full length album, originally released in 1992 on Century Media Records. This isn't the heaviest album to come out of Sweden in the early '90s. Instead it is a testament to this band's ability to experiment with their sound, create something wholly unique, and not completely lose themselves in the process.

Recommended Track: "The Sleeping Beauty"

356. Coroner – R.I.P.

This is the debut album from Switzerland's Coroner, originally released by Noise Records in 1987. The two albums that came after were much more technical than this one, and definitely more progressive and experimental in their sound. Where the second and third albums relied on tempo changes, better instrumentation, and a more doom-reliant approach to smacking the listener around, this album simply relies on overpowering the listener with a barrage of middle-finger-flipping thrash metal. When most people think of Coroner they don't think traditional thrash. They should, at the very least because this album is one of the better thrash albums of the late '80s. As the genre was getting more and more watered down by major labels looking to cash in, there stood a handful of bands, Coroner among them, keeping the flame of true, unpolished, dirty thrash burning.

Recommended Track: "Reborn Through Hate"

355. Tankard – The Morning After

The Teutonic thrash scene had their own "big three" if you will in Destruction, Kreator, and Sodom. When people talk German thrash these are always the first three bands people mention and rightfully so. But I would argue that much like the "Big Four" of American thrash, the scene in Germany did not begin and end with those bands. One such example of an often overlooked German thrash band is Tankard. For the most part, these guys had one speed – fast as lightening. Musically they were the proverbial out of control sports car driven by the owner's drunk teenage son. It was always all out, all the time. In fact, when you listen to Tankard's earliest releases today there is sort of a punk rock quality to them. So much so, that I'm a little surprised more people don't lump these guys into the crossover sub-genre. *The Morning After* was the band's third full-length album, released in 1988 on Noise Records. It's absolutely one of the better late '80s thrash records and if you've got the need for speed then feel free to gas up here.

Recommended Track: "The Morning After"

354. Enslaved - Blodhemn

Norway's Enslaved started their careers playing fist-to-the-face black metal but have evolved, seemingly with every record, to incorporate a huge, progressive sound that has been taking them further and further away from the "black metal" label. No two Enslaved records sound completely alike, and that's an awesome feat to pull off. Future albums after this one would further help Enslaved stand out from the crowd with a sound not unlike if Pink Floyd decided to invent black metal sometime in the '70s. This record was possibly the last to be rooted almost solely in the Viking/black metal tradition, yet even this album had experimentation on it that most bands labeled "black metal" wouldn't dream of at the time. *Blodhemn* (Norwegian for Vengeance In Blood) is Enslaved's fourth full-length album, originally released by Osmose Productions in 1998.

Recommended Track: "Nidingaslakt"

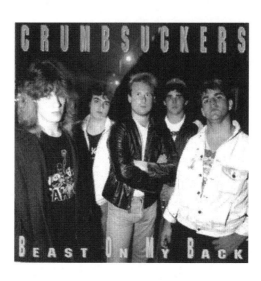

353. Crumbsuckers – Beast On My Back

When you think of crossover thrash most people immediately envision sunny California and kids skateboarding in empty pools. But the East Coast had its own great crossover thrash scene and one of the bands at the forefront was New York's Crumbsuckers. The crossover sound on the East Coast, specifically in New York City, would be, among other things, one of the catalysts to the formation of an immensely strong hardcore scene in the '90s. Crumbsuckers were one of a handful of bands that fit snugly on both metal and punk bills and helped bring together two scenes that didn't always get along very well. But entire books could/should/already have been written on the melding of hardcore, punk, crossover thrash, crust punk, etc. For brevity's sake, let's just say that Crumbsuckers were similar enough to groups like D.R.I. or Cryptic Slaughter to run in similar circles. *Beast On My Back* was the band's second and final full length album, originally released by Combat Records in 1988.

Recommended Track: "Beast On My Back"

352. Assück – Misery Index

How Assück isn't discussed more often when people talk about the greats of the grind genre I will never, ever know. Maybe it's because of their relatively small musical output? (Only two full-length albums and a handful of EPs, demos and 7"s.) Maybe it's because they were a grind band in a scene dominated by death metal and hardcore in 1990s Florida? Whatever the reason this band was absolutely killer and appealed to both the metal and hardcore kids. Their lyrical content was extremely political endearing them to the crust punk scene as well. The fact that they are beloved by so many different factions of the metal world should, alone, put them on a larger pedestal. *Misery Index* was the band's second and final full-length album, originally released in 1997 on Sound Pollution Records. This album is only 15 minutes in length. In other words, it's a sonic cyclone so brace yourself for immediate and drastic impact.

Recommended Track: "Salt Mine"

351. Ulver - Bergtatt

Bergtatt (which is the truncated version of the album title), was Ulver's debut album released in 1995 on Head Not Found. Right from the get-go these guys started playing this atmospheric, neo-folk influenced brand of metal that mixed in clean vocals, acoustic guitars, flutes, and all sorts of ethereal songwriting that, frankly, doesn't sound like black metal at all in certain passages. But be patient with it because eventually they are going to show you why they were a black metal band at heart (at least at this point in their career). This album is schizophrenic at times in the best way possible. To say that Ulver is influential would be a gross understatement. This band has had a profound impact on the metal landscape at large. But this album specifically put the black metal world on its ear because there really was very little like it floating around at the time.

Recommended Track: "Capitel V: Bergtatt - ind i Fjeldkamrene"

350. Deadguy – Screamin' With The Deadguy Quintet

Deadguy formed in the early '90s, they signed to Victory Records (at the time the biggest hardcore label in the world) and put out one amazing full-length. Then they went on a tour that apparently was legendarily bad. So bad that the singer and one of the guitar players quit the band and moved to Seattle (and later formed Kiss It Goodbye). The band was seemingly done at that point but instead of calling it quits they recruited two new members, shifted some responsibilities around and recorded for Victory their second album entitled *Screamin' With The Deadguy Quintet* in 1996. In the short period of time they were together they absolutely turned the hardcore world upside down and were one of the first bands to openly fuse metal and hardcore to form this chaotic, swirling sound. A lot of people dismissed this band after the split of the original line-up. Those people are foolish.

Recommended Track: "Free Mustache Ride"

349. Borknagar – The Olden Domain

The Olden Domain was the second album from Norway's Borknagar, and first released under the Century Black imprint of Century Media Records in 1997. This album is possibly their most important for one huge reason: It was the first where a lot of progressive elements that would define their careers moving forward began to show up. Rest assured there are plenty of blood-curdling screams and blast beats to keep this thing listed in the black metal genre. But this was the first record where they decided to take their sound on various epic and ethereal journeys. It laid the foundation for a career filled with monumental releases. This also happens to be the last album to feature Garm on vocals (he being the voice behind both Ulver and Arcturus). When we look back at black metal in the 90s it is not an understatement to say that this album will go down as one of the most influential of the genre.

Recommended Track: "The Winterway"

348. The Gathering - Mandylion

Some bands always teeter along the line of what is metal and what is not. Netherlands' The Gathering are one of those bands that has spent their entire career challenging metal fans to find the "metal" in their sound. Up until about a decade ago there was enough to go around. Their first two releases were certainly in that sort of atmospheric doom metal realm. Although their sound would drastically mellow over time there was enough "metal" in play that the band didn't seem to lose many fans as other bands might. *Mandylion* was their third full-length album, but first to ever feature Anneke van Giersbergen on vocals. It was also their debut release for Century Media, originally released in 1995. While there are some atmospheric doom elements still present on this record, it's van Giersbergen's soaring and immense vocals that make this thing stand apart from any other acts cut from the same cloth. Anyone looking for a more Gothic or esoteric experience should head for this album before most others.

Recommended Track: "In Motion #1"

347. In Flames – Lunar Strain

Lunar Strain is the debut album from Sweden's In Flames, originally released on Wrong Again Records in 1994. By the mid-'90s, the Swedish death metal scene was splintering from its original "buzz saw" roots. Bands like Dark Tranquillity and At The Gates were adding more melodic elements without compromising the brutality of the genre. Then a whole new crop of bands started showing up with everything from the occasional clean vocals to violins, and they would eventually find a leader in In Flames. If you are a newcomer to this band and are looking for the mid-tempo, non-abrasive brand of "death metal" that In Flames has been playing for the last two decades or so then you are probably going to be a little surprised listening to this record. You may not even like it because it's easily the heaviest record they've ever done and the vocals (turned in by Mikael Stanne from Dark Tranquillity) are just nastier. But with that said, this album has stood the test of time and whether you are a fan of their recent output or not this one is a must-own.

Recommended Track: "Lunar Strain"

346. Nuclear Assault - Survive

The Bay Area has long dominated discussions about the U.S. thrash metal scene. But the East Coast has held their own for a long, long time now. If you were going to create a "Big Four" of East Coast thrash metal it would probably be Overkill, Whiplash, Carnivore, and Nuclear Assault (although entire books could be written off that debate alone). *Survive* was the second full-length record from Nuclear Assault, originally released in 1988 on I.R.S. Records (which was distributed by MCA at the time). This was the album that made Nuclear Assault a household name in the metal world and it actually sat on the Billboard chart at one point. Nuclear Assault are not going to wow you with their technicality. They play a pretty straight-forward, smack you upside the head, version of thrash metal. But they do it well…really well…and this album could be used as Exhibit A in showcasing why this band has been so important to the history of U.S. thrash metal.

Recommended Track: "Brainwashed"

345. Paradise Lost - Icon

When you talk about the death/doom sub-genre or the concept of "Gothic metal" few bands should come to mind as quickly as England's Paradise Lost. *Icon* was the band's fourth full-length album, originally released by Music For Nations in the UK/Europe and Metal Blade Records here in the States in 1993. After three albums of perfecting Goth-tinged death/doom, this was the album where they showed their true pantheon of influences and flew the "Gothic metal" flag a little higher than the death metal one. That's not to say this album is lacking in heaviness. On the contrary, it has a huge, monolithic sound that is set up by some of the best and heaviest riffs this band ever wrote. Plus the vocals don't really get 'clean' on this album unless you count "shouting in key" (Nick Holmes' quote, not mine) as 'clean'. This album is one of the better doom records of the early 90s and a testament to a band successfully spreading their collective wings.

Recommended Track: "True Belief"

344. Absu – The Sun of Tiphareth

Texas natives, Absu, have always been lumped into the black metal discussions, but much like other early pioneers of the American black metal sound, so much of what they were doing wasn't really black metal at all. Thrash has played (and still does) a massive role in their sound. You could even consider them pioneers of the folk metal explosion based on their lyrical themes and some of the varied musical elements they were incorporating. Regardless of how you want to classify them, Absu have been hugely influential on not just American black metal, but the extreme metal underground in general. *The Sun of Tiphareth* was the band's second full length album, originally released by Osmose Productions in 1995. It is still, to this day, one of the more unique and influential albums of the second wave of black metal, geographic locale be damned.

Recommended Track: "A Quest into the 77th Novel"

343. Cradle of Filth – The Principle of Evil Made Flesh

There are few bands in these pages as equally loved and disliked, usually for the same reasons as England's Cradle of Filth. The super slick production, the symphonic elements such as prominent keyboards and operatic female vocals, the diminutive vocalist with the really high-pitched squeal, just to name a few. Regardless of whether you love or hate them there is no denying their influence. *The Principal of Evil Made Flesh* was the band's debut album, originally released in 1994 on Cacophonous Records. It is unlike anything else this band has released and is the one album that doesn't have the super slick production they've grown accustomed to. It's as raw and unchained as this band has ever gotten. When you look at the songwriting on this album, and when it was released, it really does deserve to be in the discussion of key second wave black metal albums that originally came out in the early '90s.

Recommended Track: "The Forest Whispers My Name"

342. D.R.I. – 4 Of A Kind

A lot of people attribute the term "crossover" in reference to a certain style of thrash to D.R.I. because, well, that was the name of their second full-length album (which also happened to be when their sound started to…you guessed it…cross over). By the time this record came out the band's sound had lost most traces of their hardcore punk roots which were so prevalent on their earliest releases. You could easily go so far as to say that this is the band's first true "thrash" record. *4 of A Kind* was their third album, originally released in 1988 on Metal Blade Records. As far as D.R.I. records are concerned it's extremely important in the band's development. If you dig '80s thrash, especially thrash with an abrasive, punk edge to it, then I highly suggest you start circle-pitting to this album as soon as possible.

Recommended Track: "Suit and Tie Guy"

341. Clutch – Transnational Speedway League

Clutch and their instantaneously recognizable sound is punctuated by Neil Fallon's insane vocals (and even crazier lyrics) alongside the reliance on a lot of wah pedal giving them a dirty Southern rock sound meets punk aesthetics. Most stoner rock bands will or have spent their entire careers in virtual obscurity, at least partially because rock radio today doesn't actually play rock music. However, Clutch is the anomaly here because they've spent almost their entire career on major labels, have had some mainstream rock radio success, and have a fan base that extends beyond the metal world. All of that started with this record. *Transnational Speedway League* was originally released in 1993 on EastWest Records (a subsidiary of the Warner Music Group). If you've never heard Clutch or simply need a refresher, this album is as good as any place to start. It's a raw effort with a frenzied and slightly insane sensibility to it, again adding to the mystique and uniqueness that is Clutch.

Recommended Track: "A Shogun Named Marcus"

340. Coven – Witchcraft Destroys Minds & Reaps Souls

Originally released in 1969 on Mercury Records, *Witchcraft Destroys Minds & Reaps Souls* is one of the first occult rock records and an underrated inspiration on the metal scene. Sonically these guys play a pretty jazzy brand of psych rock. But there's more than meets the ear, so to speak. Coven were Satan's minions long before anyone threw up the metal horns. In 1969 very few bands were openly singing about black masses (or dedicating roughly twelve minutes at the end of the album to recording part of one). So even though they may not sound "metal" by today's standards it's safe to say that this record most likely influenced its fair share of future metal musicians. In 1970 an Esquire Magazine article linking the occult underground scene in California at the time to the Manson Family murders specifically mentioned this album. Mercury promptly pulled every last copy off the shelves. Just like that this album was lost to the history books, and despite the band selling CD versions online, the original vinyl has become a massive collector's item.

Recommended Track: "Wicked Woman"

339. Brutal Truth – Need To Control

However you want to define their music, New York's Brutal Truth is one of the more influential extreme acts the U.S. has produced over the last couple of decades. Their earliest work, specifically the albums they released on Earache, have some very death metal moments. But this band was originally formed by bassist Dan Lilker, who was a founding member of Nuclear Assault, played on the first Anthrax album, and even had a black metal side project at one point. In other words, I don't think this band was ever intent on following any "scene rules" and that's what makes them so special. *Need To Control* was the band's second album, originally released by Earache in 1994. It's their last album you could ever possibly attempt to categorize as "death metal". In actuality, it is one of the best examples of how grindcore pushed the extreme metal envelope and challenged people's ideas about where one genre begins and another ends.

Recommended Track: "Godplayer"

338. Forbidden – Forbidden Evil

California's Forbidden were unfortunately victims of being over-shadowed by their own scene peers at least partly because their discography during the height of thrash metal's groundbreaking period (from roughly 1985-1991) consisted of only two studio albums. However, those two albums, this one being the first, are absolute rippers and deserve way more street cred than they normally get. *Forbidden Evil* was originally released on Combat Records in 1988. It was reissued in 1999 on Century Media Records. If you're looking for a nice little time capsule of classic late '80s Bay Area Thrash you can't go wrong with this album. Also, for those of you who like to follow the incestuous nature of music scenes, or just like a little metal trivia, please note that two musicians who played on this record would go on to play with Slayer (drummer Paul Bostaph) and Testament (guitarist Glen Alvelais).

Recommended Track: "Chalice of Blood"

337. Celestial Season – Solar Lovers

When a band starts out as a death/doom band, but eventually evolves into one of Europe's first true stoner rock bands there has to be some sort of transition record, right? Absolutely, and for Dutch act Celestial Season, who took that exact career path, this is the transition record. This is the record where their death/doom incubation was met head on with their burgeoning love of the rock riff. Despite the British doom worship and the gruff vocals there is so much more going on here than any normal doom record would allow. This album runs the gamut of emotions from touching and bleak to fierce and dangerous. *Solar Lovers* was originally released in 1995 on Displeased Records, and licensed for the States by Metal Blade Records. When we look at the evolution of both doom and stoner rock we should really be talking more about this band and specifically this record.

Recommended Track: "Solar Child"

336. Exumer – Possessed By Fire

Germany's Exumer play a pretty intense speed/thrash hybrid. This album is almost punk rock in its delivery because it's so manic and all over the place. It's literally like listening to the musical equivalent of a train traveling 200 miles an hour carrying 500 kids hopped up on so much sugar you'd think they were on crystal meth. Exumer would evolve by the second record into a sort of pseudo-Slayer worship but this one is a total maniac for sure. Exumer were one of those bands that just never got to that proverbial next level. They had enough fans in Europe but were somewhat ignored here in the States, due mostly to not having a U.S. label to back them. Maybe that was the root cause of the band originally breaking up after only two proper albums? Regardless, none of that should diminish shining the spotlight on this killer album. *Possessed By Fire* was originally released in 1986 on Disaster Records out of Germany.

Recommended Track: "Possessed By Fire"

335. Sacrifice – Torment In Fire

Torment In Fire was the debut album from Canada's Sacrifice, originally released on Diabolic Force Records in 1986. Just a few months after its initial release the album would be picked up by Metal Blade and they would reissue the record for an obviously wider distribution. When you look back at the classic era of thrash there are really very few albums that come off with as much ferocity as this one. The second album in their discography gets way more accolades. The songwriting on that second album was just as good, the production was better, and they gained a certain power and force behind their sound. But this record is just raw and primal in its delivery. It seethes evil throughout. There are even tracks like "Burned At The Stake" that have a sort of first wave of black metal vibe to them. It is, simply put, one of the most underrated thrash albums of the mid-1980s.

Recommended Track: "Burned at the Stake"

334. Gorguts – Considered Dead

Before they became known as the godfathers of strange time signature and tempo changes in the death metal world, Gorguts played death metal the way it was originated: brutal. Gorguts were originally part of the North American death metal lineage whose sole undertaking was to pummel the listener into flattened road kill. Listening to this album you knew right off the bat that there was something about this band that was a little different. That hunch would come to full fruition by the time they recorded the *Obscura* album, however it was only incubating at this point. *Considered Dead* was the band's debut full-length album, originally released in 1991 on Roadrunner. In 1991 there weren't a ton of bands who were playing it this heavy, this well. This album stands as a beacon of death metal's early stages where bands were seemingly trying to out 'heavy' each other with every release. This one was hard to surpass for sure.

Recommended Track: "Disincarnated"

333. Onslaught – Power From Hell

Everyone knows about the great punk scene in England, but I'm not really sure there was a British metal band as influenced by the likes of Discharge and Broken Bones (who were releasing music at the same time) as Onslaught. *Power From Hell* was the band's debut album, originally released in 1985 on Children of the Revolution Records. When I look back at this record I'm totally amazed that it's not considered one of the great cult metal releases of the 1980s by more sources. It was a perfect mix of metal technicality with punk fury. It was also an album that could be considered first wave black metal and an influence on the burgeoning black metal scene with how ferocious it sounds. Throw in some overt Satanic imagery and lyrics and you are left with an album that begs to be included among the likes of Venom and early Bathory in that respect. It's also one of the first albums to coin the term "death metal." (It may be the first depending on what source you trust.)

Recommended Track: "Death Metal"

332. Sarcofago - Rotting

Rotting was originally released as an EP in 1989 on Cogumelo Records in Brazil (a rather large indie label down there) and licensed in Europe by Music For Nations. Because Sarcofago had a hard time finding distribution in the States at the time this album, and really this band, never got the credit they deserved up this way. But they sure as hell had a huge influence across the pond all over Europe. Although this album could certainly still fall under that first wave of black metal banner, it is a bit of a departure from the debut album and has more of a death metal feel to it. The songs are longer and the way they structure them has more in common with bands like Possessed or Slayer than say Venom or early Bathory. But the fact remains this is a brutally awesome record so full of pure, raw aggression that it's hard to overlook its influence on the extreme metal world.

Recommended Track: "Rotting"

331. Riot – Fire Down Under

Fire Down Under was the third full length album from New York's Riot, originally released in 1981 on Elektra Records. The story of how they got to this point is pretty interesting in and of itself. They started as a straight up hard rock band, eventually opening for AC/DC, among others. They were signed by Capitol Records, dropped by Capitol, re-signed by Capitol, and then had this record put on ice by the label because it wasn't "radio accessible" and was "too heavy". By the early '80s Riot had gone through their first reinvention from a hard rock band to a band highly influenced by NWOBHM. With every subsequent release they would get a little heavier and a little heavier until their classic *Thudersteel* album, which was full on power metal at its absolute finest. Regardless of their ever-shifting musical direction, if you are looking for one of America's answers to the NWOBHM scene that was constantly exploding like fireworks all throughout the early 80s then look no further than this record.

Recommended Track: "Fire Down Under"

330. Sanctuary – Refuge Denied

Refuge Denied was the debut album from Seattle's Sanctuary, originally released in 1988 on Epic Records. This album was also produced by Dave Mustaine. (Honestly, I don't think that means anything at all except for being a nice piece of metal trivia.) The influence this album has had on the metal landscape is pretty huge. There are a ton of bands doing the retro-thrash thing these days that are simply ripping off this record. But the beauty of this album was in the fact that it's not just thrash. They throw in everything from power metal to prog rock along the way. It's one of those 'kitchen sink' records where a band is able to take these seemingly unrelated influences and weave them into something coherent. It beautifully laid the groundwork not only for future Sanctuary releases, but for Nevermore as well.

Recommended Track: "Die For My Sins"

329. King Diamond - Them

This is the third full length album released by King Diamond, originally in 1988 on Roadrunner Records. It's a concept record about two kids who 'welcome home' their crazy grandmother from a stay in an asylum. Turns out, she's not crazy, she can just commune with the evil spirits that inhabit her house. Creepy stuff happens, people die, evil wins in the end. If you were going to make this a horror movie it would be totally inspired by a lot of the psychedelic haunted house films of the 1970s. From a musical standpoint this is an interesting record as it comes off a bit like a metal opera of sorts. King has this story in mind and the rest of the band are asked to keep up as he weaves this tale he's clearly put a lot of effort into. When the rest of the band can come to the forefront a bit and at least share the spotlight it winds up being some absolutely killer heavy metal.

Recommended Track: "A Broken Spell"

328. Death – Individual Thought Patterns

Individual Thought Patterns was Death's fifth full-length album, originally released on Relativity Records in 1993. It would later be reissued (along with a handful of other Death releases) by Relapse in a super-deluxe format. By this point in Death's career main man Chuck Schuldiner had cycled through a lot of different line-ups and had spent the previous album dabbling with a lot of different prog elements. With this album those prog elements really started to dominate, yet they easily managed to maintain their heaviness at the same time. It was just another way this band was making themselves one of the most influential extreme metal acts in the world. Speaking of line-ups, this album features Gene Hoglan (about 6,000 other bands) on drums, Steve DiGiorgio (founding member of Sadus, also played in about a dozen other notable bands) on bass and Andy LaRocque (King Diamond) on second guitar. If that's not a powerhouse line-up I don't know what is.

Recommended Track: "The Philosopher"

327. Whiplash – Insult To Injury

Insult To Injury was the third full-length album from New Jersey's Whiplash, released in 1989 on Roadracer Records. This is the first album that guitarist Tony Portaro did not also handle vocals as they recruited a guy named Glenn Hansen for this album. This is also an album where they started to experiment ever so slightly with their sound and you can hear it in songs like "Dementia Thirteen" for example. Instead of the all out, raging, speed assault of the first two albums, this one takes on a more churning, less scattershot approach. Regardless of the change in vocals or the slightly slower tempos, this is one of the better thrash albums the late 1980s produced. If you are a fan of killer, mid-paced thrash from the last few years of the golden era then this album is right in your wheelhouse.

Recommended Track: "Hiroshima"

326. Sadus – Swallowed In Black

California's Sadus were one of those bands that just never fully rose from "kvlt" status because of a myriad of mitigating circumstances, and that's a shame because this album in particular is just outstanding. *Swallowed In Black* was the band's second full-length album and their first for the Roadracer imprint, R/C Records, released in 1990. While a thrash record at its blackened core, one thing that separated Sadus from a lot of their peers was this death metal-like aesthetic they brandished. The crazy, screeching vocals, the way various songs are structured, there's a lot here that lovingly mimics the burgeoning death metal scene of the day. It gives this album a dark and nasty edge that most thrash bands either never had or lost by 1990. It is a damn shame that more people didn't pick up this record in 1990 and an even bigger shame that over 25 years later we aren't talking about how important this record was to the Bay Area scene and the metal world at large.

Recommended Track: "The Wake"

325. Disrupt - Unrest

Disrupt was born out of an extremely prolific Boston punk/hardcore/crust scene in the late 1980s. They would go on to release what seemed like an endless array of 7"s, EPs, split EPs, and appeared on what seemed like another dozen or so comp albums. But their only true full-length record came in 1994 via Relapse Records. Unrest is 30 tracks of anarchist-infused punk rock mixed with some tremendously brutal crust/d-beat. Seriously this album will make you want to stick safety pins in your cheek and go burn down a McDonald's or two. It's a vicious record at times with its rabid duel-vocal assault and non-stop riffing. Its an album that proves why the early thrash scene in particular had so much in common with the crust and punk scenes. Whether you agree with their politics or not, you can't deny that this album tears it up from start to finish.

Recommended Track: "Mass Graves"

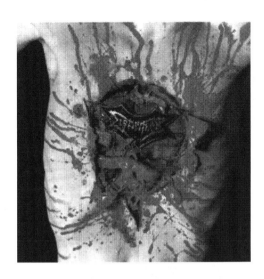

324. Dismember – Indecent and Obscene

It is not an understatement to say that the early Dismember releases are as important to the history of Swedish death metal as any from their contemporaries. *Indecent and Obscene* was the band's second full length album, originally released on Nuclear Blast in 1993. The album title comes from an article about the band after a run-in they had with British authorities regarding their previous album. This album is about as classic an example of great Swedish death metal as you are going to get. The production is top notch and the songs on here don't follow any type of death metal formula. There's actually quite a bit of experimenting going on, especially with the changes in tempo. There's also some riffing that's all over the map, going from black metal styled tremolo-picking to almost stoner rock like riffs during the slower parts. But it's all completely buried at times by the sheer brutality of it all (and not in a bad way).

Recommended Track: "Skinfather"

323. Agent Steel – Unstoppable Force

Born out the ashes of the band Abattoir, Agent Steel was a pretty unique speed/thrash band who at one point had only two full-length records to their name. (They would reunite with a different vocalist ten years after their initial 1988 break-up and wind up putting out three more records.) They had a profound impact on the L.A. metal scene, as well as touring the world as one of the premiere U.S. speed/thrash bands of the mid to late 80s. Unfortunately a two decade battle over who owns the rights to the band name and essentially two different groups touring and playing Agent Steel material over the last ten years has muddled the legacy of this band a bit. But in reality it shouldn't have, because the original line-up's output (two full lengths and one EP) was stellar. *Unstoppable Force* was the second full-length album and last of the classic line-up, originally released by Combat Records in 1987.

Recommended Track: "Unstoppable Force"

322. Exodus – Pleasures Of The Flesh

Pleasures of the Flesh is the second full-length album released by Exodus, originally for Combat Records in 1987. This is also the first album to feature Steve Souza on vocals. To be honest with you, I don't think you could find two vocalists that sounded as similar as Souza and original vocalist, Paul Baloff, sound. So the change in vocalists detracts nothing from record one to record two. (Baloff, who left the band when they were demoing this material, actually has three writing credits on this record.) Is this record as violent and raging as the debut? No. But it's a classic example of mid-tempo, late 80s thrash. Gary Holt and Rick Hunolt wrote some of their best riffs on this record as well. You'd be hard-pressed to find a ton of records that inspired more spin-offs in the thrash scene than this one did upon its release.

Recommended Track: "'Til Death Do Us Part"

321. Cathedral – The Carnival Bizarre

Lee Dorrian and crew created this band to be an homage to all the great doom bands of the '70s and early '80s. Mission accomplished. *The Carnival Bizarre* was the band's third full-length album, released in 1995 on Earache Records. Cathedral spent their entire career tweaking their sound and adding all sorts of strange twists and turns. Cathedral albums were like snowflakes, no two were alike. Out of all their records this one might be the best example of their love of stoner rock. They were experimenting with a more rock oriented sound on the previous album but after being dropped by Columbia here in the States and seeing a return to Earache they were free to experiment even more with their sound. The riffs on this album are just flat out delicious and when you can get Tony Iommi to lay down a guest guitar track, then you must be doing something right.

Recommended Track: "Hopkins (The Witchfinder General)"

320. Twisted Sister – Under The Blade

Under The Blade was the debut album from Twisted Sister, released originally in 1982 on Secret Records. Outside of the NWOBHM scene the line between hard rock and heavy metal in 1982 was still very much blurred. If you were to listen to this album for the first time now you think, 'this is a rock n' roll record.' But think about hearing a song like "Sin After Sin" in 1982. Dark stuff for a world at large that was hooked on bands like REO Speedwagon and Asia. This is the album that got the attention of Atlantic Records and got them signed to a deal that would see them go on to sell millions of records. In 1985 Atlantic would reissue this album with a completely new and polished mix. It was almost like they castrated this album as tracks like "Destroyer" were meant to be heard in their original raw and nasty form. Thankfully this album was again reissued in 2011 by Eagle Records with the original mix restored.

Recommended Track: "Sin After Sin"

319. Bolt Thrower - ...For Victory

...For Victory is the fifth full-length album from England's Bolt Thrower, originally released on Earache Records in 1994. It's the last album they would release with long-time label Earache, as the relationship would sour and the band would move to Metal Blade. By this phase in their career Bolt Thrower had actually started to pick up the tempo a bit on certain tracks. That's not to say they had returned to their grind roots, but the doom-like elements that permeated the previous two efforts were lessened. It almost sounds as if they were writing this album like they were pissed off at the world in general. The trademark Bolt Thrower guitars are ever prevalent. (I've always said that Gavin Ward and Barry Thompson are one of the most underrated guitar duos in metal history and this is one of the albums that proves why.) These five musicians together make music that is sonically crushing and this album is a perfect example of how they could continually steamroll you from one track to the next.

Recommended Track: "...for Victory"

318. Type O Negative – Slow, Deep and Hard

Type O formed out of the ashes of one of the greatest East Coast thrash bands, Carnivore, and their earliest releases still smacked of the thrash and NYC hardcore scenes that each member was so steeped in. This album in particular is a crazy hybrid of doom and Gothic metal mating with thrash and hardcore punk outbursts. With the clashing of styles on here, combined with the length of most of the songs, this album has an almost rock opera feel to it. Apparently the story it tells of infidelity, betrayal and suicidal depression is also somewhat autobiographical adding even more of this soundtrack-like style to it. *Slow, Deep & Hard* was Type O's first album, originally released in 1991 on then Roadracer Records. It's a prelude to what's to come for this band as they lay down dirge-filled riffs and entire segments of songs that resemble funeral doom at certain points.

Recommended Track: "Unsuccessfully Coping…"

317. Paradise Lost – Shades of God

At the time of this album's release, Paradise Lost was writing some of the best, heaviest and most intriguing doom metal in the world. This is easily one of their most enduring and influential albums. *Shades of God* was originally released in 1992, jointly by Music For Nations in Europe and Metal Blade in the U.S. It's the band's third full-length album and is the first to see their sound start to shift ever so slightly. The vocals, although still gruff, were not nearly as grunted and growled as they were on the first two albums. The songs also took on a much more melodic vibe. This album, amongst the first three, has the most to offer people who are either not necessarily doom fans or may be new to the genre. The guitar work on this album alone is worth the price of admission and some of the best songs this band has written came off this record.

Recommended Track: "As I Die"

316. Unleashed – Shadows In The Deep

One of the earliest masters of the Swedish sound and one of the earliest bands (outside of Bathory and a small handful of others) to jump on the Viking bandwagon was Unleashed. This band carried the flag of Swedish death metal just as well as any other band of that era (and one could argue put out quality albums for a longer stretch of time). *Shadows In The Deep* was the band's second full-length album, originally released in 1992 on Century Media Records. It's a powerful testament to how potent straight-ahead death metal can be, even after 20+ years. Unleashed, especially early in their careers, merged influences from the first wave black metal bands and early thrash bands with elements of doom. It gives them a distinct sound and has helped to make them one of the more influential (and underrated) death metal bands of all-time.

Recommended Track: "Crush The Skull"

315. Cannibal Corpse – Tomb of the Mutilated

Tomb of the Mutilated was the third full-length album from Cannibal Corpse, originally released by Metal Blade Records in 1992. I can remember the day I bought this (on cassette!) taking one look at the uncensored album cover (not shown here) and knowing this was one I was going to have to possibly hide from mom. But it wasn't until I popped that cassette in the deck that I realized I had purchased something pretty special. This quickly became a favorite death metal album for several years to come for most metal fans who heard it. The riffs often have a thrash aesthetic to them, the drumming is machine gun precision throughout, and Chris Barnes' vocals sound like they are coming directly from Satan's sewer pipes. If you're a death metal fan at all or are death metal curious you can't go wrong with this album.

Recommended Track: "Hammer Smashed Face"

314. Death Angel – The Ultra-Violence

The Ultra-Violence was Death Angel's debut album, originally released in 1987 on Enigma/Restless Records. 1987 was right around the peak of the golden era of thrash metal. There were bands releasing classic albums left and right. This was definitely one of those albums. When you take into account that the members of this band were all in their teens and early 20s when they recorded it then it becomes a little more mind-blowing. I'm still not 100% sure Death Angel would have ever topped this album even if their career hadn't originally been cut short in 1991. As it stands, this album is so visceral, so heavy, and so technically proficient that it makes several albums from their older contemporaries look fairly weak in comparison.

Recommended Track: "Voracious Souls"

313. Corrosion of Conformity – Animosity

C.O.C. started out in the hardcore punk scene and their debut album was more punk than metal. *Animosity* was their second full-length album, originally released on Death Records in 1985. This album has more in common with bands like D.R.I. and Suicidal Tendencies than any other album they would produce. The albums that followed this one would range from pure thrash to eventually some fairly radio friendly stoner rock. Truly an amazing career arc as they've seemingly come full circle since their reunion a few years ago. *Animosity* was perfect for its time though. Part thrash fury and part hardcore punk nastiness, this album is a perfect bridge for fans from both scenes to cross over freely upon. Like all the other great crossover bands of that era these guys were not afraid to share a bill or tour with anyone at all, as long as they were true to their art. A gem of an album in a discography that is as interesting as it is influential.

Recommended Track: "Holier"

312. Massacre – From Beyond

How influential were Florida's Massacre? Their members have also played in Obituary, Death, Six Feet Under, and about a dozen other well-known bands. Their vocalist, Kam Lee, is credited as far back as their earliest demos for being one of the first true death metal growlers and to this day his inhumanly brutal growl on this record is one of the best you're going to hear. *From Beyond* was the band's debut album, originally released on Earache in 1991. This is far from being the first death metal album and it may not be the heaviest, but Massacre were instrumental in helping to further a very potent Tampa scene that gave us a ton of great death metal. It's also a record that's not afraid to experiment, whether it's epic intros or the infusion of thrash elements. Overall it's a unique and wild ride that should have propelled this band onto much bigger and better things.

Recommended Track: "Cryptic Realms"

311. Saint Vitus - V

The first two Saint Vitus records are excellent but probably their most dynamic line-up came with the addition of Scott "Wino" Weinrich on vocals. Wino is a pretty damned accomplished guitarist in his own right but his vocals are about as stoner rock appropriate as they get. With Wino on vocals Saint Vitus originally recorded three albums of doom and stoner rock awesomeness. This album represents the last of the trio. *V* (as in the Roman numeral 5) is the band's fifth studio album. It was originally released in 1990 on German label Hellhound Records. This album features the trademark down-tuned, Sabbath-worshiping guitars, the elephant stampeding rhythm section and of course Wino's warbling vocals which, again, fit the songs perfectly. This album is certainly one of several Saint Vitus albums that helped spawn a 1,001 imitators that are floating around the metal scene today.

Recommended Track: "Patra (Petra)"

310. Raven – Wiped Out

Although they would go on to don athletic gear on stage and refer to themselves as "athletic rock", in their earliest recordings Raven was about as thrash as they came at that point in time. They often played at breakneck speeds rarely scene this side of punk rock. It just so happens that they came from the same scene that gave us bands like Judas Priest, Iron Maiden, and Motörhead, so they were eventually overshadowed a bit. But at the end of the day Raven's earliest recordings should be held in similar esteem as those of their bigger contemporaries. *Wiped Out* was the band's second full length album, originally released on Neat Records in 1982. This was the album that would finally "break" this band and their next release was picked up by both Roadrunner in Europe and Megaforce for distribution here in the States. This album is a non-stop, rip-roaring affair and one that's worth however much time you're willing to give it.

Recommended Track: "Faster Than The Speed Of Light"

309. Darkthrone – Under A Funeral Moon

It's well documented that Darkthrone started as a death metal band and over the first two albums morphed their sound into something blacker, if you will. This album is part of what many people consider the "Unholy Trinity" of Darkthrone's career (along with predecessor *A Blaze in the Northern Sky* and follow-up album, *Transilvanian Hunger*). These are the albums that would help set the blueprint for all black metal that was to follow. You really don't get much more influential than that. *Under A Funeral Moon* was the band's third full length album, originally released in 1993 on Peaceville Records. Everything about this album just seethes black metal – the creepy black and white cover photo, the lo-fi production, the unholy growling vocals, the bombastic song segments interspersed among the blasting madness. It's such a "kvlt" record and I really can't even begin to explain the influence this album had over all of Europe and the metal world in general.

Recommended Track: "Unholy Black Metal"

308. Pestilence – Consuming Impulse

Hailing from the Netherlands, Pestilence first came torpedoing out of Europe with a strictly thrash metal sound. However this band would undergo huge changes over the years until they were a death metal band utilizing jazz fusion influences. *Consuming Impulse* was the band's second full-length album, originally released on R/C Records in 1989. If you had to tag one of their albums as the transition record between thrash and death metal then this would be it. Vocalist Martin van Drunen (who would leave the band after this record and go on to front Asphyx) growled and snarled his way through this album, immediately giving them street cred with the burgeoning death metal scene. Meanwhile, the songs themselves lapse back and forth between death metal rumblings and thrash metal axe slinging. No matter what phase of their career you're talking about Pestilence are one of the most influential bands of the late '80s/early '90s. Their ability to bend genres to their will to pull together music that was wholly their own is commendable to say the least.

Recommended Track: "Chronic Infection"

307. Slaughter - Strappado

Over the years time has been good to Canada's Slaughter, and their legacy has grown by leaps and bounds. Not only do they hold a position alongside bands like Exciter and Voivod as one of the most heralded of metal exports from the Canadian borders, but their contributions to the formation of death metal have not gone unnoticed either. *Strappado* was the band's lone full-length album, originally released in 1987 on Diabolic Force Records. The band would call it quits shortly after this album because, among other factors, they were disenchanted with the music industry in general. The shame of that is they weren't active to see the fruits of their labor as their brand of crusty, gritty proto-death metal would go on to influence more bands than they could have possibly imagined at the time. Looking for an album that helped birth a scene and directly influence countless other albums in these pages then look no further than *Strappado*.

Recommended Track: "Nocturnal Hell"

306. Diamond Head – Borrowed Time

In 1980, Diamond Head self-released their debut album. It was a gritty, rockin' affair that caught the attention of MCA Records, who signed the band pretty quickly while touting them as "the next Led Zeppelin." In 1982, Diamond Head released their second full-length album, *Borrowed Time*. The label, and at one point the band, claim that this album should be considered their debut because the debut album was meant to be a demo. That first album may have sounded "demo quality" to a label like MCA but it was released as, and fully intended to be, their debut. Whether you consider this album their debut or not there is no denying its importance both within and outside of the NWOBHM scene. This album, despite losing some of the heaviness that made the debut album so enduring and powerful, is a beacon of traditional metal.

Recommended Track: "To Heaven From Hell"

305. Destruction – Eternal Devastation

Germany's Destruction have a long, and at certain points, convoluted history. But one thing is for certain - their earliest output will forever stand as some of the greatest thrash metal ever produced. *Eternal Devastation* was the band's second full-length album, originally released in 1986 on SPV sub-label Steamhammer. I know a lot of other very prominent bands released albums this same year but for what it's worth, in 1986, there were few albums that stood up to this one in pure, thrashing, brute force. This album actually saw Destruction start to expand their sound ever so slightly to include more technical elements. That's not to say this album is any less heavier than the debut, but they do tend to play with solos and overall compositions in ways they didn't previously. Regardless of these slight changes this is a thrash classic.

Recommended Track: "Curse The Gods"

304. Candlemass - Nightfall

This album is a classic example of early European doom and so essential in the formation of a scene that would be in full, epic force by the early 90s. When you talk about bands like Paradise Lost, My Dying Bride, even later acts like Electric Wizard, you can trace at least part of their sound back to Sweden's Candlemass, and this album is a huge reason why. *Nightfall* was originally released on the British label Active Records in 1987 and would be released in the States by Metal Blade. The first thing most people notice when listening to this album for the first time are Messiah Marcolin's vocals. They are absolutely soaring and at times just overpower everything else on the record (not in a bad way). But the guitar playing is Iommi-inspiring in its heaviness and the overall mood is just engulfing from start to finish. A must own record for anyone who considers themselves a doom fan.

Recommended Track: "Dark Are the Veils of Death"

303. Saxon - Saxon

Saxon's self-titled debut album was original released on French label Carrere Records in 1979 (later reissued by EMI). Prior to this album Saxon went through a bunch of name changes, and from what has been written, just as many stylistic changes in an effort to find themselves as a band. That comes through a bit on this record as it's not the most focused product they came up with. There are progressive elements that they would eventually abandon altogether. But in the end it always manages to find its way back to the rock and for that alone it's an endearing effort. This album sets the band on the path to metal greatness and for that reason alone deserves your consideration. Plus there are enough tracks on this album to make it a must own for fans of the NWOBHM scene and traditional metal in general.

Recommended Track: "Stallions of the Highway"

302. Bathory - Hammerheart

Hammerheart was the fifth album from Sweden's Bathory, originally released by Noise Records in 1990. The songs on this album still contained a lot of the elements that made Bathory one of the earliest progenitors of black metal. However there were a lot of elements added to this record that altered the band's style enough for everyone to sit up and take notice. Orchestral voices in the background of certain songs, a singing style that was a bit cleaner than previous efforts, epically long songs, a new emphasis on synths and effects rarely seen on previous efforts, and of course lyrics that abandon the blatant Satanism of the first four albums in favor of odes to the inhabitants of Valhalla are now all present. This is an album that helped define the whole "Viking metal" movement and is one of the more unique efforts the metal scene had seen up to this point.

Recommended Track: "One Rode to Asa Bay"

301. Motörhead - Bomber

Bomber was the third album from the legendary Motörhead, originally released on Bronze Records in 1979. So if I say Motörhead what's the first album people tend to mention? Often times it's *Ace of Spades*, which came immediately after this one. That album set off a string of records that seemed to be played only at one speed – fast and pissed. It cemented the trademark Motörhead sound they are now most famous for. That's not to say the previous three albums weren't intense. On the contrary, they were unbelievably heavy for the time period. This album is a stellar record because it's not a straight forward, all-out assault. There's a ton of rhythm to match the rock and what you get is an album, although overshadowed greatly by the two albums that came after it, is on par with them as far as songwriting and memorable songs.

Recommended Track: "Bomber"

300. Krieg – The Black House

The history of US black metal is a highway littered with bands that have come and gone, burnt bright in the night sky only to implode upon themselves. One act that has maintained their creative rise towards the pinnacle of the scene is Krieg. *The Black House* was Krieg's third album, originally released in 2004 via both Red Stream and Darkland Records. This effort sees Krieg take a step back in production values but a step forward in both songwriting and atmospherics. It's a nasty, raw, stripped-down affair that aims to throat punch the listener as quickly and as often as possible. Yet somehow the sonic violence on this album doesn't snuff out the eerie vibe that seems to run like a river right through the middle of this thing. (Complete with one of the most insane and insanely unique cover songs you'll ever hear.) Krieg has established an amazing legacy of stellar USBM and this album is a must own for fans of the genre.

Recommended Track: "Ruin Under A Burning Sky"

299. Demilich - Nespithe

To say that Finland's Demilich was a unique band with a unique album would be a massive understatement. What this band did with their lone full-length record was nothing short of mind-boggling. *Nespithe* was originally released through Necropolis Records in 1993. Forget for a second that this album had insane vocals which sounded like someone letting a 38-minute belch rip. What this band was able to do within each song was groundbreaking within the death metal scene at the time. Crazy time signature changes, downright funky grooves, and blasting madness all found their way into almost every track. It was, and still is, an album that turns the heads of both fans and fellow musicians. One has to wonder just how much influence this band could have wielded over the death metal scene if they had lasted past one album.

Recommended Track: "When the Sun Drank the Weight of Water"

298. Disincarnate – Dreams of the Carrion Kind

Guitarist James Murphy has had a hand in some truly classic releases from the likes of Death, Obituary, Testament, and a myriad of other acts. But one release that stands tall amidst these classics is the lone album from Disincarnate. *Dreams of the Carrion Kind* was originally released in 1993 via Roadrunner Records. Outside of one demo it stands as the only recorded material this band was able to muster, but the end result was some truly phenomenal, old school, US death metal. Some of Murphy's most inventive guitar work appears on this record as he's able to take each song on an interesting ride through churning and voracious death metal calisthenics. It's hard for a band to only release one album within a scene that has been responsible for so many classics and make any kind of lasting impact. Yet Disincarnate was able to do just that.

Recommended Track: "Stench of Paradise Burning"

297. Skeletonwitch – Beyond The Permafrost

Take thrash metal and blackened death metal, throw in a few nods to NWOBHM and you start to get a feel for what Ohio's Skeletonwitch is all about. They often get lumped into the same discussions as a lot of retro-thrash acts that were, and still are, kicking around. However, over their careers Skeletonwitch have really done an awesome job incorporating elements of second wave black metal and early death metal to give them a sound that is honestly just heavier than those other acts. They may not always play as fast as some of those bands and they may add more melodic elements in their song structures but they will out heavy a lot of bands kicking around today. *Beyond The Permafrost* was their second full length album, originally released in 2007 on Prosthetic Records.

Recommended Track: "Baptized In Flames"

296. High On Fire – De Vermis Mysteriis

For Oakland's High On Fire it seems every album they release is one that could rival anything else they had done prior. Their discography is just that consistently good. This album is filled with vitriol and brutality, like a very poisonous snake latched onto your jugular. It's extremely infectious. (Then again, when you're writing a concept record about the time-traveling twin of Jesus you better come up with something as memorable as the lyrical content.) *De Vermis Mysteriis* was the band's sixth full-length album, originally released in 2012 on eOne Music. If you aren't familiar with High On Fire then you are missing out for sure. Picture Motörhead if they were a thrash band with doom and stoner rock influences. It's a crazy and rabid mixture and is as good as any album for a starting point when exploring High On Fire's back catalogue.

Recommended Track: "Bloody Knuckles"

295. Christian Mistress - Possession

Washington's Christian Mistress play this entirely bad ass hybrid of hard rock and heavy metal that takes the listener back to the earliest days of metal's development, back to a time when the line between rock and metal was just barely being drawn in the sand. There's as much Deep Purple and Uriah Heep influencing this album as there is Pentagram and early Judas Priest. The husky-voiced Christine Davis is a throwback to metal pioneers like Doro Pesch of Warlock fame, but this band and album isn't completely defined by Davis. The songs as a whole are just as dependent on the killer riffs these guys are laying down as anything else. It's a really unique and special record and frankly if it had come out a couple years earlier it probably would have been even higher on this list. *Possession* is the band's second full-length album, released at the beginning of 2012. It's also their debut album for Relapse Records.

Recommended Track: "Conviction"

294. Buried Inside - Chronoclast

Canada at one point in time had arguably the best hardcore scene in the world. In the late '90s there was so much good hardcore pouring out of the Great White North it was hard to keep up. Bands like Acrid, Grade, Ire, and Chokehold, among many others, were taking hardcore music in all sorts of different and exciting directions. So that's where we start with Buried Inside because their sound is an amalgamation of all the great factions of the Canadian hardcore scene, along with influences like Neurosis and Isis. Buried Inside's sound combines the best elements of melodic hardcore with post-metal and doom metal to form this dreary and epic sounding take on hardcore music. *Chronoclast* was the band's third full length album, originally released in 2005 on Relapse Records. This album is a concept record about time and how humans have become a slave to the clock. You are going to be hard-pressed to find an album here with more poignant lyrics.

Recommended Track: "Time As Abjection"

293. Clutch – Pure Rock Fury

Pure Rock Fury was originally released in 2001 on Atlantic Records. This would be the only album they would release for Atlantic despite the band having moderate success, scoring a single on the Billboard charts with "Careful with that Mic..." This is a typical Clutch record, full of thick, meaty riffs, ridiculous lyrics, and enough head banging moments to satisfy the most finicky of fans. After Clutch released *The Elephant Riders* album they gifted us the bluesy *Jam Room* album. It looked as if they were headed towards writing more and more accessible music. *Pure Rock Fury* closely resembles their other major label efforts, however this is also the album that started them on the sonic road they are currently travelling now. That's to say, this album is the first in a now long line of powerful stoner rock records which could stand tall and out-muscle anything else being released in the genre.

Recommended Track: "American Sleep"

292. Pagan Altar – Lords Of Hypocrisy

During the NWOBHM there were a ton of bands making killer music in the UK. One band who's name kept getting dropped and who's live performances were the stuff of legend was Pagan Altar. They were possibly the most gloom and doom band of the entire scene and had arguably the closest sonic ties with the grand masters, Black Sabbath. But by the mid-80s they were a footnote, because outside of a 1982 demo they left no recorded history of their work. Fast-forward to the late 90s and Pagan Altar returned hell-bent to take all of the music they had written from roughly 1977-1984 and finally get it on record. If their music had actually been recorded when it was written their best period would have been between 1982-84. *Lords of Hypocrisy* consisted of music written during that time period, including some material that appeared on that now sought after demo cassette. In real time though this was the band's second post-reunion, full-length album released in 2004 on Oracle Records.

Recommended Track: "Armageddon"

291. Mythical Beast - Scales

Their very brief bio states this mysterious act are "part Pagan ceremony, part performance art..." That's a pretty spot on way to describe Mythical Beast. Their sound is one that would probably find a better home on the soundtrack of some psychological based horror film than it would in a dirty club somewhere. It's a very minimalistic sound, with very little percussion and guitar riffs that act more as the rhythm backbone than anything else. Corinne Sweeney's powerful voice is the main instrument of this band as the rest of this trio are there to simply set the tone for her. Some who listen to this album will probably not consider it metal in the strictest terms. But it most definitely has a home in the occult rock/psych rock thing that's so pervasive in the scene today. Formed in pre-Katrina New Orleans, the band was displaced to Austin, TX after the storm, and moved to Kansas City for awhile. It would appear that this band has broken up permanently at this point. *Scales* is their only full length album to date, originally released in 2008 on Not Not Fun Records.

Recommended Track: "Cycle/Circle"

290. Agents of Oblivion – Agents of Oblivion

One of the greatest bands to ever come out of the rich and dynamic New Orleans metal scene was Acid Bath. Once Acid Bath broke up the members scattered into different projects. One project that emerged from the ashes of Acid Bath was started by vocalist Dax Riggs and guitarist Mike Sanchez. That band was Agents of Oblivion. Agents of Oblivion are not going to 'out heavy' many metal bands. But there are few bands in these pages that write music as dark and depressing. Agents of Oblivion write music that could be defined as stoner rock, but really that feels like a cheap, backdoor way to get them under the metal banner. They are also able to fit under the psych rock banner and do pull a bit from the doom realm. However you want to describe it, this album can be as depressing as an assisted suicide. I highly suggest you queue up something upbeat immediately after listening. This self-titled album was originally released in 2000 on Rotten Records.

Recommended Track: "Endsmouth"

289. Brutal Truth – Extreme Conditions Demand Extreme Responses

Brutal Truth formed in NYC in the early 90s with a goal to play the most pissed off and unique brand of grindcore they possibly could. Like all early grindcore there are some serious death metal influences on this record, especially seeing as NYC had their own burgeoning death metal scene at the time. But despite the obvious death metal influences, especially on tracks like "Denial of Existence", this is a grindcore record through and through and a highly influential one at that. *Extreme Conditions...* is Brutal Truth's debut, full-length album, originally released on Earache Records in 1992. From the vocals that alternate between low and high pitch screams, to the drumming that's about as manic as you'll get, to the Slayer meets Carcass riffing that's going on, this is a testament to how good early grindcore could be when all the right pieces fall into place.

Recommended Track: "Ill-Neglect"

288. The Obsessed – The Church Within

The Obsessed formed in the late 70s but from their formation in 1976 until they first broke up (when front man Scott "Wino" Weinrich left the band to join Saint Vitus) they recorded some demos and an album that was supposed to come out on Metal Blade but for whatever reason never saw the light of day. Fast forward to the early 90s and Wino has left Saint Vitus to reform The Obsessed. *The Church Within* would be their final album, released on Columbia Records in 1994. Wino would go on to form Spirit Caravan and the rhythm section would go on to form Goatsnake – two killer bands in their own right. They play it slow and heavy, yet mixed with some killer hooks. They're a doom band first, but one of the originators of the modern day stoner rock scene as well. If you like your metal as closely linked to Black Sabbath as possible then you've come to the right place.

Recommended Track: "To Protect and To Serve"

287. Anthrax – Spreading The Disease

Spreading The Disease was the second full-length album from thrash legends Anthrax, originally released in 1985 on Island Records here in the U.S. This album is an important one in the history of Anthrax, if for no other reason than because it's the first with Joey Belladonna on vocals and Frank Bello on bass. Even with the line-up changes it's classic Anthrax. What you see is what you get and in this case it's thrash metal alternating from mid-paced to rip-roaring, and back again. It would be an understatement to say that their influence is still being felt today. The massive amount of neo-thrash bands that seemed to tune right into the Anthrax sound is downright staggering. Again, this album is a huge reason why.

Recommended Track: "Gung-Ho"

286. Converge – When Forever Comes Crashing

If you are talking about the late '90s especially, it's not a stretch to claim that Converge was possibly the best hardcore band in the land. Outside of Coalesce and Integrity, I don't really know if it's even close to be perfectly honest. Those three bands helped merge metal and punk rock in ways that most people thought impossible. *When Forever Comes Crashing* was the band's third full-length album, originally released in 1998 on Equal Vision Records. It should also be noted that this record was produced by Steve Austin of Today is the Day fame. Anyone who listens to this album and claims "it isn't metal" is probably too elitist to hear what the rest of us are hearing - the perfect marriage of thrash and speed metal with punk rock.

Recommended Track: "Conduit"

285. Rotten Sound - Exit

Finland's Rotten Sound started as a death metal/grindcore hybrid but by the early 2000s had morphed into a well-oiled grind machine. This album in particular would be the one to stamp them onto the grindcore map and make them a household name in a lot of metal circles. As good as their previous material was this is the album that pulled everything together. Pristine production meets amazing musicianship to form an unholy alliance of grinding madness. It's easily one of the best grind records of the 2000s and when it's all said and done we may be talking about this album as one of the ten or so greatest grind records of all-time. That's not meant to be hyperbole in any way. *Exit* was the band's fourth album, originally released in 2005 on Willowtip Records here in the States and Spinefarm Records in the rest of the world.

Recommended Track: "Burden"

284. Whiplash – Ticket To Mayhem

New Jersey's Whiplash were the type of band who could take the intensity of their live set and so easily transfer it onto record. Possibly the best example of this was their *Ticket To Mayhem* album. This album bottles up all the grit and skill of killing it in a live setting and somehow successfully gets it into a studio. Chock full of speed metal styled riffs, and the occasional atmospheric interlude, this album is an absolute gem of 80s thrash. *Ticket To Mayhem* was the band's second full-length album and was originally released in 1987 on Raodracer Records. Whiplash, for whatever reason, has kind of gotten lost in the thrash shuffle over the years. I'm really at a loss as to why more people don't recognize this band for not only how talented and influential they were but how much effort they put into making music that wasn't cookie-cutter in its delivery.

Recommended Track: "Burning of Atlanta"

283. Internal Void – Standing on the Sun

If you are a fan of traditional doom, then you have a pretty good idea already what you're in store for – slow, dirge-like riffs accompanied by a rhythm section that just pummels you at every turn, and a clean vocalist who may not be the best "singer" in the world but can take each note and drape them in funeral clothing. Internal Void formed in Maryland in the late 80s. It was a time when the doom genre was just starting to hit its stride and was growing from this cult phenomenon into a powerhouse. *Standing On The Sun* was the only release of the original line-up and the only album the band put out in the '90s before vanishing for awhile (resurfacing in the early 2000s with two albums). This album was released on Hellhound Records out of Germany in 1993.

Recommended Track: "Warhorse"

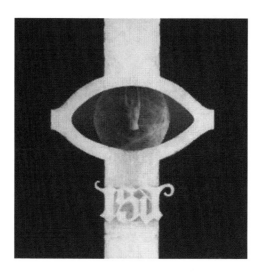

282. Enslaved - Isa

The term "progressive" is one of those oft-used terms that just doesn't have the power it used to thanks to blatant overuse. But Enslaved truly are a progressive black metal band, to the point that a lot of their more recent output doesn't even resemble black metal. But that hasn't stopped them from literally changing the game when it come to black metal as a genre. They've spent their entire career taking the genre and bending it to their creative will; flexing their songwriting muscle and proving to the world that you can write black metal songs that are amazingly produced and not devoid of beautiful melodies, for example. *Isa* was the band's eighth studio album, originally released on Candlelight Records here in the U.S. in 2004. After starting out as one of the best and brightest bands of the second wave of black metal, by 2004 their sound had grown to a point that their influence was now seeping outside the black metal world as well. From a songwriting standpoint, *Isa* was easily their most ambitious album at the time and to this day stands as one of their best.

Recommended Track: "Return to Yggdrasil"

281. Winter – Into Darkness

There are a handful of bands in these pages who've graced us with only one full-length album before vanishing for various reasons. The sting of 'what could have been' can be maddening. Arguably no other band left so much unfinished business as New York's Winter. Combining the rotting stench of death metal with the molasses-like ambiance of doom metal, and sprinkling it with bits of Celtic Frost aesthetics, Winter, much like their moniker, was an absolute force to be reckoned with. As mentioned, *Into Darkness* was their lone full-length album, originally released in 1990 on Future Shock Records. (It would be reissued two years later by Nuclear Blast, and would include their lone EP as bonus tracks.) In the ever-growing history of the death-doom sub-genre, Winter continue to stand tall as pioneers and a truly influential force, no matter how many albums they did or didn't release.

Recommended Track: "Servants of the Warsmen"

280. Running Wild – Gates To Purgatory

Named after a Judas Priest song, Germany's Running Wild play a very Priest influenced brand of thrash. The songs are mostly mid-tempo and rely heavily on the band's imagery and lyrical content. That's been the case with this band's entire career as they transitioned to a pirate-themed brand of metal in the late 80s. Prior to their 20+ year pirate phase Running Wild wrote some pretty dark and "Satanic" stuff. *Gates To Purgatory* was Running Wild's debut album, originally released through Noise Records in 1984. I'm personally convinced that if they had stuck with the formula they created on this album that we'd be talking more about this band in terms of their influence on the metal landscape. As it stands Running Wild was one of the bands that helped put German thrash on the international map and it started with this album; a brooding mix of various evil elements.

Recommended Track: "Diabolic Force"

279. Atomic Rooster – Death Walks Behind You

I can not overstate how difficult it was to take all of the great hard rock and prog rock acts of the 1970s and try to decide which ones were "metal enough" or had a big enough influence on the metal landscape to warrant inclusion. The obvious influence that Atomic Rooster had on the metal world can be seen in the number of bands that have covered the title track to this record (including Paradise Lost in 1992). But their influence extends to more than just the dark and heavy title track. *Death Walks Behind You* was the band's second full-length album, originally released in 1970 by B&C Records in the UK and Elektra Records here in the States. While this album was easily the heaviest they would churn out, later diverging into a more blues-based sound, it stands as a monument of proto-metal, shrouded in exceptional prog rock clothing.

Recommended Track: "Death Walks Behind You"

278. Godflesh - Pure

There is no denying that UK's Godflesh are easily one of the more influential bands in the history of extreme music. They helped formulate the whole "industrial metal" scene that was so popular in the '90s and early 2000s, not to mention influencing a ton of bands outside that sub genre as well. *Pure* was the band's second full-length album, originally released in 1992 on Earache Records. Their use of a drum machine pounding out these non-stop rhythms was the baseline for their entire sound at this point in their career. Meanwhile Justin Broadrick (he of one side of a Napalm Death) would play riffs that if played in a clean tone would have as much Pink Floyd influence as any heavier acts. Terrorizer Magazine named it one of their Top 100 albums of the 1990s.

Recommended Track: "Mothra"

277. The Devil's Blood – The Thousandfold Epicentre

Dutch outfit The Devil's Blood wrote music that had as much in common with King Crimson as it did Black Sabbath. They were fronted by a vocalist, Farida Lemouchi, who has some serious pipes on her. The progressive elements are what differentiate this band from other occult rock bands out there, but it was Lemouchi's vocals that made them instantaneously recognizable. Add in the fact that they called their live performances "rituals" and treated them as such (including dousing themselves in pig's blood) and what you had was one of the leading bands in the recent occult rock movement. Unfortunately, not long after this album was released, the band broke up. They released one more album, post-break up, but their demise left a lot of unfulfilled potential. *The Thousandfold Epicentre* was the band's second full-length album. It was originally released in Europe by Van Records at the end of 2011 and licensed by Metal Blade here in the States in 2012.

Recommended Track: "She"

276. Soilent Green – Sewn Mouth Secrets

Explaining Soilent Green's sound is kind of like explaining everything that your grandma threw into her stew. A little bit of this, a little bit of that, a bunch of stuff that shouldn't work together at all but somehow does. Take nasty, blasting grindcore, mix in some sludgy riffs that only New Orleans could birth and maybe even a snifter of the blues for good measure and what you get is something at least close to what Soilent Green produced. There are so many direction changes and left turns in every single song it's sometimes hard to keep up. Guitarist and main songwriter, Brian Patton may be well known as one of the masterminds behind Eyehategod, but Soilent Green is the band that he "fronts" with his propensity for writing some of the dirtiest riffs this side of Iommi. Also in this band is vocalist Louis Benjamin Falgoust, who also sings for Goatwhore. So the musical talent on this record runs pretty deep. *Sewn Mouth Secrets* was the band's second full length album, and first for Relapse, originally released in 1998.

Recommended Track: "It Was Just An Accident"

275. Dio – Dream Evil

Ronnie James Dio's voice is one of the most powerful instruments you'll ever hear. It's a canon firing blazing balls of metal straight at your ears. It's just that good and this album is one of the classic performances he gives in the studio setting. *Dream Evil* was Dio's fourth full-length album, originally released in 1987 on Warner Bros. It's a pseudo-concept record where all the songs are about dreams/fear of the dark/etc. It's the first Dio album that did not have Vivian Campbell on guitar, (Campbell, of course, being fired after his contentious relationship with Dio finally came to a head.) but Craig Goldy fit in just fine. It's also the last album to feature Vinny Appice on drums until he returned to the band in the mid-90s. Simply put, this is guitar driven, synth-laden, powerful, traditional metal at it's finest.

Recommended Track: "Night People"

274. Tankard – Zombie Attack

Along with Kreator, Sodom, Destruction and a small handful of other acts, Tankard helped make "Teutonic thrash metal" into one of the greatest sub-genres in all of metal in the mid to late 80s. This album is where it all started for Tankard. *Zombie Attack* was their debut album, originally released in 1986 on Noise Records (and licensed in the U.S. by Combat). The year prior to this record, Kreator and Destruction released their debut albums. Sodom would release their debut full-length this same year (although they had an EP out in 1984). It was during this two year stretch that the German thrash metal scene really exploded and the world took notice. When the cream rises to the top in a scene the hope is that people outside of said scene take notice. For German thrash they certainly did. Tankard is a big reason why, despite not getting the same accolades as some of their contemporaries.

Recommended Track: "Mercenary"

273. Sleep - Dopesmoker

When doom legends Sleep split with Earache in 1995 they were wooed into signing with London Records (a label owned under the Universal Music Group banner). Sleep went to work crafting this hour-plus opus that is the antithesis of what a major label would want to release. Needless to say, when they turned the tapes into London, the label refused to release it. They also refused to release a stripped down, 52-minute version. Sleep would break up in 1998 not having their final work see the light of day. Fast forward to 1999 and Rise Above Records gets permission from London Records to release the shortened 52 minute version as an album called *Jerusalem*. (There's some discrepancies as to whether this is a "bootleg" or an authorized version by the band.) Fast forward again to 2003 and this time Tee Pee Records gets their hands on the rights to the full 63-minute version of this song and releases it in its entirety, entitled *Dopesmoker*. Thus a monumental doom/stoner rock record was finally released as the band originally intended so many years earlier.

Recommended Track: "Dopesmoker" (All 63 minutes…)

272. Satyricon - Volcano

Norway's Satyricon are one of the true greats of the original second wave of black metal. *Volcano* was Satyricon's fifth full length album, originally released in 2002 on their own Moonfog Productions imprint but licensed in different parts of the world by both Capitol and Virgin Records. *Volcano* was the first album where Satyricon would add what most fans would dub "black 'n' roll" elements to their sound. The tempo of certain songs may have changed, but the darkness remains. This album seethes evil and the album cover alone does a good job conveying the nightmare-inducing quality held within. While Satyricon did incorporate some rock elements to their sound, as well as traditional metal influences, the core black metal aesthetics that they perfected in the late 90s remain strongly intact. All told, it's a fun and sinister ride from start to finish.

Recommended Track: "Fuel For Hatred"

271. Fu Manchu – No Rides For Free

We've discussed at length what a fine line it is for stoner rock bands to walk between metal and hard rock. This is music that if commercial radio stations (and the major labels that feed them) actually played music that rocked then bands like Fu Manchu would have such a wider audience. But because stoner rock bands exist in the underbelly of the rock world, the metal world gladly opens their arms to bands like Fu Manchu and gives them a proverbial home. *No One Rides For Free* is Fu Manchu's debut album, originally released in 1994 on Bong Load Custom Records. Formed originally as a hardcore punk band they would eventually evolve into one of the most prolific and powerful stoner rock bands of all-time. This album is chock full of meaty, Sabbath-like riffs, and a rhythm section that will knock you over like a blade of grass in a stiff wind. It's a powerful first chapter in a storied career.

Recommended Track: "Ojo Rojo"

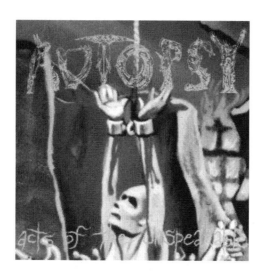

270. Autopsy – Acts of the Unspeakable

California's Autopsy are not only one of the most influential American death metal bands, but one of the first on the scene. Drummer/vocalist Chris Reifert played drums on the first Death album and after his departure from Death, Autopsy was given a unholy birth shortly thereafter. Autopsy's sound is a brutal amalgamation of doom, grind, and death metal that was entirely unique and recognizable from the outset. Autopsy should not only be credited as one of death metal's finest but also as a band that was not afraid to experiment with the death metal blueprint right from the start. *Acts of the Unspeakable* was Autopsy's third full-length album and was originally released in 1992 on Peaceville Records at the height of that label's popularity. If you are looking for some grizzly, grinding death metal, replete with plenty of gore-soaked lyrics then you could do a lot worse than this album.

Recommended Track: "Funereality"

269. Clutch – The Elephant Riders

The Elephant Riders was originally released by Columbia Records in 1998. It was the first and only album for Columbia Records that Clutch would release. The first two Clutch albums were still rooted in the hardcore punk ethos that the band was born out of. But this is the record where they got super funky on certain tracks and started to infuse some serious Blues influences. It also stands as possibly their most accessible record as multiple tracks seethe good, old-fashioned, Blues-infused rock 'n' roll. When you listen to the riffs on this album there's as much Lightening Hopkins and Muddy Waters influence as there is Black Sabbath and Deep Purple. Yet even within this wild concoction Clutch manage to out-heavy almost every other stoner rock band of that time period. Such is the beauty and dichotomy of Clutch.

Recommended Track: "The Elephant Riders"

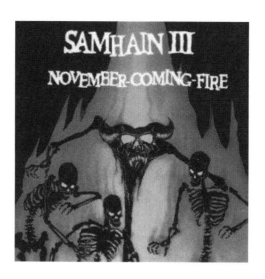

268. Samhain – III: November-Coming-Fire

Once Glenn Danzig and the rest of The Misfits called it quits in a blaze of glory he would go on to form Samhain. Samhain's sound was the perfect blend of The Misfits' horror punk and the crooning, bluesy metal of the first few Danzig albums. But, despite the dark lyrics and imagery, Samhain is also the most accessible to fans of Goth and dark wave of any project Danzig fronted. Fans of acts like The Damned and Bauhaus are going to find just as much to like on a Samhain record as metal fans are. Tracks like "Birthright" are absolute precursors to the Danzig sound and have a thrash tinge to them, while tracks like "Let The Day Begin" hearken back to the Misfits days. But there's just as much Goth rock going on as anything else. With all that said though there is enough heaviness and metal aesthetics to warrant inclusion here. *November Coming Fire* was the second full-length album released by Samhain, originally in 1986 on Danzig's own Plan 9 label.

Recommended Track: "Halloween II"

267. Testament – Souls of Black

Testament was of course born out of the Bay Area thrash scene but they were a "late bloomer" in terms of when their first albums hit the streets compared to some of their contemporaries. Nonetheless, they've had just as much influence on the metal world and they were one of the first thrash bands to sign to a major label when the majors were scooping up metal bands in the hopes of striking gold. *Souls of Black* was their fourth full-length album, originally released in 1990 for Atlantic Records. It peaked at #73 on the Billboard 200 and it is still one of the more popular thrash albums from the early 90s. Testament has undergone a slew of stylistic changes through their long career. Looking back now, *Souls of Black* stands as a sort of transition record between the aggressive thrash of the first three albums and the more melodic approach they would take on the next handful. While it may be the most melodic album of their "classic" period, there are still plenty of fist-pumping, head-banging moments.

Recommended Track: "Face In The Sky"

266. Amebix - Monolith

Amebix are rightfully credited with being one of the first bands to define the crust punk sound. Between the late 70s and their initial break-up in 1987, Amebix put out a bunch of killer music, including two full-length albums. *Monolith* was the band's second, and until 2011, last full-length album, originally released on Heavy Metal Records in 1987. This is definitely the more "metal" sounding of the first two full-lengths, but make no mistake that punk rock still lived within the blackened hearts of these dudes. This album honestly sounds like a melting pot of Bathory, Motörhead, punk legends Crass, and throw in a synth/keyboard player for good measure. This album is a perfect example of how punk rock and something resembling first wave black metal can come together to form this amazingly unique and dark sound.

Recommended Track: "Last Will And Testament"

265. The Dillinger Escape Plan – Calculating Infinity

This album would quite literally turn the entire hardcore scene upside down and, for at least a few years, make New Jersey's The Dillinger Escape Plan the darlings of the new wave of American hardcore. *Calculating Infinity* was the band's first full-length album (after releasing two EPs), originally released on Relapse Records in 1999. This would be their final release with their original vocalist and would feature quite possibly their most talented line-up. It is easily one of the ten best hardcore albums of the 1990s which is saying a lot because that was an amazing decade for hardcore music to say the least. It's an exercise in discordant music if nothing else, but really so much more than just a band adding extra notes to passages for the sake of it. It's also vicious in its delivery and utterly relentless compared to what a lot of their contemporaries were doing at the time.

Recommended Track: "43% Burnt"

264. The Obsessed – Lunar Womb

The Obsessed were a band that played doom metal yet were really born out of the D.C. punk scene, therefore giving their brand of doom a more "rock 'n' roll" flavor to it. After his stint in St. Vitus ended, Wino would eventually recruit none other than Scott Reeder (Kyuss, Goatsnake) to play bass. This new line-up, including Greg Rogers (Goatsnake) on drums, would record the *Lunar Womb* record, originally released in 1991 on Hellhound. I'm not sure if it's because of the line-up or if it's Wino's new found passion for his original band but this is an inspired effort. Some of the best songs The Obsessed has ever recorded are on this album. It's no surprise at all that this album would lead them to garner attention from Columbia Records (who would release their third album).

Recommended Track: "Brother Blue Steel"

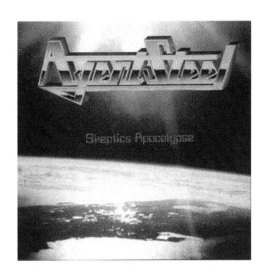

263. Agent Steel – Skeptics Apocalypse

The entire career of Los Angeles' Agent Steel can be defined by two very powerful elements. The first is that they play a highly proficient brand of speed metal. It was steeped in technicality while playing, at times, as fast as possible. The second element, and the most recognizable, are the vocals of John Cyriis. This guy could hit notes that very few other vocalists could. You could make the argument that few other other metal vocalists had the immense range that Cyriis had. But the vocal performance is just one reason to continually revisit this record. Shredding solos, pummeling drums and bass – this record just explodes in a flaming ball of speed metal madness and continues to burn bright from start to finish. *Skeptics Apocalypse* was the band's debut album, originally released by Combat Records in 1985.

Recommended Track: "144,000 Gone"

262. Deadguy – Fixation on a Coworker

For a band that put out very little actual recorded material, especially with the original line-up, it's a wonder that New Jersey's Deadguy had any impact at all, let alone the massive one they've actually had. This should give you some context as to just how amazing and how groundbreaking their sound was back in the early to mid-'90s. There were a bunch of bands that took hardcore music and brought it firmly into the metal world. I'm not sure if any of them did it with such piss and vinegar running through their collective veins the way Deadguy did. This was one angry band and their music reflects that. *Fixation on a Coworker* was the only full-length album Deadguy ever produced and it was originally released in 1995 on Victory Records.

Recommended Track: "Pins and Needles"

261. Electric Wizard - Dopethrone

Doom takes on a lot of different forms. It's not all droning, somber stuff and Electric Wizard seems to prove that on every record. They've experimented quite a bit on recent releases, but early on their brand of doom was heavily laden with enough sludge to give New Orleans a run for its money. One of the best examples of this sludge/doom hybrid, and one of the finest doom metal albums of the last twenty years, is their *Dopethrone* album. *Dopethrone* was originally released in 2000 on Rise Above Records. There are a lot of people out there who consider this Electric Wizard's best album. (Terrorizer Magazine would name it their album of the decade for the 2000s.) That's debatable, but what's not debatable is that this album would cement Electric Wizard's reputation as one of the finest doom bands in all the land. It's a mesmerizing record in so many ways and just crushingly heavy. It's like the sonic equivalent of a wool blanket on a summer day. It's downright oppressive at times.

Recommended Track: "Funeralopolis"

260. Pestilence – Testimony of the Ancients

When you are talking about progressive death metal there are certain bands that should absolutely come to mind – Death, Atheist, Cynic, Nocturnus…and of course Netherlands' Pestilence. There are few bands in the metal world that reinvented themselves on every single album the way Pestilence did. They began as a thrash-based act, transitioned to death metal, and would eventually become this progressive, jazz fusion-death metal hybrid. It was, if nothing else, a very interesting trajectory to watch unfold. *Testimony of the Ancients* was originally released in 1991 on R/C Records. This is extremely intricate and technically proficient death metal executed by a band that was at the top of their songwriting game. The progressive elements they add on this record are just a harbinger of what was to come on future releases. Here though they are subtle textures that really expand their sound in positive ways from the previous offering.

Recommended Track: "Twisted Truth"

259. Exciter – Violence & Force

Violence & Force was the second full length album from Canada's Exciter, originally released in 1984 on Megaforce Records. This was their debut for Megaforce and the album that would entrench them permanently on the metal map. (This album also lead to U.S. tours with Anthrax and Mercyful Fate as well.) Exciter play a hybrid of speed and thrash metal, the former of which they are considered one of the earliest progenitors. There are certainly songs where they are going a million miles an hour, but honestly some of the best tracks on this record include ones like "Pounding Metal" where they slow it up a bit in favor of creating a heavier vibe. However, if you like your metal going all out on raging speed alone you'd be hard-pressed to find a band that did it as well as Exciter.

Recommended Track: "Saxons of the Fire"

258. Royal Thunder - CVI

CVI was the debut full-length for Relapse Records from Georgia's Royal Thunder, released in 2012. If you are a fan, even in the slightest, of the Atlanta/Savannah sludge metal sound the metal world has been tapping into then you should be all over this record. Royal Thunder begin with vocalist/bass player Mlny Parsonz. Her voice is one of the most captivating in all of metal. She's the meeting of Sarah Vaughn and Janis Joplin with a delivery that can be so smooth and yet so biting all at the same time. Guitarist Josh Weaver is one of the most underrated guitar players in the active metal universe. He weaves together Blues-infused riffs with the precision and care of an ancient craftsman, carefully plotting each note so that nothing will escape from the final product when finished. Each song really is a swampy and dark thing of beauty. It's an album that draws from equal parts doom and stoner rock. Royal Thunder's sound on this album shifts back and forth from haunting to thunderous. (Pun intended.)

Recommended Track: "Parsonz Curse"

257. Raven – Rock Until You Drop

We've touched on this band before but it's worth noting again that out of all the bands that emerged from the NWOBHM scene in the late '70s/early '80s one band who seemingly never gets enough credit is Raven. *Rock Until You Drop* was the band's debut album, originally released in 1981 on Neat Records. As you would expect from an album released in 1981 there is a fair amount of hard rock influence that's quite prevalent. However there is no mistaking that this is a metal record and one listen to a track like "Hell Patrol" will tell you all you need to know about this band. They play it rockin' and rollin' for sure but with an aesthetic of raging heaviness that would influence an entire generation of thrash bands, and simultaneously help to formulate the speed metal genre.

Recommended Track: "Hell Patrol"

256. My Dying Bride – As The Flower Withers

From the get-go My Dying Bride's sound was a delicious hybrid of death metal, doom, Goth, and bits of traditional metal thrown in for good measure. *As The Flower Withers* is the band's debut album, originally released in 1992 on Peaceville Records. This is easily their heaviest album as there are zero clean vocals to be found. But it's more than just the vocals because the songs themselves are the closest this band ever got to the "death" part of the term death-doom. You'll not find any albums that contained tracks as manic as "The Forever People", for example. My Dying Bride is the perfect example of a band that allowed their sound to work for them and played whatever felt right. If a song called for keyboards or violins, in went keyboards and violins. If a song called for clean vocals, they weren't afraid to drop the growling. This album though, in all its brutal glory, is the perfect jumping off point for a band that has a discography filled to the brim with quality releases.

Recommended Track: "The Bitterness and the Bereavement"

255. Sodom – Agent Orange

Sodom helped put Germany on the metal map with a brand of thrash that's been described not only as a huge influence on the death metal world, but also as an early precursor to black metal as well. *Agent Orange* was the band's third full-length album, originally released by SPV imprint Steamhammer Records in 1989. Now while I would agree the first Sodom album could absolutely be considered first wave black metal, by the time this album came out they were thrashing it up like no one's business. However, when people talk about their influence on the death metal world it's totally warranted and this album is one reason why. *Agent Orange* is also an important album because it's the last album to feature Frank Blackfire on guitar. With Blackfire on guitar, Chris Witchhunter on drums, and of course Tom Angelripper on bass/vocals this would constitute in many people's minds the "classic" Sodom line-up.

Recommended Track: "Tired and Red"

254. Marduk - Nightwing

Sweden's Marduk have had a long and storied history. They've had two periods when their line-up was stable and it should come as no shock that this was when their best material was being released. One such period is with the current line-up having been together for multiple, exceptional albums. The other period of stability was between 1997-2001 and consisted of four albums that helped define just how unrelenting and blasphemous black metal could truly be. One of the albums to come out of that first period of stability was *Nightwing*, originally released in 1998 on Osmose Productions. *Nightwing* was, up until that point, their most expansive sounding album. It is divided into two parts with the second half of the album telling the historical tale of Vlad 'Tepes' Dracul. Dracul was not only the man behind the impalement of literally thousands of enemy soldiers (thus his nickname Vlad The Impaler), but was also Bram Stoker's inspiration for Dracula.

Recommended Track: "Slay The Nazarene"

253. Voivod – Killing Technology

Canada has seen it's fair share of influential metal bands emerge up there in the Great White North. However there may not be a more influential Canadian metal band than Voivod. There also may not be any Canadian bands that went through as many stylistic changes as Voivod. However, no matter what style they were playing, there were people paying attention. *Killing Technology* was the band's third full length album, originally released in 1987 on Noise Records. Voivod started their career as a thrash/speed metal band before adding all sorts of progressive elements. However in between they went through this sort of crossover phase where they were adding elements of hardcore punk to their sound as well. So take thrash, speed metal, progressive metal, hardcore punk, mix them all up into this weird smorgasbord of sounds and that pretty much sums up this album.

Recommended Track: "Ravenous Medicine"

252. General Surgery - Necrology

I'm not sure if any band got as much mileage out of one EP as Sweden's General Surgery did. They reformed in 2003 and since then have released two full-lengths and a handful of EPs and split releases. Now they are one of the most well known grindcore/goregrind bands around. But from their inception right around 1990 to their reformation they released one official EP. But that EP would put this band on the metal map. *Necrology* was originally released in 1991 on Relapse as 7" vinyl only. Relapse (North America) and Nuclear Blast (Europe) would re-issue it on CD in 1993. For an album that's only about 12 minutes in length they got about 12 years worth of mileage out of it. While the knock on this band has always been their sonic ties to Carcass, the reality more closely resembles a band that took the goregrind sub-genre, molded it in their own image, and continue to do so today.

Recommended Track: "Severe Catatonia in Pathology"

251. King Diamond - Abigail

Featuring the guitar prowess of Andy LaRocque and Mercyful Fate veteran Michael Denner and a rhythm section of Timi Hansen (Mercyful Fate) on bass and Mikkey Dee (Motörhead) on drums, the musicianship alone on this record is worth the price of admission. Throw in King's massive vocal range, and a thought-provoking concept running through the songs like a horror story and this is King Diamond at their peak. *Abigail* was King Diamond's second full length album, originally released in 1987 on Roadrunner Records. The story held within these songs center around a haunted mansion and a young couple that inherits it. They soon find out that the woman has been impregnated with the spirit of a ghost named Abigail who inhabits the mansion. It's honestly something that reads like it's out of a classic Stephen King novel, but throw in King Diamond as "narrator" and it's an exceptionally creepy affair.

Recommended Track: "The Family Ghost"

250. Riot - Narita

Narita was the second full length album from New York's Riot, originally released in 1979. For the first five months the only place you could find it was Japan. It wouldn't get a proper US releases until Columbia finally picked them up. But Columbia would drop them after a successful tour opening for Sammy Hagar. Before the album even went through its normal cycle they already found themselves without a label. The band went out and sunk their money into promoting the album themselves, including massive radio airplay at hard rock and college stations across the country. Columbia took notice and picked up the option for the next record. Honestly this band could have been America's answer to Judas Priest, instead they would constantly face an uphill battle thanks to the people that were supposed to be supporting them. Regardless of their label issues it doesn't detract from how rockin' this record is and the impact it had on a burgeoning metal scene.

Recommended Track: "Kick Down The Wall"

249. Immortal – Blizzard Beasts

When you are talking about the glorious second wave of European black metal there are a small handful of bands that should be immediately top of mind. One of those bands is Norway's Immortal. *Blizzard Beasts* was Immortal's fourth full-length album, originally released in 1997 on Osmose Productions. This album is chock full of killer riffs and some great material in general. While not as expansive in overall atmosphere as some efforts that would come later, it's the perfect bridge from their more polished recent material to their lo-fi beginnings. This would be the last album that founding member Demonaz Doom Occulta would be on guitar due to severe tendinitis in his arms. This was also the first album that Horgh would be on drums, starting a run that has now lasted over 20 years behind the kit. All told, it's a landmark album for a landmark band.

Recommended Track: "Blizzard Beasts"

248. Napalm Death – Harmony Corruption

Harmony Corruption was Napalm Death's third full-length album, originally released by Earache Records in 1990. Their previous two albums were as grindcore as grindcore can get. After their second album though they went through some major line-up changes including bringing Barney Greenway (ex-Benediction) on as vocalist and Jessie Pintado (ex-Terrorizer) on guitars. They would also head to Florida to record with legendary death metal producer, Scott Burns. In other words, this is a death metal record. There is no arguing about what genre of music it is anymore, not with 25+ years of hindsight on our side. This album sounds more like a Florida death metal album than anything else. The mid-tempo songs, Greenway's vocals, there is just so much to this album that screams death metal and forsakes their grindcore roots. But that doesn't mean it's a bad record. On the contrary, it's extremely well-written and contains plenty of classic material.

Recommended Track: "Mind Snare"

247. Trouble – Run To The Light

Trouble was marketed as a "white metal" band by their label at the time, Metal Blade, because they sang songs that reflected the member's Christian beliefs. That's a misnomer though because the music that Trouble wrote was a) heavy as a sack of bricks and b) not overly preachy. Despite the lyrical content (and in this case the album title/cover art), these guys could still bring it with an amazing Black Sabbath aesthetic combined with various '60s psych rock influences. *Run To The Light* was the band's third full-length album and final album for Metal Blade, originally released in 1987. After this album they would find themselves on a new label and with a new sound as they moved more towards a more stoner rock kind of vibe. The first two things you noticed about Trouble were the sick riffs and the vocals of Eric Wagner. Both are at the top of their game on this recording.

Recommended Track: "On Borrowed Time"

246. Diamond Head – Lightning to the Nations

Lightning to the Nations was the debut album from England's Diamond Head, self-released in 1980 on their own Happy Face imprint. There have been literally dozens of reissues of this album as the original vinyl pressing was only 1000 copies. Therein lies part of the reason this band never attained the global status of some of their peers, as they missed getting on the original gravy train that rode out of the U.K. to the rest of the world. But the real shame of that lies in the fact that this album is so powerful and so well written that even for an album the band was originally calling a "demo" it blew the doors off a lot of other bands at the time. (They considered this album enough of a demo that all of the songs would eventually be re-recorded and appear on other Diamond Head releases.) If you like big, tasty riffs and your metal in the traditional vein then Diamond Head better be on your list, especially this album.

Recommended Track: "Am I Evil"

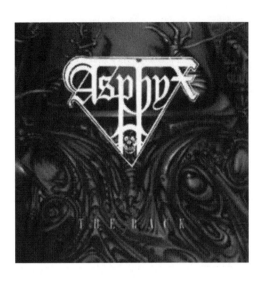

245. Asphyx – The Rack

Formed in the Netherlands in the late '80s, Asphyx didn't really come together with a solid line-up until vocalist Martin van Drunen left Pestilence and joined the band. Soon after they were signed by Century Media Records and in 1991 released their debut album, *The Rack*. His work on the first two Pestilence albums would put van Drunen in the conversation of being one of the better death metal vocalists around. His work with Asphyx would solidify that. But Asphyx wasn't all van Drunen. On the contrary, this band played a monster style of death metal reminiscent of the Swedish sound but not entirely beholden to it. They could write death metal that sounded like a chainsaw tearing down a forest, but had this penchant for slowing up the tempo and letting the music drip like molasses. On their earliest releases it was a thing of abhorrent beauty. *The Rack* is not their most polished effort but it's easily one of the most underrated death metal albums of the 1990s.

Recommended Track: "Vermin"

244. Emperor – IX Equilibrium

IX Equilibrium was the third full length album from Norway's Emperor, originally released by Candlelight Records in 1999. It was during the recording of this album that the songwriting duo of Ihsahn and Samoth heightened their musical differences. Samoth wanted to take the band in a more direct approach, while Ihashn wanted to continue with the pomp and circumstance of the symphonic black metal sound which they helped create. Ihsahn would apparently win out because this is an extremely progressive album, featuring spoken word passages, classical interludes, and a heightened usage of synths/keyboards. The final product is an album that is absolutely relentless in the way it attacks the listener. Even with the sparse interludes the listener really only has time to catch their breath before being sonically assaulted again by this wall of cacophonous sound. But don't think of it as an attack in the same way a death metal or grindcore album attacks. Think of it as something a little more refined if you will.

Recommended Track: "Curse You All Men!"

243. Sepultura - Arise

Arise is the fourth full-length album by Sepultura, originally released on Roadrunner Records in 1991. This was truly the first Sepultura album that had production values to match the songwriting. Even the previous album, which famed producer Scott Burns traveled to Brazil to help them record, did not have the production quality of this one. This time around the band came to Burns and his studio in Florida and it paid off. *Arise* moves further away from their original thrash sound, yet is still a thrash/death metal hybrid album like it's predecessor. However, in hindsight, it also clearly laid the groundwork for the groove metal these guys would start churning out with the next release. This album is also one of their best sellers, achieving Gold status in a handful of countries. It's easy to see why. It's a slick sounding album that is as accessible as death metal could ever possibly hope to be.

Recommended Track: "Arise"

242. Solitude Aeturnus – Into The Depths Of Sorrow

Into The Depths Of Sorrow was the debut album by Texas' Solitude Aeturnus, originally released in 1991 on Roadrunner Records. It mixes elements of the traditional doom first laid down by the likes of Black Sabbath and Pentagram, but melds it with this killer traditional metal/NWOBHM vibe. The vocals are soaring (and frankly some of the best doom metal has to offer), the guitars are powerful and driving, and even the little neo-classical interludes fit perfectly within the aesthetics they were going for. If you're a fan of early doom metal then you should be all over this album. It stands as one of the best (and most underrated) examples of American doom we have from the 1990s.

Recommended Track: "Where Angels Dare To Tread"

241. Whiplash – Power and Pain

New Jersey's Whiplash was one of the first East Coast thrash bands to really make a name for themselves outside of their own scene alongside the likes of Anthrax, Carnivore, and Overkill. It was their debut album that really opened a lot of eyes. *Power and Pain* was originally released on Roadrunner Records in 1985. Let me start by saying that this is a vicious album. Whiplash would never record an album as venomous and heavy as this one. That's not to knock any of their later releases because there are some great albums to choose from. But this album just has this edge to it that is unmatched by not only their own catalog, but by most of their contemporaries' releases as well. This album is fast and furious, combining elements of both speed metal and thrash metal. The vocals are borderline demonic sounding and the breakneck pace at which most of this record is played makes it sound like a bullet train straight to hell. A true thrash metal classic.

Recommended Track: "Last Man Alive"

240. Rainbow – Long Live Rock 'n' Roll

I'm pretty sure that Ronnie James Dio could have sat down and read from the phone book and it would still be one of the most metal sounding things you'd ever heard. Add to that mastermind Ritchie Blackmore on guitar and the two of them combined were an extremely formidable duo. *Long Live Rock n' Roll* was Rainbow's third full-length album, originally released in 1978 on Polydor Records. This is an important album for two reasons. The first because it contained some of their best material, including "L.A. Connection", "Gates of Babylon", and "Kill The King." Secondly this would be the final album to feature the mighty vocal talents of the diminutive RJD, who would go on to join up with Black Sabbath after his departure. Speaking of line-ups this album would also feature Cozy Powell (who had played with Jeff Beck) on drums and Bob Daisley (who would later play on a handful of Ozzy Osbourne records) on bass. Needless to say this was a powerhouse lineup making powerhouse music.

Recommended Track: "L.A. Connection"

239. Cannibal Corpse – Butchered At Birth

Butchered At Birth was Cannibal Corpse's second full-length album, originally released in 1991 on Metal Blade Records. They play, and have for the most part always played, a fist-to-the-face brand of death metal. There really is no simile or metaphor I could use to further expound on their sound. They just need to be experienced to be appreciated. In a lot of ways *Butchered At Birth* was the first Cannibal Corpse album that was truly as heavy and as brutal as the name would imply. It was their first album to grotesquely soar beyond what the average death metal band was achieving at the time, so it's not only important from an influence standpoint but also from a legacy standpoint. (It was also the first Cannibal Corpse album to face widespread censorship both for the music/lyrical content and for the album artwork.)

Recommended Track: "Living Dissection"

238. Dio – Sacred Heart

Most hardcore Dio fans would scoff at the notion that this album was somehow "lost." But the unfortunate fact remains that over time this album has become the least distributed, and least critically acclaimed out of Dio's first four studio albums. While it may have been a slight step down from the first two albums especially, there's no good reason for this thing to be lost to the metal history books. *Sacred Heart* was Dio's third album and it went all the way to #29 on the Billboard 200 upon it's release in 1985 on Warner Bros. It produced some classic songs, such as the title track, which RJD included in live sets pretty much right up until his death. Lastly, despite a growing rift with guitarist Vivian Campbell that would see him leave the band shortly after the album's release, it was an album that had some amazing songwriting. To the point there really isn't any filler on this album at all.

Recommended Track: "Like the Beat of a Heart"

237. Opeth - Orchid

Orchid was Opeth's debut album, originally released by Candlelight Records in 1995. The fact that Century Media chose to reissue this album under the Century Black banner in 1997 is interesting. It certainly isn't a black metal record, but there is an edge and a rawness to this album that would be lost over time as the band moved to a more polished and progressive sound. Make no mistake though, this is Opeth as you've come to know and love them, complete with clean, folksy interludes and a smattering of progressive rock elements. However, look no further than a track like "The Twilight Is My Robe" to see the frost-covered fingerprints of the Swedish metal landscape in 1995 all over this release. Even the peaceful interludes like "Silhouette" that dot this album have a darker, more sinister feel than most of what they would produce later on. After over twenty years and almost a dozen albums later, this still stands as one of the best albums Opeth ever produced. It's certainly one of their heaviest and most grim efforts if nothing else.

Recommended Track: "The Twilight Is My Robe"

236. Exhorder – The Law

The Law was Exhorder's second and final album, released in 1992 on Roadrunner Records. Exhorder's first album was a blazing mixture of thrash and hardcore punk. By the time this record came out they moved away from their punk/crossover routes into a style of thrash that includes all of those elements we would later use to recognize as "groove metal." But what we now consider "groove metal" was, at the time, a reflection in a dirtied mirror of what was going on in Exhorder's home scene in New Orleans. Bands like Crowbar, Eyehategod, and a little later on, Soilent Green and Acid Bath were all experimenting in different ways with sludge and other extreme elements, which when combined with thrash gives you this "groove" sound. It's a bit of an oversimplification of Exhorder's musical transition, however it would not be a stretch to say they were, by this time, the perfect storm of both their own tastes and that of their scene.

Recommended Track: "I Am The Cross"

235. Anathema - Serenades

These days England's Anathema are not a metal band. Simply put, they play this ethereal brand of atmospheric alt rock mixed with some prog elements. It's a far cry from their debut album to say the least. It has also been a completely natural progression for them as they went from a heavy death/doom sound to a more progressive brand of doom, to where they sit today. But where it all started was with this album. *Serenades* was their debut full-length, released in 1993 on Peaceville Records. Let's make no mistakes here, this is the heaviest album Anathema ever released. How heavy? How about heavy enough that they toured with Cannibal Corpse before its release. If you are familiar with their recent endeavors let that sink in for a second. This is the only album to feature Darren White on vocals, as he grunts and growls over and through some fiercely depressive and ethereal doom metal. Without hesitation, a true classic of the genre.

Recommended Track: "They (Always Will) Die"

234. Neurosis – Enemy of the Sun

Oakland's Neurosis originally released *Enemy of the Sun* in 1993 on Alternative Tentacles. (This would be their final release for A.T. as they would move to Relapse Records for their next effort.) The album starts off with a sample from the film, *The Sheltering Sky*, which starred Debra Winger and John Malkovich as an American couple about to spend an extended amount of time traversing the Sahara region. The sample, which starts with, "Are you lost...Yes..." is the perfect set up for this album. The film is gorgeously shot, yet portrays a story that is downright bizarre and at times brutally depressing and unnerving – that pretty much sums up this record as well. It's so gorgeous and lush yet so psychotic at the same time. Trust when I tell you there was nothing at the time of this album's release that sounded anything like this record. It not only sent Neurosis on this amazingly prolific and influential career trajectory, but it literally changed the paradigm of extreme music for anyone who heard it.

Recommended Track: "Raze the Stray"

233. Extreme Noise Terror –
A Holocaust in Your Head

England's Extreme Noise Terror are thought of as godfathers by two different camps. The crust/d-beat camp often site this band as one of the innovators of the genre. Same goes for fans of grindcore. Neither of them would be far off, especially with this album. Punk kids dig these guys in equal number it would seem as metalheads, although by the time this album was released they already played heavier and nastier than most punk rock records of the day. *A Holocaust in Your Head* was Extreme Noise Terror's debut album, originally released in 1989 on Head Eruption Records. Its dual-vocal assault and breakneck pace will immediately hearken to the earliest days of grindcore. The super political lyrics and their punk rock aesthetics would also lend to the idea that they are one of the earliest crust punk bands as well. I would argue they didn't 'start' either genre, but there's no denying their influence and it all started with this album.

Recommended Track: "Deceived"

232. Cathedral – The Ethereal Mirror

England's Cathedral started their career as a gritty doom metal band and would, over time, evolve into this rockin' outfit who wrote songs that could have easily played well to commercial radio. Somewhere they needed to transition though and their second and third efforts were the ones that served as the bridges. *The Ethereal Mirror* was the band's second full-length album and was originally released in 1993 on both Earache and Columbia Records. Although this album is more accessible and experimental than their debut it's probably not what Columbia was hoping for. For one, Lee Dorrian is the antithesis of the archetypal rock front man in the best possible way. The irony about this album is Columbia came knocking probably one album too soon because their sound would continue to move away from heavy doom and more towards stoner rock. Regardless, this album stands as a stellar testimony to where they came from and where they were going.

Recommended Track: "Enter The Worms"

231. The Accused – The Return of...
Martha Splatterhead

The Accused were, for lack of a better term, a crossover act. They were born out of a rich Seattle punk rock scene but by the time this first full-length was released had already started adding a lot of serious metal elements to their music. Punk rock riffs would be buttressed by some killer thrashing giving this album a completely fresh sound at the time, and one a lot of bands would go on to copy. When this album hit record players and tape decks in 1986 it was something way more aggressive than a lot of punk kids were used to and something way more scattershot than a lot of metal kids were used to. That's a beautiful thing and its influence can still be felt today. This album was originally released through Subcore Records, but would be re-released in 1987 as the first ever release for Earache Records.

Recommended Track: "Wrong Side of the Grave"

230. Nuclear Assault – Game Over

When bass player and founding member, Dan Lilker, left Anthrax right after the release of their debut album he set out to form his own thrash project. I can only assume that he was driven to make something faster, heavier and more technically proficient than his former band. Even if he didn't it was mission accomplished with the debut album from Nuclear Assault. Adding yet another jewel into the crown of East Coast thrash, Nuclear Assault came rumbling out of New York City in the early '80s writing some of the fiercest metal that scene had produced up to that point. *Game Over* is the band's debut, originally released by Combat Records in 1986. To say that 1986 was a watershed year in metal music would be an understatement. Obviously the first album people think of from that year is Metallica's *Master of Puppets*. But over on the other coast, around the same time, the thrash scene there was also producing some gems, with *Game Over* maybe being the best of the lot.

Recommended Track: "After The Holocaust"

229. Unleashed – Where No Life Dwells

Unleashed were a huge contributor to the Swedish death metal scene for a couple different reasons. The first, and extremely important, reason being they were one of the first bands this side of Bathory to embrace Viking culture/Norse mythology as legitimate lyrical content. The second, and probably most important, reason was because they are damn good at what they do. *Where No Life Dwells* was Unleashed's debut album, originally released in 1991 on Century Media Records. This album had everything that made Swedish death metal so good at the time – a ripping guitar sound, the ability to change tempos at the drop of a hat, shredding solos, a vocalist with one of the best guttural voices of his era, and a sound that was so deep and cavernous it could swallow you whole. This album is one of the benchmark releases of the Swedish death metal scene and I'm constantly amazed at how underrated this band and this album truly are.

Recommended Track: "If They Had Eyes"

228. Samhain - Initium

When punk legends The Misfits blew up in 1983, the side project that front man Glenn Danzig was planning, Samhain, became his focus. In 1985, Samhain released their debut album, *Initium*, on Danzig's own Plan 9 label. This album is a pretty direct extension of what The Misfits were doing at the end of their amazing run. However the lyrics were a little bit darker, the live shows a little bloodier, and the music a little heavier. The punk aesthetics are still very much there, but again, the overall vibe and musical direction of this album is much heavier than anything The Misfits were doing, often removing catchy hooks in favor of driving rhythms. If you're a fan of punk, Goth rock, or really any form of early '80s metal you should give this album a go for sure. It's not going to be the heaviest or darkest record found here, and frankly isn't as good as the first couple Danzig records. But it's still a great testament to a time period where, for a few years anyway, the musical worlds of The Misfits and Danzig collided.

Recommended Track: "Macabre"

227. The Obsessed – The Obsessed

The history of The Obsessed is a complex one, which we've covered a bit in previous entries. That long lost album that Metal Blade Records was supposed to release in 1985? This is it essentially. In 1990, Germany's Hellhound Records (a label that doesn't get enough credit for their role in the history of doom metal/stoner rock) would release the debut, self-titled album from The Obsessed that Metal Blade had passed on after the band had appeared on a Metal Massacre comp. Realizing that The Obsessed wasn't dead after all, Scott "Wino" Weinrich would quit Saint Vitus and move back east to revive his original project. Metal Blade did a lot of things right back then but history has shown they dropped the ball on this one. This album is one of the closest things you are going to get to classic Black Sabbath without actually listening to classic Black Sabbath. A true stoner rock/doom tour de force.

Recommended Track: "Freedom"

226. Cryptic Slaughter – Money Talks

Cryptic Slaughter might not be the first crossover thrash band, but they were right there when it all started going down out on the West Coast. In a scene that would combine hardcore/punk rock and thrash metal into this amazing combination of angst and speed, it resonated with a lot of kids looking for something to be pissed at. *Money Talks* is the second full-length album originally released in 1987 on Metal Blade Records. Cryptic Slaughter were one of a handful of bands that Metal Blade would sign who would be key in the formation of the crossover genre. Arguably, these guys may have been the heaviest of the lot. Super fast riffing, combined with jackal like screams about a world gone to pot, are punctuated by breakdowns that only offer brief respites until they gear back up to kick your teeth in again. It's a rabid record and one that still resonates today.

Recommended Track: "Freedom of Expression?"

225. Atheist – Piece Of Time

The whole idea of technical death metal was not a foreign concept when Atheist released their debut album. In fact, by the time this album finally got a proper release, Atheist were one of a handful of death metal bands who were changing the paradigm of what was acceptable to call "death metal." *Piece of Time* would originally be released in 1990 on Active Records out of the UK. Atheist and their fans would have to wait another six months for this album to be properly released in the States when they finally signed a licensing deal with Metal Blade Records. Whenever you mention Atheist's name you immediately get comments like "progressive death metal" and "jazz fusion." While both of those monikers would fit the band in due time this album is their purest in terms of the death metal aesthetic. However, the foundation was there for what was to come. Intricate time signature changes, rapid fluctuations in tempo, the occasional synth, and sheer death metal brutality were all on display.

Recommended Track: "Piece of Time"

224. Exodus – Bonded By Blood

Bonded By Blood was the debut album by Exodus, originally released on Torrid Records before being re-released by Combat Records after the band was picked up by the label in 1985. This album was actually completed and ready for release a year earlier but there were problems with the artwork, album title, and the label in general. When it finally saw a proper release, *Bonded By Blood* was gifted to the metal world at a time when the Bay Area was at their pinnacle. Metallica and Possessed would release genre defining albums within a 12 month window of this album's release, and bands like Death Angel and Testament would be close behind. The work that Exodus was doing at this time rivals it all for excellence. This album is also notable for being the only studio album Exodus would release with Paul Baloff on vocals and to contain songs co-written by former member Kirk Hammett.

Recommended Track: "Metal Command"

223. Saint Vitus – Mournful Cries

Formed in Los Angeles in the late 1970s, Saint Vitus were one of the few bands at the time carrying the torch of Black Sabbath inspired doom metal. 30 years ago you didn't play doom metal because the chicks dug it. You didn't play doom metal because it would win you popularity contests. So when a band like Saint Vitus came along playing down-tuned, sludgy jams that made your innards rumble, it was pretty unique for the most part. *Mournful Cries* was the band's fourth full-length album, originally released in 1988 on SST Records. This album is chock-full of all of those elements mentioned above. It's a heavy, dirty, molasses-like and just comes at you like a possessed steamroller. The dragon thing on the front cover is a pretty epic representation for this album, as the band rumbles across the countryside, breathing fire and laying waste to everything in their path.

Recommended Track: "Dragon Time"

222. Voivod – Rrröööaaarrr

Canada's Voivod started out as a band heavily influenced by the hardcore/punk scene and their debut album could actually fall into the crossover genre we've discussed so much. The album that came after this one was a much more technical and progressive offering than anything that came before it. This album would fall somewhere in the middle of the two. *Rrröööaaarrr* was the second full length album released by Voivod, originally on Combat Records in 1986. The hardcore/punk elements are absolutely still present on this record but there's also a distinct progression towards a more metallic/thrash-based sound. On top of that Voivod would add their trademark ability to shift the paradigm just enough so that no other thrash record sounded like this one in 1986. It was then, and still is today, the bastard love child of thrash and punk in so many disturbing ways.

Recommended Track: "Slaughter in a Grave"

221. Sarcofago – I.N.R.I.

In 1987, Brazil's Sarcofago would release their debut album, *I.N.R.I.* through the Cogumelo label. Its influence over the death and black metal worlds can still be felt today. The first thing you'll notice about this album is the fact that the band appears to be wearing "corpse paint" long before anyone in Europe (not named King Diamond or Tom G. Warrior) was doing it. Second, and most important, is the music held within. This album certainly has proto-death metal and thrash influences all over it. But at the end of the day you'd be hard pressed to find an earlier example of what we now call first wave black metal anywhere else in the world at this time. It's evil, gritty extreme metal and the amount of blast beats alone on this thing put it in a category with very few other bands in 1987. The vocals are downright demonic, the riffs are picked in seemingly double-time, and the bass is a thunderous blast of noise. More credit should be given to this band and this record when discussing the earliest beginnings of both black and death metal.

Recommended Track: "Satanic Lust"

220. Warlock – Burning The Witches

It could be argued that Warlock, were really Germany's answer to the NWOBHM movement from a musical standpoint, especially on this album. *Burning the Witches* was the debut album from Warlock, originally released in 1984 on Mausoleum Records. It's a shame to think that due to poor distribution and a lack of overall label support that more people didn't hear this album upon its initial release. If Warlock did have proper distribution from the start we'd be talking about them as one of the most important metal bands of the early '80s, as opposed to the immensely underrated act they are today. As it stands this album is extremely influential, especially in their homeland where Warlock remained very popular right up until their demise. Fans of driving, melodic, traditional heavy metal could certainly find worse albums to start their day with than this masterwork.

Recommended Track: "Burning the Witches"

219. My Dying Bride – The Angel and the Dark River

The Angel and the Dark River was My Dying Bride's third full-length album, originally released on Peaceville in 1995. It can honestly be described as something along the lines of beauty through heaviness. It's a gorgeous, lush album, complete with waves of instrumentation. But it's also one of the most somber and depressing albums you'll ever hear. Almost every song crawls along, dragging the listener through a maze of sounds, replete with violins, synths, and some of the best doom riffs you'll ever hear. This is also the first My Dying Bride album where all the vocals are clean. Honestly, that adds to the misery of it all. Aaron Stainthorpe's vocals are so pleading and so bereft of any hope whatsoever. It's a fascinating and fantastic addition to their sound when coupled with the signature oppressive doom My Dying Bride has become famous for. Needless to say this is not the type of music you throw on at a party, unless you and your guests plan on finishing the night with a bucket of special Kool-Aid.

Recommended Track: "The Cry of Manknd"

218. Mercyful Fate – In The Shadows

Right when they were really hitting the heights in both popularity and creativity, Mercyful Fate called it quits. Band members went their separate ways with King Diamond taking half the band with him to form his namesake project that would release some solid albums in their own right. But after two comp albums that brought to light previously unavailable recordings (1987's *The Beginning* and 1992's *Return of the Vampire*) and a weird split album that former label Roadrunner slapped together featuring previously released material from both bands, Mercyful Fate decided to get back together properly. Four-fifths of the original line-up (original drummer Kim Ruzz would not join the band) would come together to release their third proper full-length album. *In The Shadows* was originally released in 1993 on Metal Blade Records, their first of several albums throughout the '90s for the legendary label, and a return to the fold for one of metal's greatest bands.

Recommended Track: "The Bell Witch"

217. Trouble – The Skull

The Skull was the second full-length album from Chicago's Trouble, originally released in 1985 on Metal Blade Records. It's the album, that along with their debut, helped define a burgeoning U.S. doom scene. It's a darker album than their first and at least part of that has to be associated with front man Eric Wagner's struggles with substance abuse, not to mention band turmoil that would see a couple members depart shortly after this album's release. As with all Trouble albums though, the lyrical content is once again chock full of religious overtones. Doom metal was born on the back of "the Devil's note" and dark lyrics that could be misinterpreted as "Satanic". Yet Trouble had no problem bringing the heavy with lyrics that ultimately delivered a positive message. In the long and storied history of American doom metal this album still ranks as a genre-defining classic.

Recommended Track: "Pray For The Dead"

216. Samael – Ceremony of Opposites

Samael albums prior to this one should be considered second wave black metal or maybe blackened death metal. Pretty much everything that has come after this record has been this sort of industrial/Goth metal – heavy on synths, clean vocals, an overall sound that lacks a lot of their early aggression, etc. Somewhere between two worlds lives this album. *Ceremony of Opposites* was the third album from Switzerland's Samael, originally released on Century Media Records in 1994. It lacks some of the black metal aesthetics of their predecessors, and instead those aforementioned synths show up while they experiment with a slightly more melodic brand of songwriting in general. But it is still a heavy, nasty, blasphemous affair. If anything this album still screams to be classified as blackened death metal at the very least. Regardless of classification, *Ceremony of Opposites* is possibly one of the most underrated albums that Century Media put out in the 1990s.

Recommended Track: "Baphomet's Throne"

215. D.R.I. - Crossover

Based in California, by way of Houston, Dirty Rotten Imbeciles started out as a hardcore punk band and a damn good one at that. But by their second album they had started to add more metallic leanings to their sound. This melding of the punk and metal worlds into a new brand of thrash metal would of course be called "crossover" or "crossover thrash." Now whether or not this album title is where everyone got the name is really kind of up for debate. It's an easy beacon to recognize and certainly is an apropos title for what's held within. Regardless of the origin, the title says it all. *Crossover* was D.R.I.'s third full length album, originally released by Metal Blade Records in 1987. Albums that would follow this one would lean even more on metal and start to fade further away from the band's punk roots. This album is honestly the perfect match of the two styles, wedded in unholy matrimony.

Recommended Track: "Tear It Down"

214. Saxon – Denim and Leather

One of the most important and influential bands to come out of the NWOBHM scene would be Saxon. They were, at one point in time, one of the biggest heavy metal bands in the world. In their native UK and Europe, especially, they would dominate the album charts, headline massive festivals and tour endlessly. When Ozzy Osbourne first left Black Sabbath and went on tour with his "Blizzard of Ozz" band he opened for Saxon. Read that again: Ozzy opened for Saxon. They were that big. Their first four albums helped to put them there, this one being the last of the batch. *Denim and Leather* was originally released in 1981 on Carrere Records out of France. This is an album filled with arena-like anthems, and a massive, sweeping sound. It was written to be played as loud as your stereo could go and to bang your head from start to finish.

Recommended Track: "Princess of the Night"

213. Dismember – Like An Everflowing Stream

In the early '90s there was very little that was "melodic" about Swedish death metal. If it was done right it was a brutal, gut-punching wall of cacophony. One of the bands that helped perfect the "Swedish sound" was Dismember. Originally released in 1991 on Nuclear Blast Records, *Like An Everflowing Stream* is born from hellfire and a blitzkrieg-like approach to death metal. Tracks like "And So Is Life" and "Skin Her Alive" (which nabbed the band an indecency charge from the British government upon the album's entry into the U.K.) are driving, buzz saw guitar-filled barrages. This album rarely lets up and is one of the better death metal debuts you are going to find pretty much anywhere or at any time. It can't be understated that when we talk about some of the greatest Swedish death metal records of all-time this album should fall somewhere into the discussion.

Recommended Track: "And So Is Life"

212. Darkthrone – Transilvanian Hunger

Few bands in the metal universe have the type of legacy and "kvlt" standing that Norway's Darkthrone have. Whether it's being one of the leaders of the second wave of black metal, the last decade plus they've spent successfully reinventing themselves, or their minimalist, reductive approach to making music, Darkthrone have always been a band that has risen above the majority of criticism anyone ever attempted to heap on them. *Transilvanian Hunger* was the band's fourth full-length album, originally released by Peaceville Records in 1994. After their debut release, which of course had a more death metal sound, the band would release three albums considered by many to be their "Unholy Trinity" of second wave, black metal masterworks. For most of society this album is simply white noise with someone growling over top of it. And while that may be true in a sense, it was a black metal landmark and an album that cemented Darkthrone as one of the powerhouses of black metal's glorious second wave.

Recommended Track: "Skald av Satans sol"

211. Obituary – The End Complete

The End Complete was Obituary's third full length album, originally released by R/C Records in 1992. Obituary was one of a handful of bands at that time making Roadrunner arguably the largest underground metal label in the world. This is Obituary's best selling album and I've seen varying sales figures that put it at over half a million sales worldwide. This album is the third album in what I've dubbed the "Obituary trilogy", which comprises the first three Obituary albums. Those albums came out one right after the other over a four year period and each one is a masterwork of the death metal genre. When you make that much good music in such a short period of time good things are bound to happen for you. Obituary's sound has always incorporated that swampy, sludgy edge to it and yet still manages to pummel listeners on every track. They are such a unique addition to the scene and it's no wonder their influence is still felt today.

Recommended Track: "The End Complete"

210. Paradise Lost - Gothic

Gothic was the second full length album from Paradise Lost, originally released in 1991 on Peaceville Records. To this day it still stands as both a genre and career-defining album. Where their debut was much more death metal-centric, this album takes a huge leap creatively. First and foremost, doom becomes the centerpiece on the mantle for these guys. Throw in everything from strings, to operatic female vocals, the first appearance of "clean" lead vocals, and just an overall dreary vibe and what you've got is one of the first doom albums to embrace the Gothic subculture. The influence of this record can be felt everywhere from doom to symphonic black metal. It's a potent album that really should be avoided if you are feeling glum. But, if you can stay off the suicide watch list then I highly suggest you get involved with this album immediately.

Recommended Track: "Gothic"

209. Deicide - Legion

If you are ever looking for a band that plays uncompromising, relentless, blasphemous death metal with plenty of Satanic lyrics and imagery, your search should start with Deicide. *Legion* was the second full length album from Florida's Deicide, originally released by R/C Records in 1992. *Legion* is chock-full of brutally proficient death metal. In fact, I'd go so far as to say this may be the most technical album that Deicide ever produced. There's some repetition on this record but it actually serves as a nice break in between the intricate riffing and the Slayer-like guitar solos that permeate throughout. This album is like a thousand Satanic tanks running roughshod through your town. While Glen Benton and company would cause a stir on so many different fronts, no one could ever say this band didn't back it up with their music.

Recommended Track: "Satan Spawn, The Caco-Daemon"

208. Pestilence – Malleus Maleficarum

Malleus Maleficarum was the debut record from Pestilence, originally released in 1988 on Roadrunner imprint R/C Records. If you had to pinpoint what genre this album falls into your best bet would be thrash metal. But there are elements of death metal all over this thing, especially Martin van Drunen's vocals, which straddled the line between raspy thrash singer and acidic death metal vocalist. But more than just vocals this album was way heavier than the average thrash record. This album falls somewhere in that gray zone between thrash and death metal that bands like Possessed, Sepultura, and Kreator hung out in. There would also be those elements that when you look back on their career arc with 20/20 hindsight you can see how they were headed into a sort of prog-like state. Regardless of how you want to classify this album it's not only one of the best albums of Pestilence's career but it's one of the best extreme metal albums of the late '80s.

Recommended Track: "Bacterial Surgery"

207. Witchfinder General – Friends of Hell

To say that Witchfinder General is one of the most influential bands of their era is a bit of a misnomer. Their true influence wasn't felt until long after they were gone. Witchfinder General is considered a NWOBHM band almost by default. They were from the UK and recorded their first two albums in the early '80s. Therefore by pure happenstance they are lumped into the conversation when talking about NWOBHM bands. They wrote music pulling in elements of the contemporary, traditional metal sound, but no band from that scene worshiped at the altar of Black Sabbath the way this band did. The result would be this proto-doom sound that set in motion a burgeoning British doom scene. *Friends of Hell* is Witchfinder General's second full-length album, originally released on Heavy Metal Records in 1983. It would be the final album of the classic era as they would break up shortly after its release.

Recommended Track: "Last Chance"

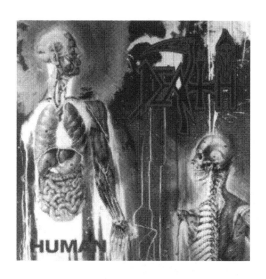

206. Death - Human

Human is Death's fourth full-length album, originally released by Relativity Records in 1991. In the later years of their illustrious career, Death would be credited with being one of the pioneers of progressive death metal. If you were looking for where that started then look no further than this album. The three albums prior to this one are absolute metal classics. But this was the album where Death really started to expand their sound in ways they only hinted at on previous efforts. The almost constant and complex time signature changes, the beefed up bass lines, even the lack of gore-drenched or overly political lyrics were all signs Death was transitioning away from their traditional death metal roots. There's no denying Chuck Schuldiner is one of the greatest guitar players in metal history. Frankly, he's also one of metal's most potent songwriters as well, and it's showcased perfectly on this album.

Recommended Track: "Suicide Machine"

205. Graveyard – Hisingen Blues

Sweden became the hotbed for yet another movement in the metal underground in recent years. This time the Swedes dominated the retro/occult rock thing that quickly replaced stoner rock as the bread being buttered by those who worship at the altar of the Black Sabbaths, Blue Cheers and Deep Purples of the world. One of the best bands to come out of this scene was Graveyard. *Hisingen Blues* was Graveyard's second full-length album, originally released by Nuclear Blast Records in 2011. This album has everything that those who swear they are 'born too late' have come to love. Deep, bluesy vocals? Check. Heavy, catchy as hell riffs? Check. Special attention paid to making sure the rhythm section isn't just background noise, the way Sabbath perfected? Check. Eyebrows may be raised by those not expecting to see this album ranked this high. However, when it's time to look back on the rebirth of proto-metal, we'll be speaking Graveyard's name with reverence.

Recommended Track: "Ain't Fit To Live Here"

204. Amon Amarth – Twilight of the Thunder God

Death metal and Sweden go together like peanut butter and jelly, and one of the best Swedish death metal bands in the world right now is Amon Amarth. They get lumped into the "Viking metal" category because…well, pretty much every song they write is about Vikings or Norse Mythology. There are few bands in the world who dig as deep into Norse history and mythology for lyrical material as this band does. There are also few bands carrying the torch of melodic Swedish death metal as this band does. *Twilight of the Thunder God* was the band's seventh studio album, originally released by Metal Blade Records in 2008. As amazing as the first six albums were it really wasn't until this album that Amon Amarth became the household metal name that they are today. The title track is still a favorite metal anthem in their live sets, and the rest of the album has produced some truly memorable tracks.

Recommended Track: "Twilight of the Thunder God"

203. Witchcraft - Legend

Sweden's Witchcraft has always been an extremely riff-oriented stoner rock band, using the likes of Black Sabbath and Pentagram as their guides. But on their fourth album, *Legend*, they decided to expand their sound in several ways. *Legend* was originally released in 2012, and was the first album they released for Nuclear Blast. The move to a bigger label clearly afforded them a bigger recording budget as the band moved away from their "vintage sound" to something that was a little more polished and streamlined. However, big line-up changes after an extensive hiatus, including the addition of a second guitar player, made sure that 'polished' did not equal 'tame'. The riffs and overall heaviness in songs like "Deconstruction" and "Flag of Fate" are some of the best of their somewhat brief careers. Despite the slicker production, Witchcraft returned themselves to the top of the stoner rock/proto-doom heap with this album.

Recommended Track: "Deconstruction"

202. Exhumed – Gore Metal

Gore Metal is Exhumed's debut full-length album, originally released on Relapse Records in 1998. I've seen this album classified as goregrind, but at the end of the day what's goregrind but death metal with grosser imagery and lyrics? Let's put it this way, if you consider bands like Carcass and Impetigo as being part of the greater pantheon of death metal then certainly Exhumed is as well. At the end of the day all you need to know is that *Gore Metal* is a fast-paced, thrill ride of an album that never relents for one second. It was the album that introduced the world to a band that took death metal back to its decrepit roots. The vocals sound like someone gargling broken glass, the rhythm section is almost perpetually maintaining a galloping blast, and the riffing is superb. Simply stated this is one of the best death metal albums of the late '90s.

Recommended Track: "Open the Abscess"

201. Horseback – Half Blood

Imagine if a shoegaze or doom outfit decided to hire a black metal vocalist, added some keyboards and started writing songs designed specifically for 1970s horror films. That should give you a decent idea of what we are working with here. The music of North Carolina's Horseback is not easily digestible, but if you let it be it's downright trance inducing. *Half Blood* is Horseback's second full-length album, originally released by Relapse Records in 2012. Horseback was formed by guitarist extraordinaire, Jenks Miller. Miller's full-time gig is playing guitar in alt country/indie folk outfit Mount Moriah. So one thing to keep in mind when listening to Horseback is that Miller has zero allegiance to any particular genre and that's possibly what makes this band such a breathe of fresh air…fresh, drug-laced, nightmare-inducing air.

Recommended Track: "Ahriman"

200. In Solitude – The World.
The Flesh. The Devil

There are a lot of bands these days looking for that "traditional metal" sound. Those that are doing it right are not only shining a new light on a lot of the traditional metal bands of the late '70s/early '80s but are taking that sound into a new realm. Sweden's In Solitude were one of the best at capturing that sound of long ago and their second full-length album, *The World. The Flesh. The Devil* is an absolute tour de force of traditional metal. *The World. The Flesh. The Devil* was originally released in 2011 and served as their debut for Metal Blade Records. I've seen comparisons to Mercyful Fate, among others, and those comparisons are not far off. Their sound on this album is a thrash-tinged, heavy rock affair that hearkens back to a time when metal didn't have to be brutally heavy to give you that unsettling feeling that the universe has a dark side to it.

Recommended Track: "Serpents Are Rising"

199. Blood Ceremony – Living With The Ancients

Canada's Blood Ceremony are a throwback of the highest order. Female vocals, organs, and flute combined with a proto-metal power trio to form this very dark and surreal sound. Each of their albums sounds like it was recorded thirty or so years ago, yet maintains this modern heaviness. If you were to mistake this band for some early purveyor of traditional British doom I wouldn't fault you. Plainly stated, it's sinfully delicious music. *Living With The Ancients* was the band's second full-length album, originally released in 2011 on Rise Above Records and licensed for releases here in the U.S. by Metal Blade Records. It was the album that really 'broke' the band in many ways and opened them up to a much wider audience. If you're a fan at all of the great occult rock bands of yesteryear then I highly recommend checking out this album.

Recommended Track: "Night of Augury"

198. Fu Manchu – The Action Is Go

Fu Manchu is never going to wow you with technicality or even heaviness. But they have, for a long time, written some of the catchiest, most bad ass, fuzzed out stoner rock you'll ever hear. *The Action Is Go* was the band's fourth full-length album, originally released by Mammoth Records in 1997, at the height of stoner rock's ascension. The late '90s were a magical time for stoner rock in general. There are so many great records from that era and this is one of them. This is also the first album to feature Brant Bjork on drums. Bjork is somewhat of a legend in the stoner rock realm and his contributions to every record he sits in on is noticeable. Probably the biggest take away from this record though is that it has the same drive and energy of their live sets. That can't be understated either. If you like your rock to actually rock then I highly suggest you check out this entire album.

Recommended Track: "Evil Eye"

197. Primevil – Smokin' Bats at Campton's

Primevil released only one album, *Smokin' Bats at Campton's* in 1974. They would vaporize shortly after this album, which would be lost to the ages until about 20 years later when it was finally released on CD. So, it's actually reasonable to ask the question: How could a band that released only one album and never really made it out of the Midwest have such an impact on the metal world to justify being placed in the Top 200 of this list? I'm not sure if bands like Kyuss, Nebula, or previous entry Fu Manchu ever listened to this band (or even heard of them) but this album is absolutely one of the godparents to today's stoner rock scene. Tracks like "Leavin" and "Pretty Woman" are absolutely killer jams that showcase an era where it all started for the stoner rock sound.

Recommended Track: "Leavin'"

196. Reverend Bizarre – In the Rectory of the Bizarre Reverend

Finland's Reverend Bizarre write the type of throwback doom reminiscent of acts like St. Vitus and Candlemass, complete with really fantastic clean vocals and sludgy, almost never-ending riffs. But they also have this dreariness reminiscent of their British counterparts, specifically My Dying Bride (minus the violins of course). This band writes doom metal that makes you want to pronounce it: "dooooooooooooooom metal." *In the Rectory of the Bizarre Reverend* was the band's debut album, originally released in 2002 by Sinister Figure. It would eventually be re-released by Season of Mist (which included the *Return To The Rectory* EP). Reverend Bizarre is a band that saw a growing popularity with each album only to call it a day at the height of it all. Regardless, we are going to look back at this band as one of the best doom metal bands of the last 20 years, and this album is a big reason why.

Recommended Track: "Burn In Hell!"

195. Rotten Sound - Cursed

It would not be an understatement to say that Finland's Rotten Sound may be the best active grindcore band in the world today. Their last decade plus worth of releases have put them in the discussion of who's the greatest grindcore band of all time. But this particular album is the sickening icing on what's been a pretty brutal cake. *Cursed* is the band's sixth full length album, originally released in 2011 by Relapse Records. It is an absolute tornado of pummeling sounds, including some of the best grindcore vocals around. It's a non-stop barrage from start to finish, with 16 songs clocking in at about 27 minutes. That's kind of ridiculous in the best way possible. Grindcore, even for a lot of metal fans, is an acquired taste. It's easily some of the most abrasive music in the world and sometimes even makes its cousin death metal look like child's play. However, Rotten Sound, and this album, are essential listens.

Recommended Track: "Hollow"

194. Megadeth – So Far, So Good… So What

If you were to make a list of the Top 10 most influential metal bands of all-time you'd be hard-pressed to leave this band off the list. *So Far, So Good…So What* was Megadeth's third full length album, originally released in 1988 on Capitol Records. There will be multiple Megadeth albums on this list and all of them in the Top 200. This album has the unfortunate fate of being sandwiched in between two of the greatest metal records ever made, thus its overall impact on the metal world is somewhat muted now. But even if Megadeth had a bad day at the office it is still better than what most thrash bands were coming up with in the late '80s. While this album lacks the overall atmosphere of its predecessor, and the cohesion of the follow up, it still stands as one of the better thrash albums of the second half of the decade.

Recommended Track: "Set The World Afire"

193. Triptykon – Eparistera Daimones

Eparistera Daimones was the debut album from Switzerland's Triptykon, originally released in 2010 on their own Prowling Death imprint (but licensed worldwide through Century Media Records). When Tom G. Warrior first talked about this project to the press he explicitly said that the material on this album was originally intended to be the next Celtic Frost release before their abrupt implosion. The dirge-like guitars dragging out their notes like the world itself is tearing apart, the bombastic rhythm section filling the air with heaviness, and Warrior's patented snarling vocals all come together in epic wonderment. Tracks are explored to their fullest with no track, sans one instrumental, clocking in at under five minutes in length. If Warrior set out to prove that he could create unique, poignant music without the help of his previous band mates then mission accomplished. This album is one of the better debut albums to hit the metal world in the last decade.

Recommended Track: "A Thousand Lies"

192. Cephalic Carnage – Exploiting Dysfunction

Calling themselves "Rocky Mountain Hydro Grind", Cephalic Carnage play a style of music best described as a bastardized form of grindcore. Grind is at least the foundation of what they do but death metal, doom, sludge and various experimental elements dot their musical landscape. Their album, *Exploiting Dysfunction,* was really the debut of a chaotic and schizophrenic sound they would build an entire career off of. This album was their second full length and originally released in 2000 on Relapse Records, their debut for the label. The oft-kilter time signature changes, the mashing together of influences as varied as jazz and death metal, the occasional spoken word passage, it was (and still is) a very unique take on the genre.

Recommended Track: "Hybrid"

191. Ozzy Osbourne – Bark at the Moon

After the tragic death of guitarist Randy Rhoads in an airplane crash, Ozzy Osbourne would take about a year to find a proper replacement and get back into the studio. In the interim he put out a live album, *Speak Of The Devil* (which was an album of all Sabbath covers and Ozzy firing a shot across Tony Iommi's bow). But in 1983 he returned with his third studio album, *Bark at the Moon,* released on Epic/CBS. Former Ratt guitarist Jake E. Lee took over on guitar and while he shines in certain places (the ripping solo at the end of the title track comes to mind), he's no Randy Rhoads. Then again, no one was or is. It's a synth-heavy album that sounded somewhat atmospheric for mainstream metal in 1983, and one can't deny the influence this album had on the metal community at large when it has sold over three million copies worldwide. This album even has the almost stereotypical '80s metal story behind it of a guy murdering three people and claiming this album drove him to it. (see: James Jollimore)

Recommended Track: "Bark at the Moon"

190. Pentagram – First Daze Here Too

First Daze Here Too is the second comp album Relapse Records would release of lost Pentagram recordings, this one coming five years after the original in 2006. The album consists of tracks recorded between 1971 and 1976, before they would completely dissolve for the first (but not the last) time. Although this collection exhausts the vaults a bit and isn't as solid as the first grouping of vintage songs, it's a must own for fans of '70s hard rock and proto-metal. There are certain tracks that are absolute standouts like "Much Too Young To Know" and "Wheel of Fortune." If you were an A&R person back then, could you listen to either of those songs and not sign this band immediately? Some of these songs are so far and away better than the vast majority of mainstream rock albums from that era that it honestly boggles the mind how this band didn't catch a break sooner than they eventually would.

Recommended Track: "Much Too Young To Know"

189. Amon Amarth – Fate of Norns

Fate of Norns was the fifth full-length album from Sweden's Amon Amarth, originally released by Metal Blade in 2004. This album continues the more plodding and doom-laden death metal they had begun to toy with on previous albums. Some of the tracks on here are extremely methodical in their delivery and give a somewhat darker aura than the previous three albums especially. That's not to say it's necessarily heavier than past efforts, but there is a sort of gloominess to this album that hangs over it like a pall. If anything it takes the stories they pen about Viking lore and gives them an entirely new dimension. Add to that the fact the songwriting itself is top notch and what you get is one of the best Swedish death metal albums of the 2000s. Amon Amarth still dip into this album in the live setting, specifically with the epic number, "The Pursuit of Vikings". They've put out some stellar records since this one, but this might have been the album that really sealed their place amongst the greatest Swedish death metal bands of all time.

Recommended Track: "The Pursuit of Vikings"

188. Coalesce – Give Them Rope

Coalesce is anything but generic. Their brand of metallic-infused hardcore is so technically diverse it borders on the bizarre at certain points. Yet at the same time their music is so oppressively heavy and in your face that when you listen to this album straight through there is almost an element of danger to it. *Give Them Rope* was the debut full-length for Coalesce, originally released in 1997 on Edison Recordings. When this album came out it not only knocked the entire hardcore scene on its collective ass but attracted a lot of attention from metal kids for it's sheer brutality and technical proficiency. One listen to this album straight through and you'd swear at certain points it was a death metal record. It's just that heavy. While this band would unfortunately spend almost as much time breaking up and reuniting as they would recording music, there is no denying the amazing legacy they've left behind thanks in part to albums like this one.

Recommended Track: "Have Patience"

187. Witchcraft – The Alchemist

The Alchemist is the third full length from Sweden's Witchcraft, originally released in 2007 on Rise Above Records. Where the first two albums were straight ahead, guitar driven, '70s loving, rock n' roll, this album expands their sound quite a bit. One example you could liken this album to is *Sabbath, Bloody Sabbath* by Black Sabbath. The first four Sabbath albums were nearly perfect, doom-infested rock n' roll. Then came *Sabbath, Bloody Sabbath,* an album that saw Sabbath add all sorts of instrumentation and explore song structures that they hadn't really played with on previous albums. *The Alchemist* is Witchcraft's *Sabbath, Bloody Sabbath.* The heavy neo-psych rock of the first two albums is alive and well but they toy with organ and flute on certain tracks, and add jazzy elements throughout the album that slice apart the really heavy portions with more mellow interludes. It's an overall diverse album and one that expands on the band's sound in fantastic ways.

Recommended Track: "If Crimson Was Your Colour"

186. Converge – Jane Doe

Converge have always been the type of band that can combine an extremely varied group of influences into an immensely violent package. You've never heard a band so influenced by someone like Fugazi play this viciously before. *Jane Doe* was the band's fourth full length album, originally released in 2001 on Equal Vision Records. This album seamlessly blends the ferocity of the metal/punk hybrid they perfected on the first three albums with the art rock ethos they would shift to on future efforts. The result is not only one of the best hardcore albums of the 2000s, but an album that quite literally launched the careers of a thousand knock-offs. The influence this album is still having on the hardcore/metalcore scenes today is immense. The much heralded Terrorizer Magazine out of the U.K. named this their top album of 2001.

Recommended Track: "Homewrecker"

185. Godflesh - Streetcleaner

After leaving Napalm Death, Justin Broadrick would attempt to create a project that would "out heavy" everything that came before. It would not be hyperbole to call England's Godflesh one of the most influential metal bands of the last 25 or so years. *Streetcleaner* was the debut full-length from Godflesh, originally released on Earache Records in 1989. It was the album that would set in motion a decade of influential releases and a career that would even see them sign to a major label at one point. It's also by far the most "metal" Godflesh album you will come across as all of their efforts following this one would dip further and further into industrial experimentation. The number of "post" bands that hail this album as an influence is simply uncountable at this point, and is a testament to an album that has stood the test of time with aplomb.

Recommended Track: "Like Rats"

184. Dissection - ReinkaΩs

In the early 1990s, as black metal was starting to really take the metal world by storm, Dissection rose up to produce two of the greatest "blackened metal" albums of the decade. Dissection were an unholy mix between black metal and the adjacent Swedish death metal scene that fans of both genres could wrap their arms around. By the end of 1997, band leader Jon Nödtveidt would be found guilty of being an accessory to murder. He would serve roughly seven years in a Swedish prison and upon his release in 2004 he'd reform Dissection. In 2006 they would release their third and final full-length album, *ReinkaΩs*, which was released here in the States through The End Records. Much to the chagrin of some long-time fans, gone were a lot of the symphonic elements of previous albums. However what was left over was one of the best melodic Swedish death metal albums of the 2000s. Sadly, less than six months after the release of this album Jon Nödtveidt would take his own life, effectively ending the band forever.

Recommended Track: "Starless Aeon"

183. Blood Ceremony – Blood Ceremony

This self-titled masterpiece is the debut album from Canada's Blood Ceremony, originally released in 2008 on Rise Above Records. Blood Ceremony are an occult rock band who play a style of music that sounds as if it was recorded 35 years ago, yet is amazingly timeless. The use of flute, organs, and haunting female vocals (and on this album some viola as well) layered atop some mammoth, Sabbath-like riffing gives Blood Ceremony a retro sound that most bands of this ilk only dream of achieving. This band has been described as everything from doom metal to "heavy prog rock," to things like "witch rock". But whatever you want to call it, this album is as much a blueprint for a black mass as it is a metal record. It's an eerie yet catchy grouping of songs that stick with you long after the record player has come to a stop.

Recommended Track: "Master of Confusion"

182. Bethlehem – Dictius Te Necare

In the '90s, as black metal started to explode, bands were looking for new and inventive ways to 'out evil' one another. One band that definitely took black metal down a very dark path, and simply doesn't get enough credit for it today, is Germany's Bethlehem. Bethlehem managed to put out what is arguably one of the most important black metal albums the '90s ever produced. (Although don't tell them that as they refuse to call their brand of aural torment anything other than "dark metal".) *Dictius Te Necare* is Bethlehem's second full-length album, originally released in 1996 on Red Stream Records. The first Bethlehem record is a solid affair. But this album is one of the darkest, most depraved, most self-loathing albums you'll ever hear. Inside the cover of the CD booklet it reads, "This album is dedicated to all suicide victims." If you were to put this album on repeat and spend an entire night with it you might end up as one of the people this thing was dedicated to. It is as oppressive and depressive a record as you will ever hear.

Recommended Track: "Tagebuch einer Totgeburt"

181. Horseback – The Invisible Mountain

Upon first listen to the debut album from North Carolina's Horseback there's a good chance you will be thrown into this mystical world where genre walls are annihilated and the possibilities of what could be labeled as "metal" are endless. It is, at times, an inspiring album that will require several listens, virtually non-stop, for weeks on end. The crazy, fuzzed out, psych rock is delicious enough, but throw in crazy, scathing, black metal-like growls that just kind of hang in the back of the mix and it's apparent that something very special is afoot. This album is one of a small handful that took the black metal aesthetic and married it to other genres in the most beautiful and grotesque shotgun wedding you'll ever see. It is not out of the question that 10-15 years from now when we talk about the most important metal albums of this decade we will be mentioning this band and this album. *The Invisible Mountain* was originally released in 2010 on Relapse Records.

Recommended Track: "Invokation"

180. Rotting Christ – Non Serviam

Non Serviam was the second full-length album from Greece's Rotting Christ, original released in 1994 on Unisound Records. Close to a decade later it would be reissued by The End Records and get a proper release here in the U.S. Until that reissue it was pretty much a 'lost album' with the previous effort coming out on Osmose and future efforts coming out via Century Media. So needless to say, even some Rotting Christ fans unfortunately overlook this album and that's criminal. Rotting Christ always had Gothic elements woven into their brand of blackened metal, complete with synths and a somewhat mellower approach in general. They weren't afraid to slow things down to a reasonable marching pace and drop some almost stoner rock like riffs in for good measure. Not every song had to be a million miles an hour to gain the desired, cryptic effects.

Recommended Track: "Non Serviam"

179. Acid Bath – Paegan Terrorism Tactics

New Orleans' Acid Bath defy label categorization. They mashed together this unwieldy list of influences which included, but was not limited to, thrash, hardcore, doom metal, death metal and, of course, sludge. The vocals waver back and forth between Dax Riggs' amazing voice and the screams of both he and guitarist Sammy Pierre Duet. All the while, Duet and company are laying down some of the catchiest, most groove-laden, extreme metal you'll ever hear. *Paegan Terrorism Tactics* was the second and final album that Acid Bath would release. It would be issued through Rotten Records in 1996. Sadly, this would be the last Acid Bath album due to the untimely death of their bass player, Audie Pitre, in a car crash just two months after its release. Because of their short lifespan as a band and that there are only two full-length albums to show for it, this band is starting to become a forgotten gem. A cult act, if you will. That's simply unacceptable and hopefully more people begin to rediscover the genius of Acid Bath.

Recommended Track: "Bleed Me An Ocean"

178. The Sword – Age of Winters

Some bands it seems were just born to split the metal world right down the middle with the lovers and haters squarely on either side of the aisle. Enter Texas' The Sword. *Age of Winters* is the debut album from The Sword, originally released on Kemado Records in 2006. The press push for this album was huge before it even hit the streets. That, of course, instantly irked the metal elite. You can't be "kvlt" if MTV comes knocking. Those that snubbed their noses at this band from day one would have you believe it was just a bunch of hipsters and some non-metal label trying to cash in on the retro-metal revival that had already gone full bore by 2006. Maybe? Frankly, who cares? In this space we are looking solely at the music, and in this instance the music slays. The riffs and the overall heaviness of this album is undeniable in its greatness. This is Sabbath Worship of the highest order and anyone who calls themselves a fan of the stoner rock genre should be all over this album.

Recommended Track: "Winter's Wolves"

177. Brutal Truth – Sounds of the Animal Kingdom

From the get go Brutal Truth was an important band in the grindcore scene and helped solidify it as a genre that stood apart from death metal, especially here in the U.S. New York in the early '90s was seeing a death metal renaissance and the NYDM "sound" was starting to creep into everything that city was producing. Then came Brutal Truth and they started to slowly separate themselves from the pack, culminating in this album. Some people will forever categorize this band as death metal. But in reality this band, and especially this album, are as grind as you can get and the impact this album has had on the grind scene can still be felt today. *Sounds of the Animal Kingdom* was the third full-length from Brutal Truth, originally released in 1997 on Relapse Records.

Recommended Track: "Dementia"

176. His Hero Is Gone – Monuments To Thieves

One band that was the epitome of how heavy and downright brutal crust punk could be was Memphis' His Hero Is Gone. In the '90s there was no better crust punk band in the world. This band is immensely important to every heavy musician who ever heard them. Their brand of unrelenting crust bordered on thrash and death metal at certain points as it rumbled and thundered its way through highly political content. Each song read like a battle cry for any marginalized group or person against the mainstream world that would see them held down. The vitriol in the lyrics was matched only by the equally vitriolic music. His Hero Is Gone would never write a love song, unless it was the love of revolution, a revolution they delivered the soundtrack to with each album. *Monuments To Thieves* was the band's second full-length album, originally released on Prank Records in 1997.

Recommended Track: "Monuments to Thieves"

175. High On Fire – The Art of Self Defense

High On Fire has been in the business of producing their unique brand of stoner/doom for awhile now. Matt Pike and crew initially set out to take the absolute heaviest parts of Sleep and make ears bleed. I'm not sure if there are many bands in this world who have the bowel-rumbling, earth-shaking affects that this band have. High On Fire write music that sounds like an army of elephants driving tanks through a minefield. Even when they slow it up their sound is this constant battering ram of heaviness. *The Art of Self Defense* was their debut album originally released on Man's Ruin Records in 2000 and re-released by Tee Pee Records in 2001 with new artwork and a couple bonus tracks. It would not be an understatement to say that this album is one of the best debuts the 2000s would give us, and an album that just adds to California's legacy for producing doom bands that consistently give a unique take on the genre.

Recommended Track: "10,000 Years"

174. Celtic Frost - Monotheist

After a long hiatus the two main members of Celtic Frost (guitarist/vocalist Thomas Gabriel Fischer and bass player Martin Eric Ain) finally broke musical bread in the early 2000s and started piecing together their comeback record. It would take much longer than most people expected but *Monotheist* was finally released in 2006 via Century Media Records. Where the earliest Celtic Frost material utilized a lot of thrash and traditional metal elements mixed with proto-black and death metal, this album takes all of the darkest and most doom-laden aspects of that early output and expounds on them. It's a sludge fest where even on tracks played with a quicker tempo the riffs are pounded over and over into your skull. But there's also experimentation on this album, such as the female vocals, clean vocals, and various programming. But those experimental interludes are really just a brief respite from the pounding the rest of this record is going to deliver to you.

Recommended Track: "Progeny"

173. Pig Destroyer - Terrifyer

Virginia's Pig Destroyer have been laying waste to both stereos and live audiences for quite some time now. This album however is arguably still their best effort. *Terrifyer* was originally released by Relapse Records in 2004. It's 20+ tracks of non-stop, sonic carnage, and a second disc with an immensely disturbing 30+ minute DVD of a track called "Natasha". This album is just a little bit faster, a little bit heavier, and a little bit more morbid than previous releases. This is also the album where the production value soared through the roof. You'd think that for grindcore you would want your albums to sound gnarly. However, the crystal clear production on this record only seemed to heighten the intensity of it and added an entirely new musical dimension to their sound.

Recommended Track: "Scarlet Hourglass"

172. Nebula – Let It Burn

Guitarist/vocalist Eddie Glass, bassist Mark Abshire, and drummer Ruben Romano made up one of the most stunningly powerful trios of the last 25+ years ,and that is not superfluous talk. These guys honestly redefined what a "power trio" could do with good, old fashioned, hard rock/proto-metal. *Let It Burn* was Nebula's debut EP, originally released in 1997 on Tee Pee Records. A year later Relapse would scoop up the album and re-release it with two bonus tracks which had been recorded in a different session. I highly recommend you seek out the Relapse version because the two bonus tracks they tacked on might just be the two best songs on the record. That's not a knock on the original six tracks because they absolutely shred. At the end of the day, when we look back on the golden years of '90s stoner rock it is not out of the question to call this one of the most important albums of the era.

Recommended Track: "Devil's Liquid"

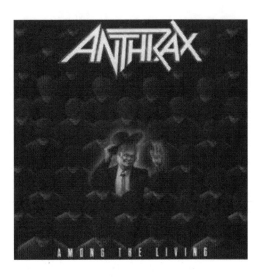

171. Anthrax – Among The Living

Among The Living was Anthrax's third full-length record originally released in 1987 on Island Records. This was the record that got the press and fans talking about how they were one of the "Big Four" of thrash. It features a bunch of songs they still perform live to this day and was really the first time they received heavy airplay on MTV. So it makes sense that this remains possibly their most influential album. One could also make the argument that this is their heaviest album as well. The rhythm section is at the forefront of the mix giving it an extra gut-punch that other Anthrax albums have lacked. It also remains one of their best-selling albums of all time after it peaked at #62 on the Billboard album charts.

Recommended Track: "I Am The Law"

170. Amon Amarth – Once Sent From The Golden Hall

Once Sent From The Golden Hall was the debut full-length album from Amon Amarth, originally released in 1998 on Metal Blade Records. If you were going to give this album some context in comparison to other Amon Amarth records this is probably their least polished and most aggressive album. It was recorded at legendary Abyss Studios with Peter Tagtgren behind the board and this album has a certain crustiness and rougher edges than future efforts. The production, in conjunction with the songwriting, makes the record sound meaner than possibly any other Amon Amarth record since. The Viking themes and melodic, Swedish riffs are still present but the overall vibe of this record is much more foreboding. This is also the only Amon Amarth record to feature Martin Lopez on drums, as he would leave to join Opeth full-time.

Recommended Track: "Friends of the Suncross"

169. Witchcraft - Firewood

Firewood was the second full length album from Sweden's Witchcraft, originally released in 2005 on Rise Above Records. Fast forward over a decade later and the retro-occult rock vibe is again a huge player in the metal world. At the time of this album's release, it was not. What Witchcraft was doing sounded simultaneously retro and fresh. When we look back at the scene as it stands now this album could easily be considered a benchmark. Witchcraft have altered their style on almost every record. For example, the album released after this one was more experimental and psych rock focused. But this album is the one which most closely resembles the forefathers of metal, such as Black Sabbath, Blue Cheer, and early Pentagram. (In fact the hidden track on this album is the Pentagram classic, "When The Screams Come".)

Recommended Track: "Chylde of Fire"

168. Enslaved - Eld

One of the first bands of the glorious second wave of black metal who opened the doors for expanding black metal's sound was Norway's Enslaved. *Eld* was the band's third album, originally released by Osmose Productions in 1997. All of Enslaved's material prior to this album was pretty straight forward black metal. All of the albums since this one have been more and more progressive with each release, first incorporating even more Viking themes then evolving to progressive, post-black metal. *Eld* would be a transition of sorts. Make no mistakes, first and foremost, this is a black metal record. But, as the sixteen minute, opening track would attest, this band was not fearful of experimenting. Their incorporation of clean (almost moaned or chanted) singing with more progressive riffs and song structures would start to separate them from a lot of their contemporaries pretty early on, starting with this record.

Recommended Track: "Hordalendingen"

167. Sepultura – Beneath The Remains

Sepultura is obviously Brazil's most famous metal export. Their influence over both the thrash and death metal scenes is pretty hefty (as is their eventual influence over the nu metal scene...). *Beneath The Remains* was Sepultura's third full-length album, originally released in 1989 on Roadracer Records. The two albums that preceded this one were raw, unfiltered works that took the fury of thrash and tangled it with the power of death metal. But it wasn't until this album that Sepultura would rise to their full potential. With legendary producer, Scott Burns, behind the board this was also the first Sepultura album to claim decent production. The cleaner production did nothing to lessen the intensity of the material as the band rips through nine tracks of death metal-infused thrash. While future releases would delve into Brazilian and tribal elements, this album stands as the perfect marriage between two of metal's most popular sub-genres.

Recommended Track: "Inner Self"

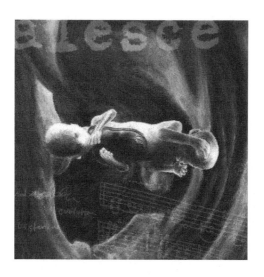

166. Coalesce – 0:12 Revolution in Just Listening

0:12 Revolution in Just Listening was the third full-length album Coalesce released, emerging originally in 1999 on Relapse Records. This was the band's debut album for Relapse which would open them up to an entirely new audience as well. By the time this album was recorded Coalesce was almost like the Fleetwood Mac of the hardcore scene. In other words, the band members weren't getting along and this album was supposedly recorded with each musician in separate sessions. Regardless of the inner turmoil this band was constantly facing, including way too many break-ups and line-up changes, Coalesce still remains quite possibly the greatest band to ever come out of the U.S. hardcore scene. Their unique style and brutal heaviness alone would spawn a thousand knockoffs. This album is an absolute beast. Clearly whatever strife was going on with the band members it comes across brilliantly in the music.

Recommended Track: "What Happens on the Road Always Comes Home"

165. Uriah Heep – Very 'eavy, Very 'umble

Uriah Heep are one of the unsung heroes of the proto-metal world. They certainly don't get the praise or credit like some of their British contemporaries – Black Sabbath, Deep Purple, etc. However their brand of progressive, bluesy hard rock (early on) and hard-charging rock n' roll (later in their career) absolutely played a decent sized role in the formation of '80s metal. It might seem easier and more apropos to choose an album like *Demons and Wizards* or *Look At Yourself* for this list as they are much more straight forward hard rock. But despite the occasional acoustic ballad or blues number it's really this, their debut album, that sets the tone for this band's career and remains a towering influence to this day. It was originally released in 1970 on Vertigo Records in the UK and Mercury Records in the U.S.

Recommended Track: "Dreammare"

164. Opeth - Deliverance

Deliverance was Opeth's sixth studio album, originally released in 2002 on Koch Records here in the States and Music For Nations in Europe. Opeth's brand of progressive death metal is split between massive, almost symphonic, sweeping passages juxtaposed with some of the most beautifully peaceful interludes you'll ever hear. A lot of the early Opeth material is pretty unrelenting in its heaviness. As they became more cerebral in their songwriting they naturally sacrificed some of it, but this album was still quite tenacious in its delivery. At certain moments it delivered some of the most vicious music that Opeth would produce. (Unlike the companion record, *Damnation*, released in 2003, which was virtually devoid of any death metal passages.) Like most of their efforts this album is simply brilliant.

Recommended Track: "Master's Apprentices"

163. Cannibal Corpse – Eaten Back To Life

Eaten Back To Life was Cannibal Corpse's debut album, originally released in 1990 on Metal Blade Records. Unlike all of their later releases this album has a sort of thrash aesthetic to the songwriting. A lot of the riffs on this album feel like they were blueprinted after all the great thrash of the late '80s, especially the stuff coming out of NYC at the time. But when you add in the blast beats and Chris Barnes' growls this is about as death metal as you're going to get. If this album was released later in their career we'd be talking about what a 'departure' it was from their signature sound. It comes off as a band doing some self-exploration, but it's still an extremely deviant vibe. When compared to what else was being released in 1990 it still stands as one of the heaviest albums of the year.

Recommended Track: "Born in a Casket"

162. Electric Wizard – Come My Fanatics…

Electric Wizard's brand of doom is a mixture of molasses, thunder and avalanches of heaviness that bury you in a tomb of distortion. Their sound is unmistakable and the equivalent of a thousand elephants stampeding through a minefield during an earthquake. *Come My Fanatics…* was the band's second full-length album and to this day stands as one of their heaviest releases. It was originally released in 1997 on Rise Above Records. It is, without argument, one of the heaviest doom records ever made and easily one of the better records the '90s produced. In true doom metal fashion this album is almost an hour long, yet only contains six tracks. The reissue tacked on two bonus tracks and pushed the total time over an hour in length. Guitarist, Jus Oborn, is a master at taking songs and bending and stretching them to his will so expect certain riffs (all of them godly) to be pounded into your brain like a hammer into a nail.

Recommended Track: "Return Trip"

161. Black Widow - Sacrifice

If you were to sit down with this album with zero
knowledge of who Black Widow were you would probably
laugh at their inclusion on this list. Acoustic guitars,
saxophone, flute, piano, strings; there's a lot on this record
that does not scream 'metal' at you. When you start to
concentrate on the lyrics though you start to get an idea of
why I'm including these guys. The use of Satanic and
occult imagery in rock music in the 1960s and 1970s was
most prevalent in the U.K. However, few bands embraced
it the way this band did. Almost every song on this record
sounds like they are trying to conjure up some demon
from a lost dimension. *Sacrifice* was the band's debut
album. It was originally released in 1970 on CBS Records.
It's a psych/prog rock record more than anything else but
it's been cited as a major influence on the metal scene,
including a tribute album featuring Italy's Death SS and
Japan's Church of Misery among others.

Recommended Track: "Come to the Sabbat"

160. Eyehategod – In The Name of Suffering

Eyehategod perfected the blues riff meets hardcore punk sensibility. Then they buried it behind a wall of fuzz, feedback and misanthropic vocals and came away with a sound so amazingly unique and brutally overwhelming. Looking out across the metal landscape it's easy to see their influence dripping off of every corner of the scene like the inside of a molasses factory after an explosion. Eyehategod just might go down as one of the 15 or 20 most influential metal bands of the last 30 years when it's all said and done. *In the Name of Suffering* was originally released in 1992 on a tiny French label called Intellectual Convulsion. The band was quickly scooped up by Century Media Records who would immediately re-release this album with new artwork. Out of all of Eyehategod's releases this one does the best to showcase their hardcore/crust punk roots. It's, at times, the fastest and certainly the rawest album they ever produced.

Recommended Track: "Depress"

159. Asphyx – Last One On Earth

Since the late '80s Europe has been hemorrhaging great death metal like it's nobody's business. When you have an entire continent giving you great product it could be very easy to overlook some classic material. One European death metal band that is criminally underrated is Netherlands' Asphyx. *Last One On Earth* was the band's second full-length album, originally released in 1992 on Century Media Records. This would unfortunately also be the last album (for about 15 years) that vocalist Martin van Drunen would record with them. Asphyx most closely resembles bands like Bolt Thrower and Obituary in that they weren't afraid to slow down the pace and add in some doom elements. Yet they also weren't afraid to crank it up to 11 and play like their collective hair was on fire either. Between van Drunen's vocals (which were supposedly recorded without his knowing he had already been fired by the band) and the riffs on this record, it has rightfully maintained its place amongst the classics of the genre.

Recommended Track: "Last One On Earth"

158. Venom – At War with Satan

There is simply no denying that England's Venom are one of the most influential metal bands of all-time. *At War With Satan* was the band's third full-length album, originally released in 1984 on Neat Records in Europe and Combat Records here in the States. This album was a departure from their previous releases in that the title track is an almost 20 minute opus that takes up all of Side A. The entire album is a sort of concept record about a fictional battle between the armies of Heaven and Hell, and clocks in at about 39 minutes long (and half of it is one song). That's slightly ridiculous for any band but extra ridiculous for a band that built their rep on songs which consistently set the world on fire in three minutes flat. With that said, Side B to this record contains five absolute scorchers that stand up pretty well against the rest of the classic line-up's catalog. While the title track may be the closest Venom ever got to being "progressive" the band's trademark aesthetics are firmly intact.

Recommended Track: "Women, Leather and Hell"

157. Exhorder – Slaughter In The Vatican

Slaughter In The Vatican was the debut album from Exhorder, originally released in 1990 on R/C Records. The early '90s saw thrash metal start to move in all sorts of interesting directions. Exhorder were one of the bands that took thrash metal to a very different place from whence it came. They combined thrash riffing with death metal styled drumming and a hardcore punk aesthetic to form a style of thrash that was effective whether played face-ripping fast or slowed down to a nice meaty pace. If you are curious to see one of the many directions thrash was heading by the dawn of the '90s then look no further than this album. Maybe it's because they only put out two records before imploding, but to me Exhorder is criminally underrated and this album showcases some of their best material.

Recommended Track: "Homicide"

156. Neurosis – Times of Grace

Times of Grace was the sixth album from Neurosis, originally released in 1999 on Relapse Records. It was their second album for Relapse and their first after widening their fan base touring with the likes of Pantera and a stint on one of the first incarnations of the Ozzfest. The style of this album is more direct in its bombastic nature than on previous releases. Specifically the two albums that came right before this one, which pushed so many envelopes in their experimentation and ability to create unsettling atmospheres. Conversely, the way some of the songs on here are structured are also very much a foreshadowing of the two albums that would come after this one, which would see the band take a much more melodic approach. In reality, what you get with *Times of Grace* is this sort of crossroad where varying stages of their career converge to form this truly amazing vortex where your concept of "metal" is both tested and confirmed all at the same time.

Recommended Track: "Under the Surface"

155. Lucifer's Friend – Lucifer's Friend

Originally released in 1970 on Phillips Records (but not given a proper release in the U.S. until 1972), the self-titled debut album from Germany's Lucifer's Friend is a case study in rock n' roll music that would give rise to the earliest days of metal. You can absolutely hear the likes of early Judas Priest and Saxon, for example, in this record. It's almost uncanny. However, after this record the band would shift gears (multiple times) and add in some psychedelic, jazz fusion elements that would culminate in them using a 30-piece backing band on their fourth full length. While those albums all have their merits, for our metal purposes this is the album to look to. If you're a fan of the hard rock/proto-metal of the early '70s or you're just looking to expand your knowledge of metal history a bit, this album is a must for further examination.

Recommended Track: "Lucifer's Friend"

154. His Hero Is Gone – Fifteen Counts of Arson

In 1997 His Hero Is Gone unleashed their debut full-length album on legendary punk label Prank Records. *Fifteen Counts of Arson* was the perfect name for this blistering array, each track encompassing its own little miniature riot. "I…Fight…Every…Day!" was a poignant lyric for this band and more than fitting for their musical style. The entire album is only about 25 minutes in length with a handful of tracks coming in at under a minute. This grindcore aesthetic combined with a punk rock attitude made His Hero Is Gone an absolutely vicious live act, which translated very well to record. His Hero Is Gone were adept in mingling the bulldog riffing of crust punk with an almost doom like atmosphere to create a style of music that was appealing to a wide range of extreme music fans. The punk kids loved their politics. The metal kids loved their ferociousness. Everybody loved the finished product.

Recommended Track: "Professional Mind Fuckers"

153. Cryptopsy – None So Vile

None So Vile was the second full-length album released by Canada's Cryptopsy, originally in 1996 on Wrong Again Records. It would later be reissued by Displeased Records and then eventually by Century Media. This is also the last album for about a decade to feature original vocalist Lord Worm. To say a vocalist makes or breaks a death metal band would be a bit of a stretch. However, it probably isn't a coincidence that after this guy departed they spent years trying to reformulate their sound. When you evaluate this band's career, *None So Vile* still stands as one of, if not their best effort and a near masterpiece of the technical death metal. This album is a must-own for anyone who calls themselves a fan of the genre.

Recommended Track: "Slit Your Guts"

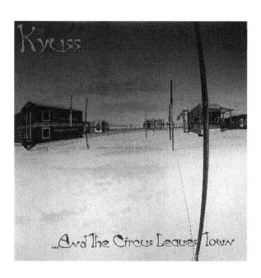

152. Kyuss - ...And The Circus Leaves Town

...And The Circus Leaves Town is the fourth and final full-length album released by stoner rock legends, Kyuss, appearing on Elektra Records in 1995. The band would split up for good a few months after this album was released due to internal strife. This album has a much less psychedelic approach to the songwriting than on previous efforts. Sonically it might even be a bit closer of a relative to the first Queens of the Stone Age record as guitarist Josh Homme was clearly headed in that direction in his songwriting. But all of the key elements to the Kyuss sound are still present – the heavy riffs churning over and over like some witches brew, John Garcia's smoked out delivery, and a thunderous rhythm section. At the end of the day, because of the internal struggles of the band, it's almost unfair to compare this record to previous efforts. Yet taken on its own merits this is a stellar album and head and shoulders above all competition at that time.

Recommended Track: "Gloria Lewis"

151. Mercyful Fate – The Beginning

Mercyful Fate is easily one of the most influential metal bands of all-time. Not only was their sound instrumental in helping in the formation of thrash metal, but their overtly Satanic lyrics and King Diamond's get up are considered huge influences on the formation of black metal as well. Easily the best of the three comp albums Roadrunner would roll out was *The Beginning*. It was originally released in 1987, just two years after the band split up. It consists of the four-track, *Nuns Have No Fun* EP, along with three tracks from "The Friday Rock Show" (a BBC radio show), and "Black Masses" which was a B side from the "Black Funeral" single. The re-master of this album, which Roadrunner also put out, would also include a version of the track "Black Funeral" that would appear on a comp called *Metallic Storm*. You will find precious few compilation albums in these pages, but this is one that is absolutely worth the price of admission.

Recommended Track: "Doomed By The Living Dead"

150. Acid Bath – When The Kite String Pops

New Orleans' Acid Bath was an absolute force to be reckoned with. I'm personally convinced that if their bass player hadn't died in a car accident we'd be talking about this band as one of the most influential of the last 25+ years. *When The Kite String Pops* was the debut album from Acid Bath, originally released on Rotten Records in 1994. When this album first came out it was an absolute revelation. When I tell you there was nothing like it, I'm not exaggerating. Hell, there still isn't anything out there that sounds like this album. Picture grindcore, sludge, thrash, and even what we would now call "post-metal" elements, all tossed together and seasoned with vocals that were both maniacally screamed and beautifully sung. On paper it's an absolute mess that shouldn't work at all, yet sonically it was damn close to perfection.

Recommended Track: "The Blue"

149. Amon Amarth – Versus The World

Versus The World was originally released on Metal Blade Records in 2002 and is the fourth full-length album from Sweden's Amon Amarth. The three albums prior to this one are stellar. But on this album Amon Amarth add a darker, more atmospheric vibe to their sound which they would carry with them and build upon for the next decade or so. This is the album that really grew their fan base, especially here in the States. There's a reason why a bunch of songs from this record are still part of their live set, as it contains some of their best material, including, "Death In Fire" and "Down The Slopes of Death". When you reexamine this album you'll find that there isn't a weak track to be found. If you're looking for the album that really adds a cold and dark Norse atmosphere to their sound then this one is it.

Recommended Track: "Death In Fire"

148. Satyricon – Nemesis Divina

There are a handful of bands that have risen out of the second wave of black metal that transcend the genre. One of the more influential bands to rise out of black metal's second wave was Norway's Satyricon. This album is a big reason why. *Nemesis Divina* was Satyricon's third full-length album, originally released in 1996 on the band's own Moonfog Productions imprint and re-released to a worldwide audience by Century Media. It marks the end of an era of sorts for Satyricon as they would start to incorporate industrial, and eventually, rock elements to their sound with varying degrees of success. It would not be a stretch to call this album their most ferocious, darkest, and most technically proficient record in their storied catalogue. It's also one of the greatest examples of how amazingly fantastic true Norwegian black metal could be.

Recommended Track: "Mother North"

147. Carnivore - Retaliation

Peter Steele was, of course, the mastermind behind Goth metal geniuses Type O Negative. But prior to the vampire-like imagery and the doom-laden dirges there was the crossover thrash of Carnivore. *Retaliation* was the second and final album Carnivore would release. It originally hit the streets in 1987 via Roadrunner Records. Shortly after this album's release the band would go their separate ways. Fans will notice the similarities between this album and the first Type O Negative record. Certainly there are massive differences as well, but it's not a stretch to listen to this album and hear the beginnings of Type O Negative – the satirical lyrics, the bass heavy sound, the occasional sludgy breakdowns, Steele experimenting with actually singing instead of just screaming, etc. The writing was on the wall, so to speak, but this album also simultaneously stands as an absolute classic of the thrash genre.

Recommended Track: "Angry Neurotic Catholics"

146. Autopsy – Mental Funeral

The impact the state of California has had on the metal world is absolutely astronomical. Thrash, death metal, crossover thrash, crust punk, doom metal, you name it this state has delivered some absolute titans of their respected genres. One band that emerged from The Golden State to become a truly influential force in the death metal world is Autopsy. This act immediately established themselves as one of the best death metal bands in the U.S. upon their arrival. Their sound borrows from the thrash-like feel of early Death and Possessed records, but also added a distinct doom influence as well. They are a fantastic amalgamation of a lot of extreme music and this album is still one of their best. *Mental Funeral* was Autopsy's second album, originally released in 1991 on Peaceville Records.

Recommended Track: "Dead"

145. Hellhammer – Apocalyptic Raids

All over Europe in the '80s metal bands were experimenting with taking metal to more and more extreme places. Playing faster, heavier, and meaner became a passion and an art for a lot of aspiring musicians. One group of musicians who perfected extreme metal in those early days was Celtic Frost. Before Frost there was Hellhammer. In 1984, just a few months before they would break-up and two core members would go on to form Celtic Frost, Hellhammer released their *Apocalyptic Raids* EP. Four songs of some of the earliest blackened death metal you will ever find. Absolute extremity that even the metal press had no idea what to do with it, as it was pretty much universally panned at the time. But the joke was on them as the influence of these songs long outlasted the magazines that lambasted them. In 1990 Noise Records would re-issue this EP with two bonus tracks, entitled *Apocalyptic Raids 1990 A.D.* Both versions are worth owning for fans of early death and black metal.

Recommended Track: "Triumph of Death"

144. Sleep – Sleep's Holy Mountain

The classic Sleep line-up contains the masterminds behind both High On Fire and Om. That alone should tell you the talent this band possessed. After a couple releases on smaller labels, Sleep decided to send a demo of their newest material to Earache Records. Earache loved it so much that they signed the band and released the album as is, with no further studio tinkering. *Sleep's Holy Mountain* would be released in the U.S, in early 1993 and is their second full-length album. It's easy to see why it has had such a profound influence over the stoner rock and doom scenes over the years. The blatant Black Sabbath and Blue Cheer worship was palpable and their penchant for recording in a similar style to those bands lent a retro feel to what they were doing. A true gem within the stoner rock/doom metal lexicon.

Recommended Track: "Dragonaut"

143. At The Gates – The Red In The Sky Is Ours

The Red In The Sky Is Ours was the first full-length album from Sweden's At The Gates, originally released in 1992 on Peaceville Records. If your only real experience with At The Gates is anything that came after this record then this one may be a bit of a shocker at first. It's a death metal record but not in the way that At The Gates were to come to be known and beloved. It's a wild (and successful) attempt at creating some very avant garde death metal. Strange and off-putting atmospherics, bizarre bass lines, violin at one point, and yet all of it mashed together with the progressive death metal that would one day become the band's trademark. It's a dark and often ethereal record in a way their future efforts are not, and those of their contemporaries would often struggle to match.

Recommended Track: "Windows"

142. Cirith Ungol – King of the Dead

King of the Dead was the second album from California's Cirith Ungol, originally released in 1984 on Enigma Records. It's considered by many to be their best album and with good cause. It's a heavy blend of '70s rock and traditional metal. Tracks like "Master of the Pit" and "Cirith Ungol" are some of the best examples we have of American, traditional metal. While thrash had already taken off here in the States by the time this album came out, it didn't stop it from being a huge influence on those bands who first heard it. It's an album that also seamlessly brings in snippets of early doom metal as well. Simply put, this album is aces. From the meaty riffs to the screeching and potent vocals, Cirith Ungol are a criminally underrated band. Unfortunately for them the tastes of the record buying population here in the U.S. would shift to speed metal, thrash, and eventually death metal and other extreme forms. By the time traditional metal came back in vogue these guys were unfortunately long gone.

Recommended Track: "Cirith Ungol"

141. Atheist – Unquestionable Presence

Florida's Atheist were one of the bands that pioneered everything to do with technical death metal. Their first two albums, especially, are classics of the genre. *Unquestionable Presence* was the band's second full-length, originally released in 1991 on Active Records. This album was shrouded in darkness as their original bass player died in a car accident right before recording started. Yet they would soldier on and somehow produce a slightly heavier and more focused album than the previous effort. Atheist were definitely not afraid to push the boundaries of what was "acceptable" for a death metal band at a time when experimenting in the genre was sometimes met with disdain by those looking for a certain sound. Atheist were not every man's death metal but they were certainly the thinking man's death metal. If you are looking for an album that blends technicality with brutality almost to perfection then you could do a lot worse than this one.

Recommended Track: "Unquestionable Presence"

140. Blasphemy – Gods of War

If you were to listen to Canada's Blasphemy with zero prior knowledge of this band (or see any corpse paint laden band photos) your first inclination would probably be to lump them into the grindcore category. You would not be far off. With a ten track album that clocks in at under 20 minutes, and a penchant for blast beats on top of blast beats this band's blackened death metal could have played well on a tour with the earliest incarnations of Napalm Death. *Gods of War* was the band's second and final album, originally released in 1993 on Osmose. It's lofi production and steady wall of cacophonous noise is an acquired taste for even the truest of the true. But at the end of the day there were a whole lot of aspiring metal musicians who grabbed their cassette copy of this thing back in 1993 and sat in awe of the ferocity spewing from their stereo speakers.

Recommended Track: "Emperor of the Black Abyss"

139. Bolt Thrower – The IVth Crusade

The IVth Crusade was Bolt Thrower's fourth album originally released in 1992 on Earache Records. Their first three albums were not only heavy, they were fast. Really fast in certain spots. This was the album where they started to slow it up a bit and add a more death/doom element to their sound, which became their calling card for the following twenty years. Tracks like "As The World Burns" and the title track are perfect examples of where Bolt Thrower puts more emphasis on one main riff that snakes its way through the entire song. This addition of doom elements made their sound even heavier. You don't have to play fast to pummel people. Steamrollers don't go above something like five miles an hour but they'll crush you like a grape, and so will Bolt Thrower with this album.

Recommended Track: "The IVth Crusade"

138. Dissection – The Somberlain

The first two Dissection albums, prior to the incarceration of main man, Jon Nodtveidt, (for being ruled an accomplice to a murder) were groundbreaking affairs that would have a drastic effect on not only the melodic death metal scene of their homeland but on the black metal scene as well. *The Somberlain* was Dissection's debut full length album, originally released on No Fashion Records in 1993. (Later to be re-released by Nuclear Blast in 1997.) This album is a genius blend of the frost bitten tremolo picking and icy blast beats of black metal with some amazing harmonic riffing characterized in the classic "Gothenburg sound." Yet at no point does this album sound forced. It's as if they took two musical parents and allowed them to naturally create a beautiful musical baby that would grow up to become an influential leader amongst his/her peers.

Recommended Track: "Black Horizons"

137. Destruction – Release From Agony

Blending thrash with elements of what we now consider black metal, the German version of thrash was often more aggressive and darker than most of what was coming out in other parts of the world. One of the bands at the forefront of the German thrash scene was Destruction. *Release From Agony* was the third full length album from Destruction, originally released in 1988 on SPV's Steamhammer label. This album is important in the history of this band as it's the first to feature a second guitar player. Moving from a power trio to a four-piece was an interesting transition, as they had success from a songwriting standpoint in their prior incarnation. But the addition of a fourth member allowed them to experiment a bit and fill out some of their songs with more intricate soloing. The end result was both transfixing and potent.

Recommended Track: "Sign of Fear"

136. Trouble – Psalm 9 (Trouble)

Originally a self-titled album for Chicago's Trouble, the band would release another self-titled album in 1990 and the name of this release would be officially changed to *Psalm 9*. This album was originally released in 1984 on Metal Blade Records. Along with releases by the likes of Saint Vitus and Candlemass around the same time, it helped formulate the doom metal genre that we know and love today. Only, unlike those other bands, Trouble wasn't afraid to dip into the burgeoning thrash metal scene for inspiration as well. In fact, some tracks, like "Assassin", are more thrash than doom for the most part. But at it's core this album is the beginning of a long run of doom/psych rock albums that would set Trouble apart from much of the competition.

Recommended Track: "The Tempter"

135. Entombed - Clandestine

Clandestine was Entombed's second full-length album, originally released by Earache Records in 1991 in Europe and early 1992 in the U.S. It's a brutal and pummeling album that combines in-your-face death metal with an eerie vibe that most bands at that time just couldn't nail down. This album is important for several reasons, no the least of which is the songwriting was more experimental than on their debut release. They proved on this record that, as a band, they didn't need to go 100 miles an hour to show how dark and ominous they could sound. They were able to achieve that through a somber tone that runs throughout the entire record. It's a great example of a band expanding their wings a bit to see how high they can soar. Yet, at the same time, it is also still a crushing example of early Swedish death metal.

Recommended Track: "Stranger Aeons"

134. Megadeth – Killing Is My Business... And Business Is Good

Killing Is My Business...And Business Is Good was Megadeth's debut album, originally released in 1985 on Combat Records. If you're a metal fan the history of this band is one you are familiar with. Dave Mustaine was Metallica's original lead guitarist. He helped write half their first album and was booted to the curb. Shortly thereafter Megadeth started wreaking havoc. This album was written with, in Mustaine's words, the intention of being heavier and faster than anything he had written with Metallica. You can debate all you want on whether this album is heavier but it's certainly just as fast and as dark as anything Metallica was writing. Dave Mustaine has always been an extremely technical guitar player. So the guitar work on here is a definite plus and one of the selling points. Also Dave Ellefson is one of the most underrated bass players in metal history. His performance is also a selling point. This album is a worthy first step for one of the greatest bands in metal history.

Recommended Track: "Looking Down The Cross"

133. Morbid Angel – Blessed Are The Sick

Few bands that came crawling out of the Florida swamps have been as important to the metal world as Morbid Angel. *Blessed Are The Sick* was Morbid Angel's second full-length album (technically third if you count the album that went unreleased until after this one came out), originally released in 1991 on Earache Records. This album was a bit more experimental than its predecessor. The tempo changes from blistering fast to a more mid-paced affair added an extra element of heaviness to it at times. The vocals were all over the map with varying styles of death growls and the occasional spoken passage. There are several great examples here of how they were combining things like double bass drum with these sludgy riffs. Such an amazing juxtaposition in sounds this band would come to perfect. When they slow it down to an amazing, sloth-like effort at certain points it just seethes heaviness.

Recommended Track: "The Ancient Ones"

132. Opeth – My Arms, Your Hearse

My Arms, Your Hearse was the third full-length album for Opeth, originally released in 1998 by Century Media's Century Black sub-label here in the States and Candlelight Records in Europe. This is an immensely important album in the Opeth pantheon. First and foremost, it was the first Opeth album to get a proper international release. This was also the first time Opeth experimented with a concept record. The songs are loosely bound together by a story of a man who dies and spends the afterlife following his beloved around and getting perturbed because he thinks she didn't mourn him enough (yet in reality she just can't cope with his loss - an afterlife soap opera of sorts). Lastly, this album is immensely important because out of their first three this one is possibly the heaviest and certainly the most focused of the lot. It's the album that would lay the groundwork for their coming masterpieces.

Recommended Track: "Demon of the Fall"

131. Kreator – Extreme Aggression

Kreator, along with Sodom and Destruction (and for some Tankard), helped to put Germany firmly on the metal map with a brand of thrash metal so dark and so evil sounding that to this day many consider these bands hugely influential in the formations of both death and black metal. That's not a stretch at all, especially death metal. It wasn't just Kreator's barking vocal style, but the way they structured many of their songs that would help lend to the death metal "sound" we are so familiar with today. Those three bands, along with U.S. acts like Possessed, are the reason that bands experimented with playing faster, louder and heavier. It was a natural extension of what these bands were churning out in the mid-'80s. *Extreme Aggression* was the fourth full-length album from Kreator, originally released in 1989 on Noise Records.

Recommended Track: "Betrayer"

130. Mayhem – De Mysteriis Dom Sathanas

De Mysteriis Dom Sathanas is the debut full length album from Norway's Mayhem. By the time it was finally released, two original members would be dead and their bass player would be in jail. Entire books have been written about this band and their shenanigans. For those who don't know here's the Cliff's Notes: Original vocalist, Dead, committed suicide in 1991. Bass player Varg Vikernes murdered guitarist Euronymous in 1993. Multiple members had partaken in burning down thousand year old churches all over Norway. Stories about skull necklaces, cannibalism, and sordid live shows abound. Through it all this album was finally released in 1994 on Euronymous' own Deathlike Silence label. It would be reissued by Century Media under their Century Black sub-label. Even if this band's history wasn't so infamous this album would have to be considered a landmark in the black metal genre and a must-own for anyone who calls themselves a black metal fan.

Recommended Track: "Freezing Moon"

129. Motörhead - Motörhead

I'm not sure if there is any other band in the world that is as equally loved in both punk and metal circles as Motörhead. They are not only a precursor to the NWOBHM and thrash metal scenes but they were clearly drawing from all the great '70s British punk on their first couple of albums. This album I'd classify as a punk rock record as much as a metal one simply by sound alone. This was Motörhead's debut album, originally released in 1977 on Chiswick Records. It is actually the second album Motörhead recorded, because their first attempt, recorded in 1976, would be rejected by their label. Despite the obvious punk rock tendencies, tracks like "Iron Horse/Born To Lose" show a distinct psych/hard rock sound not all that distant from what Lemmy's former band, Hawkwind, was doing. It's track like this one, along with the early works of bands like Judas Priest and AC/DC that would help create the NWOBHM sound that would go on to spawn an entire worldwide musical movement.

Recommended Track: "Motörhead"

128. At The Gates – Terminal Spirit Disease

As the Swedish death metal scene evolved, the trademark "buzz saw" sound started to fade and a more melodic vibe crept into studios all over the country. Gothenburg was the epicenter of the melodic death metal movement and the "Gothenburg sound" would eventually forever emblazon itself upon the metal lexicon. One of the bands responsible for procreating this new wave of Swedish death metal was At The Gates. *Terminal Spirit Disease* was the third full-length album from At The Gates, originally released in 1994 on Peaceville Records (licensed through the Futurist label here in the U.S.). The album itself is really a six song EP with three live tracks to round out the disc, and one of those six songs is an instrumental piece featuring piano and cello. Despite the brevity of recorded material on this album it stands as a landmark for Swedish metal in general, and especially for melodic death metal.

Recommended Track: "The Swarm"

127. Testament – Practice What You Preach

It's well documented, here and in other places, that the Bay Area thrash scene was exponentially prolific. Testament was one of many bands to carry the Bay Area torch and they've done well by it for over 30 years. *Practice What You Preach* was the band's third full-length album, originally released in 1989 on Megaforce Records and licensed through Atlantic Records. Don't underestimate the impact that working with a major label had on this band. To this day it is still one of their best selling album and has almost reached Gold status here in the U.S. alone. Bands like Metallica and Iron Maiden have skewed our sensibilities for just how hard it is for a metal band to sell half a million records. For this band to be close on a couple different albums is pretty impressive. While this album lacks some of the aggression of their first two records, it still contains a large number of classic Testament songs worth experiencing as much as possible.

Recommended Track: "Practice What You Preach"

126. Carnivore - Carnivore

Carnivore's self-titled, debut album was originally released in 1985 on Roadrunner Records. Where the follow-up has a more crossover styled sound, this album is straight ahead, 100% thrash metal. It's also a much darker and more aggressive album than its predecessor. Tracks like "Predator" and "Thermonuclear Warrior" are absolute beasts that showcase how heavy this band could actually be when they were playing it somewhat serious. With that said this album is still wrought with Peter Steele's ridiculous brand of humor, if not in the songwriting itself at least in some of the lyrics. Regardless what your thoughts are on lyrical content there is no denying this is possibly one of the most underrated thrash albums of the '80s. It's a powerhouse album and a stellar debut for a band whose influence far exceeds its output.

Recommended Track: "Predator"

125. Witchfinder General – Death Penalty

The roots of doom metal obviously start with Black Sabbath. But the early '80s had a plethora of bands that you could count as the "first wave" of doom metal. A bunch of which emerged out of the NWOBHM scene in the UK including Witchfinder General. *Death Penalty* was Witchfinder General's debut album, originally released in 1982 on Heavy Metal Records. First and foremost this band never got the credit they deserved when they were still an active band in the early '80s. This album in particular is stellar. The music lies somewhere between the hard driving rock n' roll that UK metal bands built a foundation on, and a somewhat blatant worship of Ozzy-era Black Sabbath. The end result is a crushing display of proto-doom metal of the highest order, and an album that helped launch a scene that is still thriving today.

Recommended Track: "Death Penalty"

124. My Dying Bride – Turn Loose The Swans

Turn Loose The Swans was the second album from England's My Dying Bride, originally released in 1993 on Peaceville Records. To say that this album is a masterpiece of the death/doom sub genre would not be an overstatement in the least. My Dying Bride were always the most "Goth" of the British doom bands, combining heavy doses of violin and piano with dirge-like guitars. Their vocalist, Aaron Stainthorpe, would come and go between death growls, melancholic clean vocals, and spoken word passages. This was the first album to bring all of those trademark elements together successfully. The opening and closing tracks don't even utilize guitars, let alone growling vocals, and the use of violin first became prominent on this album. There are pieces that come off as pseudo neo-classical in the way they are penned, and that's the beauty of My Dying Bride. Their sound is as timeless as some of the great Classical composers who've influenced them.

Recommended Track: "Your River"

123. Eyehategod – Take As Needed For Pain

Eyehategod are a whiskey soaked, Molotov cocktail of a band, and in their heyday one of the most important bands in all of American metal. Their sound combined elements of thundering doom metal with a bluesy, Americana music vibe to create this unique hybrid that was something akin to Black Sabbath on meth. No band wrote riffs like this band. The dirtiest, nastiest riffs you'd ever hear, with a rhythm section as groovy and funky as they were heavy, and a vocalist who honestly sounded like he was constantly on the final bender of a long string of them. Their live sets were just downright dangerous. From this album forward they were able to capture that vibe, harness it into something definable, and in essence create a signature sound that bands are still attempting to duplicate today. *Take As Needed For Pain* is the second full length album by Eyehategod, originally released in 1993 on Century Media Records.

Recommended Track: "Blank"

122. Napalm Death – From Enslavement To Obliteration

In essence, grindcore is simply the bastard child of death metal and punk rock and possibly no band exemplified that in the genre's earliest days better than Napalm Death. Their sound in those early days was an endearingly sloppy affair with layers upon layers of blazing fast, hyperactive drums, bass and guitars slapped together in a whirlwind of sonic violence. All topped off with the screeches and screams of vocalist Lee Dorian. It was unlike anything, any death metal fan had heard before and despite the somewhat lo-fi nature of their sound it was absolutely brilliant. *From Enslavement to Obliteration* was the band's second full-length album, originally released by Earache Records in 1988. It stands as the last album with Dorian (Cathedral) on vocals and Bill Steer (Carcass) on guitar. It also remains one of the greatest grindcore albums ever recorded.

Recommended Track: "Lucid Fairytale"

121. Danzig - Danzig

While Glenn Danzig was fronting Samhain he was approached by producer Rick Rubin to front an "all-star" rock band. Danzig decided he'd sign with Rubin's label but only if he kept at least part of his own band intact. That band would become Danzig. The first Danzig record was, in a way, an extension of the last Samhain record as more than one song was originally intended for the former outfit. But the overall sound and vibe of the band was drastically different. Gone were the "devilocks" and stage blood, and the music itself shifted from a punk/metal hybrid to straight blues-based heavy metal. On those early records, Danzig pulled from Black Sabbath and other proto-metal giants like Blue Cheer and Deep Purple but mixed it with all the darkest elements of old school Delta Blues. The result was a fairly potent brand of metal that was distinctively their own. Danzig's self-titled, debut album was originally released in 1988 on Def American Records.

Recommended Track: "Soul On Fire"

120. Cryptic Slaughter - Convicted

California's Cryptic Slaughter took the aggression of both thrash and punk rock and combined them into a nuclear explosion of sound and fury. It was a thing of beauty and something that fans of punk, thrash, speed metal, and grindcore should be all over. *Convicted* was Cryptic Slaughter's debut album, originally released by Metal Blade Records in 1986. As far as debut albums go you'd be hard pressed to find one as downright violent. This band is criminally underrated, even though there's been a resurgence in rediscovering their work over the years. (Relapse Records even gave the first two albums the reissue treatment.) But at the end of the day this band was so influential in the crossover genre that it just simply can't be understated. This album took a punk rock aesthetic in recording and combined it with the sheer ferocity of extreme metal to create a lasting impression on several different scenes.

Recommended Track: "Low Life"

119. Carcass – Necroticism – Descanting The Insalubrious

Necroticism – Descanting the Insalubrious is the third full-length album from England's Carcass, originally released in 1991 on Earache Records. Carcass were one of the many extreme metal bands that helped cement Earache's reputation as one of the best metal labels in the world, as well as one of the bands to help shine a light on a UK death metal scene that was exploding by the early '90s. This album was the first to feature Michael Amott on second guitar and it would be, by far, the most progressive album Carcass had written up to that point. It has a certain old school, death metal feel to it and features a lot more solos and mid tempo work than previous efforts. It's the Carcass album that stretched the definition of what a Carcass album could be, yet maintained all of the key elements from the first two albums making it a must own for fans of extreme metal.

Recommended Track: "Incarnated Solvent Abuse"

118. Amorphis – The Karelian Isthmus

The Karelian Isthmus was the debut album from Finland's Amorphis, originally released by Relapse Records in the U.S. (licensed to Nuclear Blast in Europe) in 1992. As far as death metal debuts go, this is one of the better ones. Even on their debut album Amorphis played a very progressive brand of death metal. There were clear influences flowing across the border from Sweden, especially with the guitar tone they have on this record. But they weren't afraid, right off the bat, to mix up tempos and play with more melodic elements in their songwriting. Certain tracks will blast you in the face with heaviness, yet other songs have almost doom-like elements and mix in twin guitar melodies. What you have in the finished product is a death metal record that, frankly, was ahead of its time and had its own major influence on the death metal world.

Recommended Track: "Black Embrace"

117. Slayer – Seasons In The Abyss

When you are talking about the most influential heavy metal bands of all-time, no conversation is complete without the mere mention of Slayer. They are giants of the genre who helped usher in thrash metal while also aiding in the formation of both death and black metal. Their influence knows no bounds. *Seasons In The Abyss* was Slayer's fifth full-length album, originally released in 1990 on the Def American label. Two records prior Slayer released an album we will eventually see ranked very high on this list – *Reign In Blood*. The follow up was an album that slowed it down a notch and was the most progressive release of their career at that point. This album, was an interesting hybrid of both the *Reign In Blood* magic and continuing to explore other avenues for their sound. When it worked, on tracks like "War Ensemble" or "Dead Skin Mask" for example, it was metal gold.

Recommended Track: "War Ensemble"

116. Repulsion - Horrified

It's difficult to only release one album and still be considered a massive influence for so many other acts. But that's exactly what Michigan's Repulsion have done. Genres are built over time. However, there are those albums that you look at and say to yourself, 'there really was little to nothing like this anywhere else in the world at that time.' This is one of those albums. *Horrified* was originally recorded in 1986 but would not see more than a demo release until Earache sub-label, Necrosis, released it worldwide in 1989. In 1986 grindcore certainly wasn't a thing yet. Even by the time most people first heard this album in 1989 it was a revelation. It's played with the speed of crossover thrash, punk, and even registers as fast as some second wave black metal. Yet it was as heavy as bands like Possessed and Death who had just helped to launch this new death metal genre a few years earlier. Needless to say it was an atom bomb of an album, laying waste to everything in its path.

Recommended Track: "Slaughter of the Innocent"

A BLAZE IN THE NORTHERN SKY

115. Darkthrone – A Blaze In The Northern Sky

Out of all the bands that first emerged from the black metal scene in Europe in the late '80s/early '90s possibly no band has had a better run than Darkthrone. They've spent their career reinvigorating themselves and are far and away one of the most influential black metal bands of all-time. *A Blaze In The Northern Sky* was Darkthrone's second full-length album but the first of their career you could actually call black metal. After starting out as a death metal band, Darkthrone shifted gears, donned some corpse paint, and began a series of records that some have dubbed an "Unholy Trinity." This album is a distinct mile marker for a genre that was really just starting to come into its own. Peaceville Records originally released this album in 1992, but not before originally refusing to do so upon first hearing it. Apparently, it was just that raw, that uncompromising, and that brutal…and it still is.

Recommended Track: "In the Shadow of the Horns"

114. Amebix – Arise!

Crust punk is sort of a nebulous description for any band that mixes together elements of anarcho-punk, d-beat, and various forms of metal. It's a crazy little niche of the extreme music world and one of the very few that can bring an equal number of punk and metal kids out to shows. Amebix were one of those bands in the early days of metal that would draw equally from both sides of that fence. *Arise!* was the band's debut album, originally released in 1985 on Alternative Tentacles. Although their second album, *Monolith*, would be much heavier and more "metallic" than this album it stands to reason that without the distinct punk aesthetic permeating this album we may not have the crust scene we do today. At this early stage in their career Amebix may have still been considered a 'punk' band but if you listen to this album in the context of when it was released there are very, very few punk bands that were playing it this heavy and this dark.

Recommended Track: "Fear of God"

113. Obituary – Cause of Death

Cause of Death was Obituary's second full length album, originally released in 1990 on R/C Records. Their debut was nothing short of a masterpiece, but it was this album that really put them on the map. It was also the album were Obituary would perfect their down-tuned, sludgy version of death metal that sounded like it crawled right out of the Florida swamps. It makes perfect sense that this was the album they chose to cover a Celtic Frost song, a band that heavily influenced their sound. This album is also an interesting one for Obituary fans as it's the only album to feature hired gun, James Murphy, on lead guitar. There is absolutely no reason for death metal fans to not own this record. John Tardy's vocals are the stuff of nightmares, the rhythm section is absolutely pummeling, and the guitars bleed heavy. It's truly a landmark album in the history of death metal and deserves whatever accolades it gets.

Recommended Track: "Chopped In Half"

112. Entombed – Left Hand Path

Left Hand Path is the debut album from Entombed, originally released in 1990 on Earache Records. When Entombed was at the top of their death metal game they had very few peers around the world, let alone in their own scene. They've spent the last couple decades exploring the 'death 'n' roll' thing. However, when it comes to Swedish death metal this band will always be synonymous helping define a country's metal scene for an entire generation of fans. The beauty of this album is that to this day it still sounds as heavy as a sack of rusty nails to the face. It's one of the best death metal records the '90s or Sweden has given us, and that's saying a ton because both the decade and the country have done more for death metal than can be stated here.

Recommended Track: "Drowned"

111. Bathory – Blood Fire Death

Blood Fire Death was Bathory's fourth full-length album and was originally released in 1988 on the Music For Nations sub-label, Under One Flag. Bathory founder and primary songwriter, Quorthon, was not afraid to experiment with his music. His work under his own name can easily testify to that, and he would spend a large chunk of the second half of Bathory's career experimenting with the band's direction. But those first four albums are thrash-influenced, proto-black metal of the highest order. It was on this album Bathory really started to mix things up, adding in ethereal elements which would define later works. When it all came together what we were left with was one of the first pure black metal records and a testimony to one man's vision in pushing extreme music to extreme boundaries.

Recommended Track: "The Golden Walls of Heaven"

110. Morbid Angel – Altars of Madness

Altars of Madness was Morbid Angel's debut album, originally released in 1989 on Earache Records. At one point, U.K.'s Terrorizer Magazine gave this album the #1 ranking in their Top 40 Death Metal Albums of all-time list. Clearly the influence of this album is immense. They would come to be known for highly technical yet amazingly brutal death metal, complete with lyrics revolving around the Lovecraft pantheon and guitar riffs/solos that were just absolutely mind-blowing. This album though takes all of that and runs it through a wood chipper at about a hundred miles per hour. To say this is their rawest effort wouldn't be doing it justice. It is as technically proficient and intense as any of their classic albums that would immediately follow, yet was delivered in a way that was as unrelenting as barbed wire being rubbed across a rug burn.

Recommended Track: "Maze of Torment"

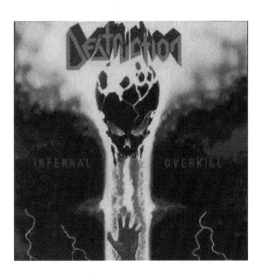

109. Destruction – Infernal Overkill

Destruction are one of the seminal thrash bands to rise out of Germany in the early 1980s. Borrowing their brand of thrash from the likes of Venom, Motörhead, and to a lesser extent Mercyful Fate, Destruction would go on to become one of the most highly-touted and influential bands to rise out of the German scene. However their debut album is often overlooked when their full catalog is discussed and that's downright criminal. *Infernal Overkill* was originally released in 1985 on the Steamhammer/SPV label. Not only is it one of the best thrash records of the mid-1980s, but it's an album that has its place amongst the first wave black metal classics that helped spawn that genre. It's a non-stop barrage, going from song to song with virtually no let up in tempo or intensity and Schmier's vocals alone are just completely unholy.

Recommended Track: "Bestial Invasion"

108. Bolt Thrower – In Battle There Is No Law!

One of the greatest gifts to metal the UK has ever given us is Bolt Thrower. When you talk about death metal bands there are few throughout the genre that hold a candle to this band. *In Battle There Is No Law!* is Bolt Thrower's debut album, originally released in 1988 on a label called Vinyl Solution. Bolt Thrower's entire career has been predicated not on how fast they play but simply how heavy they play. They had never been the fastest death metal band in the world because they didn't need to be. Instead they were simply one of the heaviest bands in the world utilizing a sound that churned and burned from track to track. But on their debut album their thrash/crust/punk roots were showing more than at any other point in their career. These influences are on full display here, making it a unique Bolt Thrower experience, but also making it possibly the most vitriolic release of their storied career.

Recommended Track: "Denial of Destiny"

107. Possessed – Beyond The Gates

Who invented death metal? The answer to that question could fill a book, and books have already been written on the subject. One of the bands that certainly had a huge hand in the formation of death metal was Possessed. *Beyond The Gates* was their second, and final, full-length album, originally released by Combat in 1986. This album took a decidedly different turn from the first, as their approach was much more thrash-centric. The band themselves will tell you they were trying for a more "accessible" sound. There is some truth to that. This album doesn't possess the ferocity and downright evil vibe the first album maintained. However it's only "accessible" to a wider metal fan base, not the general music buying populace. At the end of the day this is still a giant of a thrash album that not only helped to cement the Bay Area as the king of all US thrash scenes, but helped cement Possessed's legacy as well.

Recommended Track: "The Heretic"

106. Rainbow – Ritchie Blackmore's Rainbow

Ritchie Blackmore's Rainbow was Rainbow's debut album, originally released in 1975 on Polydor Records. It found immediate success, climbing to number 30 on the Billboard 200 chart in the States and going to number 11 on the UK charts. Blackmore was infamous for firing musicians at the drop of a hat and all eight Rainbow studio albums feature a different line-up. That alone is an impressive feat. For this album the bluesy nature brought in by former Elf members was on full display. It's also possibly their most hard-charging rock n' roll album with Dio on vocals. When we talk about bands that helped formulate heavy metal we often neglect to include Rainbow in the conversation. Part of the reason is their formation came long after that of bands like Black Sabbath and Deep Purple. Make no mistake though, Rainbow's influence on an entire generation of future metal musicians is huge.

Recommended Track: "Man On the Silver Mountain"

105. Kreator – Endless Pain

Endless Pain was Kreator's debut album, originally released in 1985 on Noise Records. It's a blistering debut complete with an unrelenting assault of shredding guitars and unholy, growled vocals (split evenly on this album by guitarist, Mille Petrozza and drummer, Jurgen Reil). The dual vocalist aspect is an interesting one to explore. The Petrozza fronted songs all have a proto-black metal vibe to them, while the Reil fronted songs have a more proto-death metal feel. Maybe that's splitting hairs but there is a distinct difference in the way the band approached each vocalist. You are going to be hard-pressed to find a thrash metal album as intense as this one. There isn't a single moment of let up on this thing. If their aim was to come out of the gates firing, then mission accomplished. It's easily one of the better thrash metal debuts from that era and set the stage for the immense efforts that would follow it.

Recommended Track: "Flag of Hate"

104. Saxon – Wheels Of Steel

Wheels of Steel was the second full-length album from England's Saxon, originally released in 1980 on EMI Records. This was the album that broke Saxon to a wider audience, even scoring them an appearance on the British music program, *Top of the Pops*. It's also, arguably, still their best album. There are few albums from that era that can simultaneously stay fresh with every listen, and yet perfectly capture a snapshot in time of the NWOBHM scene. Aggressive and powerful at certain points, yet melodic and harmonious at others, this album produced a bunch of tracks the band still perform live including, "Motorcycle Man" and the title track. You have to be doing something right if you can slay festival crowds with tracks that are over thirty years old. Fans of metal done the old ways should be all over this album.

Recommended Track: "Wheels of Steel"

103. Sodom – Persecution Mania

Persecution Mania was Sodom's second full length album, originally released in 1987 on the Steamhammer/SPV imprint. Sodom's debut album was the real culprit in their being considered a key player in the first wave of black metal alongside such titans as Venom and Bathory. On this album there would be a marked shift in creative output. That's partly because of the addition of new guitarist, Frank "Blackfire" Godznik. His playing added a level of technicality to their sound that, frankly, was lacking on their debut. Sodom are easily one of the greatest European thrash metal bands of all-time. There's no debating that. This album, along with the follow up, *Agent Orange*, are two of the most influential thrash albums to ever come off the European continent. The speed at which this album is played, the amazingly technical solos, the occasional vocal affects, the battering ram drummer, everything about this record is thrash perfection.

Recommended Track: "Enchanted Land"

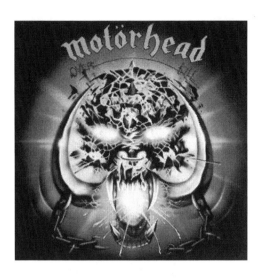

102. Motörhead - Overkill

Overkill was the second full-length album by Motörhead, originally released on Bronze Records in 1979. Where the first record leaned heavily on the UK punk rock scene for influence, this is the first Motörhead release that you can really call a metal album and not feel guilty about it. That's not to say the punk influences weren't prevalent. They're still there (they never really went away), but there is a definitive rock 'n' roll vibe to this album. That would eventually translate into albums that were faster and heavier than this one, but few that matched the influence and importance of this record. Very little was expected of the band when they formed and even after the mild success of the first album they were ready to pack it in at one point. So when they were signed to the independent Bronze Records it was originally only for a singles series the label was producing. The single was their cover of "Louie, Louie". Bronze was impressed enough to sign them to a full deal and the rest is metal history.

Recommended Track: "Overkill"

101. Death - Leprosy

Leprosy was Death's second full-length album, originally released by Combat records in 1988. Chuck Schuldiner was something of a metal vagabond in the first half of the decade, floating in and out of Florida, even spending a brief period in Canada. After the release of Death's debut, Schuldiner would move back to Florida for good. Why is this important? First, this album would consist of an entirely new lineup. Second, it would be the first Death album recorded at Morrisound Studio in Tampa. Both of these factors would play into this record's overall sound. Death's debut album was a raw, nasty slab of proto-death metal. It was almost grindcore in its production values. On *Leprosy* we get our first Death record with more streamlined production and enhanced technicality. *Leprosy* would lay the groundwork for some of the band's more progressive elements that would take center stage by the following decade, and to this day stands as one of the most important death metal records of all-time.

Recommended Track: "Pull The Plug"

100. Black Sabbath – Never Say Die!

Never Say Die! was Black Sabbath's eighth studio album, originally released in 1978 on Warner Bros. By the time they sat down to write this album Ozzy had already quit the band for a long enough period that they brought in a new singer, Dave Walker. Bill Ward sings the closing track, "Swinging The Chain," because Walker helped write it and Ozzy refused to sing it. The band was a mess at the time, constantly stoned or drunk and the tour that followed this album was a disaster as Van Halen (on their first world tour), by all accounts, blew them off the stage pretty much every night. Ozzy would be fired about a year after this album was released and both he and Black Sabbath would go on to record classic albums. With that said this album is not as bad as most people remember it being and there are enough moments on here to warrant it not only being on this list but just cracking the Top 100.

Recommended Track: "Johnny Blade"

99. Electric Wizard – Witchcult Today

Born out of big riffs, bong hits, and a potentially unhealthy love of occult/horror movies, Electric Wizard is easily one of the greatest doom metal bands to ever grace our stereos. Their brand of doom is actually rooted in the same sonic sludge that gave us all those great bands from the New Orleans scene, only toss in a '70s aesthetic and you've got a band that sounds like Black Sabbath played on the wrong speed on your record player (in a good way). *Witchcult Today* is the band's sixth full length record, originally released in 2007 on Candlelight Records here in the US and Rise Above Records in Europe. It's not often that you find a band release arguably their best record on their sixth effort, but Electric Wizard were never a band that played by the rules anyway.

Recommended Track: "Satanic Rites of Drugula"

98. High On Fire – Surrounded By Thieves

Surrounded By Thieves was the second full-length album released by High On Fire. It was originally unleashed in 2002 through Relapse Records. The artwork for the album is a personal favorite. The cover, tray card, and booklet all feature these drawings of warriors either fresh from or on their way to battle. They are some weird hybrid of Viking myths and Fantasy ethos. That pretty much sums up what you hear on this album. It is the sound of bizarre and frightening armies going into battle eight times over. It's a relentless assault of a record and it's almost sociopathic in how much it pummels listeners. It's not hyperbole to say that in a decade or so when we look back at the 2000s we will be calling this album one of the most important American metal records of that decade. The history of this album has not yet been completed.

Recommended Track: "Hung, Drawn and Quartered"

97. Anthrax – Fistful of Metal

Fistful of Metal was the debut album from New York's Anthrax, originally released in 1984 on Megaforce Records. 2/5 of the band was fired shortly after its release and it stands as the only album to feature Dan Lilker on bass and Neil Turbin on vocals. Lilker would, of course, go on to found Nuclear Assault and Brutal Truth among other projects. Turbin is sort of a forgotten figure in the history of this act, but what should not be forgotten is his performance on this album. When examining the history of Anthrax there is no other album that sounds like this one. It has a hard rock edge to it at certain points which they would trade in almost immediately for the full-on speed/thrash assault of future releases.

Recommended Track: "Metal Thrashing Mad"

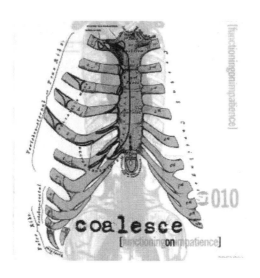

96. Coalesce – Functioning on Impatience

Coalesce has always been one of the more unconventional bands to come out of extreme music. Their sound is a bizarre amalgamation of punk and metal influences played with an almost acid jazz like craziness. Wild time signature and tempo changes, unholy and throat scorching vocals, bass played like it's lead guitar, and a live show so crazed as to have literally almost killed people. This band has always been the lead dog in innovation in the hardcore world. There are none heavier, none more cantankerous in their delivery, and none better. *Functioning on Impatience* was Coalesce's second full length album, originally released in 1998 on Second Nature Recordings. By the time this album hit the streets Coalesce was the buzz word on every hardcore kids lips and the metal kids were starting to take notice too. Filled with a special kind of vitriol this album is a message to pretty much everyone who ever doubted this band or spoke poorly of them. It was basically a two word statement, and you could probably guess what they were.

Recommended Track: "You Can't Kill Us All"

95. Marduk – Plague Angel

Sweden's Marduk are easily one of the most influential black metal bands to come out of the storied second wave. But by the early 2000s they, frankly, had started to grow a bit stagnant. However metal history is filled with revitalizations and this album certainly falls into that category. *Plague Angel* is Marduk's ninth studio album, originally released in 2004 on Regain Records. The importance of this album begins with the entry of a new vocalist, featuring the unholy talents of Mortuus. One of the most underrated front men in all of black metal, Mortuus' vocals gave this album a certain level of darkness the band hadn't achieved in quite some time. Every song is played with an intensity as high as a million suns scorching the Earth to pieces. This is, without question, one of the best black metal albums of the 2000s, and a triumphant return to the top of the black metal heap for Marduk.

Recommended Track: "The Hangman of Prague"

94. Leaf Hound – Growers of Mushroom

England's Leaf Hound put out just one album before disbanding for over thirty years, but that album is an unearthed gem of '70s proto-metal. *Growers of Mushroom* was their 1971 debut, originally released on Decca Records. There's a saying about seminal alt/indie rock pioneers, The Velvet Underground. It's something along the lines of, 'they didn't sell a lot of records but everyone who bought a record started a band.' This album may be the heavy metal equivalent of that saying. They may have been a one-and-done band and it might not have sold a ton originally, but it would seem that everyone who heard this album in 1971 was touched by it in one way or another. If you are looking for albums that specifically had an effect on the future stoner rock scene you'd be hard pressed to find an album outside of Black Sabbath's catalogue that is as much a direct ancestor as this one. It's also clearly an album that had an influence on the doom and NWOBHM scenes that would crop up less than a decade after its release.

Recommended Track: "Freelance Fiend"

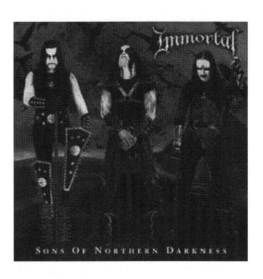

93. Immortal – Sons of Northern Darkness

Sons of Northern Darkness was the seventh studio album from Norway's Immortal, originally released in 2002 on Nuclear Blast Records. It was the final album they released before they initially decided to call it quits. They must have been saving the best for last because this is hands down not only one of the best black metal albums of the 2000s, but quite possibly of all-time. Seeing as the first six albums they released were all stellar, that's saying a lot. They not only outdid themselves, they outdid pretty much everyone else too. This album is a deadly combination of the raw, unadulterated blackened fury they perfected early on, with the more thrash influenced sound they crafted directly leading up to this record. It's a brutal, demonic affair that, at times, sounds like it's emanating straight from the bowels of hell.

Recommended Track: "Tyrants"

92. Iron Maiden – Brave New World

One of the greatest metal bands of all-time decided to kick off a new decade with a new album and the return to the fold of two former members. *Brave New World* was Iron Maiden's twelfth studio album, originally released on EMI in 2000. Not only was this not some halfhearted comeback record, this blew the doors off the last two albums that Bruce Dickinson sang on a decade prior. His voice was golden on this record. Meanwhile, the three guitar attack did not sound bloated or out of place at all and Steve Harris (bass) and Nicko McBrain (drums) were as sharp as ever. There were progressive elements that continued what they were doing on albums like *Seventh Son...* and *Somewhere In Time* yet they were still writing killer riffs and catchy choruses. This album was nothing short of a triumphant return for a band whose legacy is unparalleled.

Recommended Track: "The Wicker Man"

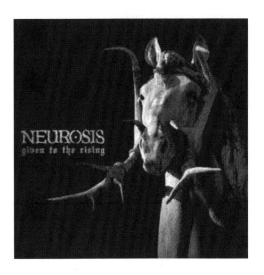

91. Neurosis – Given To The Rising

Given to the Rising is Neurosis' ninth full length album, originally released on their own Neurot Recordings imprint in 2007. Neurosis spent the first half of the 2000s taking their sound down a mellower path, removing the harsh vocals almost completely and making two albums that took their ethereal elements to new heights. This album was a return to the days when Neurosis could beat you down with heaviness and massive riffs just as much as disorient you with their blend of sonic mysticism. It was an unexpected gut punch. There are still those tracks that lean more on atmosphere than heaviness where you have this sort of floating sensation, carried along by discordant notes strung throughout the song. At the end of the day though what makes this one of the best albums the 2000s produced was the return to what buttered a lot of Neurosis fan's bread – the pure auditory bludgeoning that the band could hand out in apocalyptic proportions.

Recommended Track: "Given To The Rising"

90. Emperor – Prometheus: The Discipline of Fire & Demise

They only put out four full-length albums over the course of roughly a decade before vanishing from the spotlight, but Norway's Emperor are quite possibly the most influential band to come out of the storied second wave of black metal. This is their final recorded gift to the metal world. *Prometheus: The Discipline of Fire & Demise* was Emperor's fourth and final full-length album, originally released here in the States on Candlelight Records in 2001. It stands as the most progressive and technical album of their discography. It's truly an album that pushed the envelope not only for the band but for the black metal genre in general. Clean/whispered vocals fill the entire album, the use of programming and synthesizers was heavier than on any other record they had ever done, and the overall songwriting took on a much more prog rock type of approach. It's as unique a black metal album as you will ever find.

Recommended Track: "The Eruption"

89. Nasum – Inhale/Exhale

After years of releasing splits, demos, and EPs, Sweden's grind masters, Nasum, released their debut full-length album, *Inhale/Exhale* on Relapse Records in 1998. With this album they usurped the throne as the greatest grindcore band in the world at that time. This album knocked the entire grindcore scene on its ass. The production, which the band handled most of themselves, was crisp, and the songwriting was deadly in how relentless it was. It's a brutal, brutal affair that took a lot of people by surprise as they were not very well known at the time outside of their native Sweden. Nasum would go on to release four full-length albums. Unfortunately in 2004, vocalist/guitarist and founding member, Mieszko Talarczyk would perish in the tsunami that engulfed Thailand while vacationing.

Recommended Track: "Time To Act!"

88. Rotting Christ – Thy Mighty Contract

Thy Mighty Contract was the debut full-length album from Rotting Christ, originally released on Osmose Productions in 1993 (and re-released in 1997 on the Century Black sub-label after the band signed with Century Media). While the band would spend the next decade or so taking their sound and expanding it into progressive/symphonic/non-metal territories, their debut is an onslaught of extreme metal from start to finish. Maybe it's because in their earliest days Rotting Christ were somewhat isolated from other equally talented extreme metal acts, but whatever the reason they emerged with an album that is inherently all their own. This album is a combustible and unique blend of black metal, melodic death metal, and even some doom thrown in for good measure.

Recommended Track: "Exiled Archangels"

87. Deep Purple - Fireball

Before Deep Purple became international superstars they were writing some of the best hard rock/proto-metal in the world. *Fireball* was the fifth full-length album they released, originally for Warner Brothers (here in the States) in 1971. At the time of its release this would be the first Deep Purple record to go to #1 on the UK charts. However, history has not been kind to this album and certain band members (Ritchie Blackmore in particular) have come out saying they don't particularly like it. Despite that though this album remains an absolute classic. It's a slight regression back to a more blues-based sound, but Deep Purple continued to push the proto-metal envelope. To this day it stands as one of the best examples of how British hard rock would eventually evolve into the NWOBHM scene. Deep Purple helped lay down the blueprint for that scene which in turn helped smash open the floodgates of heavy metal.

Recommended Track: "No, No, No"

86. Opeth – Blackwater Park

Blackwater Park is Opeth's fifth studio album, originally released in 2001 on Music For Nations/Koch Records. It was the first album that saw Opeth work with Porcupine Tree front man, Steven Wilson, in the producer's chair. The fact that the music on this album started to drift even further away from their blackened death metal roots and into more progressive territory may or may not be related to working with Wilson. But regardless of what came first, the sound or the producer, he was the right producer for the sound. While this album is as dark and mysterious as anything else they released prior, it's also an album that has this sort of soaring element to it. Not unlike a bird taking off from a barren tree in the dead of winter. It is an album as beautiful as it is haunting.

Recommended Track: "Bleak"

85. Slayer – South of Heaven

South of Heaven was the fourth studio album from thrash titans, Slayer, originally released on Def Jam/American Recordings in 1988. After years of playing faster and more aggressive with each album, Slayer decided to purposely shift gears. The result was a more atmospheric effort than previous releases. This album also was just as influential in formulating the band's already amazing legacy. It's still beloved by the vast majority of a fan base that made this album Gold not long after its release. While this might not be your first choice of Slayer records you pull off the shelf when you need a fix, it's still an essential record. The influence this album had on the metal world at large is still being felt today.

Recommended Track: "Mandatory Suicide"

84. Voivod – War and Pain

War and Pain was Voivod's debut album, originally released in 1984 on Metal Blade Records. From Day 1, Voivod really didn't sound like any other thrash bands. Their reliance on NWOBHM and hardcore punk influences were nothing new. Combining the two with progressive elements, especially later in their careers, was straight out of left field and has become their calling card. This album is probably their most straight forward effort. The progressive elements that would inhabit future albums were fleeting. Instead it is clearly born out of a marriage of punk rock and the more extreme bands coming out of Europe, specifically Mercyful Fate, Venom, and Bathory. The powerful pieces that made those bands stand above their peers being wed to a hardcore punk aesthetic almost makes this album sound like a poor man's Motörhead at certain points. It's an album that put the rest of the thrash scene on notice.

Recommended Track: "War and Pain"

83. Metallica - ...And Justice For All

...And Justice For All was Metallica's fourth studio album, originally released in 1988 on Elektra Records. You should all know by now what preceded this album. Three amazing records, the death of Cliff Burton - one of the greatest metal bass players of all-time - and the hiring of Jason Newsted to replace him. By the time this album hit shelves in the summer of '88 this band was already huge, and the fact that it was declared Platinum within a relatively small period of time after its release will attest to that. Despite having to overcome historically suspect production, it's an album that helped continue this band's rise to the top of the metal heap, cementing their place as one of the most influential metal bands of all-time.

Recommended Track: "One"

82. Cathedral – Forest of Equilibrium

When Lee Dorian left Napalm Death because he was unhappy with the direction they were taking, he decided to take things in a completely different direction as well. It must have been somewhat refreshing for Dorian to go from the breakneck speed of those early Napalm Death recordings to the slowed tempos and the doom and gloom of Cathedral. From the first Napalm Death record to the first Cathedral record you probably couldn't find two bands on further ends of the BPM spectrum. *Forest of Equilibrium* is Cathedral's debut album, originally released in late 1991 on Earache Records. It's a bludgeoning record that just buries you in these dreary, molasses-like riffs. Easily the heaviest Cathedral album within their discography, the stoner rock sound they would eventually shift to was embryonic at best on this release. A true doom masterpiece and one of the best doom albums the '90s would produce.

Recommended Track: "Ebony Tears"

81. Bathory – The Return......

The Retrun...... (or *The Return of the Darkness and Evil,*
which is the actual full name of the record) was Bathory's
second full length album, originally pressed in 1985 by
Black Mark Productions. Bathory had set the metal world
on high alert with their debut and *The Return......*
continued that upward spiral through the rafters and
cementing their legacy as one of the first black metal
bands in the world. This album really was a return of sorts
to the darkness and evil of which they spoke. The
breakneck pace at certain points, accompanied by
Quorthon's snarls, and a guitar tone that would lay the
ground work a decade later for all things black metal, was
just the tip of the iceberg. While this album still contained
plenty of thrash metal elements, especially in some of the
soloing, there is no denying that it's ten times as extreme
as pretty much every thrash metal album that preceded it.

Recommended Track: "Born For Burning"

80. Eyehategod - Dopesick

In certain ways no other bands match the disruptive and exhaustive beauty of the sonic chaos that Eyehategod has created. This album is their sludge metal masterpiece. *Dopesick* is the band's third full-length album, originally released on Century Media in 1996. There is no such thing, in my opinion, as a 'bad' Eyehategod record. Their first two albums were rooted in the blues meets punk ethos that would help define exactly what sludge metal was and is. Their later efforts take doom metal on alcohol-fueled tangents, stretching the limitations of what people thought they knew about this band. This album combines all of that in a fury of sick riffs, sicker vocals and a chaos that seems to hover over the entire thing like a storm cloud waiting to burst. From the very beginning of this album, with the sounds of breaking glass and tortured screams, to the last piece of feedback-drenched mayhem, it is a blueprint for all other bands hoping to delve into the sludge realm.

Recommended Track: "Dixie Whiskey"

79. Judas Priest – Sad Wings of Destiny

Judas Priest had two very distinct phases of their career. I call it "B.L." and "A.L." or "Before Leather" and "After Leather." I'm not necessarily talking about the album, *Hell Bent For Leather* (as it was called in the U.S.), but it was around that album and *British Steel* the band started donning the studs and leather outfits that would come to rule the metal world for years. Their sound would evolve with the style. The "B.L." period was marked by a hard rock approach, including blues and psych rock elements. While the foundation of their metal mastery was always present, it wasn't until they strapped on the leather outfits that they went "full metal" so to speak. When you look at the history of Judas Priest you really can't compare albums from the '70s to the '80s. Almost a different band in a lot of respects. This album was the first essential album of the "B.L." period. *Sad Wings of Destiny* was released in 1976 on Gull Records.

Recommended Track: "Victim of Changes"

78. Kyuss – Blues for the Red Sun

Blues for the Red Sun is the second full-length album from California's Kyuss, originally released in 1992 on Dali Records. Though the album didn't sell a ton upon release, this would go down as one of the most influential stoner rock albums of all-time. Kyuss was a rock band, first and foremost. Their brand of rock just happened to be super heavy, down-tuned, and with a sound so enormous at times that regular rock radio stations shied away from them. Kyuss (and especially this album) are direct descendants of all the great heavy, psych, acid rock, etc., acts that were also largely ignored by mainstream radio while helping formulate what we know today as heavy metal. This is the first of several truly essential Kyuss albums. Josh Homme's guitar playing here annihilates everything in its path, and the entire album comes off like a crazy acid trip in the middle of the Sonora Desert.

Recommended Track: "Green Machine"

77. Terrorizer – World Downfall

For almost two decades the legend of Terrorizer grew from the single album, *World Downfall*. This was Terrorizer's debut full-length, originally recorded in 1989 and released through Earache Records. By the time the band got it together to release this album they had already disintegrated. Drummer, Pete Sandoval, had already started recording the first Morbid Angel album. So not only would this be their first and only album for roughly 20 years, but it wasn't supported by any kind of tour or label promotion. Terrorizer, as mentioned, would all go their separate ways after the release of this album. Sandoval back to Morbid Angel (along with David Vincent who sat in as a studio musician), and Jesse Pintado eventually joining Napalm Death. Regardless of their standing with other, more notable projects, what they put together was equivalent in talent to their reputations. It's a brutal cacophony of grinding madness and easily served as one of the great early grind records to ever come from US soil.

Recommended Track: "Storm of Stress"

76. Emperor – Anthems to the Welkin at Dusk

Anthems to the Welkin at Dusk is Emperor's second full-length album, originally released in 1997 on the Century Black imprint here in the U.S. and by Candlelight Records in Europe. Synths and various forms of sonic experimentation were far from unknown to the black metal scene by 1997. But Emperor were so good at experimentation – the addition of classical and progressive elements, the back and forth between gruff and soaring, clean vocals, yet all of it wrapped in a blanket of blast beats and tremolo picking. With this album they were able to take the entire black metal scene on their collective back and drag them kicking (and often times whining) into the next century. On the back of this album Emperor wrote that they play "…Sophisticated Black Metal Art exclusively". There could be no truer statement in describing this album.

Recommended Track: "Thus Spake The Nightspirit"

75. Blue Cheer - Outsideinside

Blue Cheers's influence on the formation of heavy metal as we know it today is extraordinary. They are, in my mind, the unsung heroes of the proto-metal movement. *Outsideinside* was the second full-length album released by San Francisco's Blue Cheer. Originally released on Philips Records in 1968, this would be the last album recorded with the original power trio. Blue Cheer was born out of the same Haight-Ashbury scene that had given the world artists like Jefferson Airplane and The Grateful Dead. According to some interviews with the original members these three dudes were more likely to be found picking fights alongside Hells Angels than passing the peace pipe with their fellow "hippies." That comes across loud and clear in their music. It's Blues-inspired rock but it's so much louder, heavier, and more intense than anything else being played at the time.

Recommended Track: "Just A Little Bit"

74. Celtic Frost – Into The Pandemonium

Fans looking for an exact replica of *Morbid Tales* or *To Mega Therion* wound up being sorely disappointed in this album. But we do not shy away from albums where a band took a left turn. This album is one of those instances. *Into The Pandemonium* is the third full length album from Swiss outfit Celtic Frost. It was originally released through Noise Records in 1987. The first two Frost albums were brutally heavy explosions of first wave black metal, melded with early doom. Classics for sure. While there are tracks on this album, such as "Inner Sanctum" or "Babylon Fell" that still maintain that trademark Celtic Frost sound, this was the first album where they started to experiment in ways fans just could not have expected. Elements of Goth rock and classic heavy metal are all over this record, including Tom G. Warrior's occasional moans that would replace his barking vocal style. Shifting styles or not, this is a must own for extreme metal fans.

Recommended Track: "Babylon Fell"

73. Danzig – Danzig II: Lucifuge

The first Danzig record was so unique for the time. It really stood out, especially seeing as Glenn Danzig and his new band went even further away from his punk roots. The melding of blues and traditional metal with doom elements was so effective. Maybe it was finally touring as Danzig that helped them hone their craft, but whatever the reasons, this album is lights out from beginning to end. There's isn't a weak song on this thing, zero filler. It's also an album that took the seething evilness of its predecessor and amped it up a couple notches. It's a slightly heavier, slightly more intense affair and to this day it still contains some of Danzig's best material. Over 25 years after its release it still stands as a truly classic album. *Danzig II: Lucifuge* was originally released on the Def American label in 1990.

Recommended Track: "Tired of Being Alive"

72. Deicide - Deicide

Originally called Amon, the band changed their name to Deicide after signing with Roadrunner Records. Deicide was the more fitting moniker as the band has built a career on Satanic and anti-religious messages which have brought them everything from being banned to bomb threats. Utilizing elements of thrash metal, crossover thrash, and first wave black metal woven into a tapestry of brutal death metal, Deicide have always been one of the heaviest death metal bands of their era. Their debut is a brutal assault to the senses, from almost non-stop blast beats to crazy riffs that seem to cover the entire fret board in one song, and of course Glen Benton's unholy wails. Sheer death metal brutality, played flawlessly from start to finish. *Deicide* was originally released in 1990 on Roadrunner's R/C imprint.

Recommended Track: "Dead By Dawn"

71. Pentagram – First Daze Here
(The Vintage Collection)

Pentagram's history is a long and convoluted one. The documentary film, *Last Days Here*, can do a better job telling that story than I could in such a limited space. Essentially, this band recorded some killer material in the early to mid-1970s that never saw the light of day. They would eventually reform with an entirely different line-up in the mid-1980s and record their debut album after something like 15 years post formation. This album was the first compilation to feature that classic '70s material. *First Daze Here* was originally released in 2001 through Relapse Records. No album prior to this one had ever compiled all of this classic material, recorded between 1972-1976, and distributed it to a worldwide audience in a format that was entirely approved of by the band themselves. It cemented the band's place alongside such legends as Black Sabbath, Deep Purple, and Blue Cheer as being a band that was instrumental in the formation of heavy metal as we know it.

Recommended Track: "Forever My Queen"

70. Cirith Ungol – Frost and Fire

California's Cirith Ungol formed in the early '70s, but it wasn't until 1980 that they would release their debut album, *Frost and Fire*. It was originally issued on their own Liquid Flames Records before Enigma would reissue it after signing the band. It would also be reissued by Metal Blade in 1999. While Cirith Ungol are sometimes portrayed as one of the earliest progenitors of American doom, that really only applies to the two albums directly after this one. This album is a hard rock/traditional metal album, not unlike what the NWOBHM scene was churning out. Although Cirith Ungol never played as fast or as heavy as many of the bands that followed them, the influence this album had on the West Coast metal scene is unmistakable.

Recommended Track: "Frost and Fire"

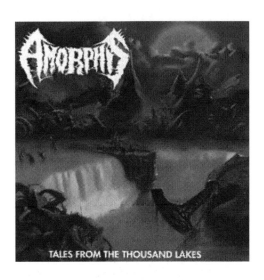

69. Amorphis – Tales From The Thousand Lakes

Tales from the Thousand Lakes was Amorphis' second full-length album, originally released through Relapse Records in 1994. This was the first album where clean vocals, psychedelic elements, and traces of what we now call "folk metal" started to take over the Amorphis driver's seat. After this record all of those elements would dominate their discography. Still, this album had a major impact on the death metal community. There are tripped out, folksy parts that stop you in your tracks. But there are also some seriously brutal doom elements that were added to their sound that emphasize just how heavy they could get. This was one of a very small handful of albums in the early '90s that really showed the world how far you could push the limits of death metal and still call it death metal, and out of those albums it was by far the best of the lot.

Recommended Track: "Black Winter Day"

68. Black Sabbath – Technical Ecstasy

In Black Sabbath lore, it is fair to say this is one of the two most underrated albums they ever produced. Originally released in 1976 on Warner Brothers Records, *Technical Ecstasy* was the band's seventh full length album. It was also the album where a) Ozzy started to lose interest, b) their drug use was taking over, especially for certain members and c) they started to tour with younger, hungrier live acts, namely taking a young AC/DC with them on tours of Europe and Australia. That's all a bad combo that would end up seeing the band completely implode while recording their next album, *Never Say Die!* While this album may not stand tall against the first five or six Sabbath albums, it's still a classic. Tracks like "All Moving Parts (Stand Still)", "Gypsy", and "Dirty Women" have riffs and base lines running through them that are quintessential Tony Iommi/Geezer Butler, and the overall performance is still steeped in the doom-laden heaviness that Sabbath built an empire upon.

Recommended Track: "All Moving Parts (Stan Still)"

67. Bolt Thrower – Realm of Chaos: Slaves To Darkness

Bolt Thrower's debut album was more crust punk than death metal. However, after signing to Earache Records the band would release their second full-length album, *Realms of Chaos: Slave To Darkness*, in 1989. With this album they would start to move towards what would become the signature Bolt Thrower sound – down-tuned, sludgy riffs, a rhythm section that squashes your skull, and a death/doom hybrid that would become instantly recognizable over time. This album was their transition from their crusty punk roots to the doom-infused death metal they would become famous for. Take the blast beats and speed of grindcore, match it up with classic, late '80s death metal and throw in touches of crust punk and you've got a pretty good barometer of what this album is all about.

Recommended Track: "Through the Eye of Terror"

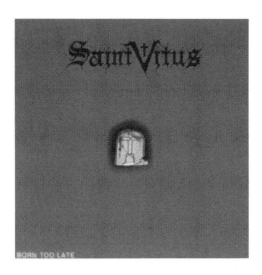

66. Saint Vitus – Born Too Late

Born Too Late was the third full-length album from Saint Vitus, originally released through SST Records in 1986. This album holds a special place in the hearts of many Saint Vitus/doom fans. Not only was the addition of Scott "Wino" Weinrich on vocals a sensational move, but the guitar work of Dave Chandler (which was always the real driving force behind this band, no matter who was on vocals) was absolutely stellar. There are riffs on this album that are not only torn from the Tony Iommi playbook but could be additions to it. When you think of the plodding, thundering nature of the heaviest doom in the land this should be one of the first albums that comes to mind. There was little, if anything, that sounded like Saint Vitus when this album hit the streets, and 30+ years later the impact this album had on the burgeoning doom scene was profound.

Recommended Track: "Dying Inside"

65. Testament – The New Order

Compared to some of their Bay Area contemporaries, Testament was a little late to the thrash game as Metallica, Megadeth and Slayer all had multiple albums out by the time they released their debut. *The New Order* was their second full-length album, originally released in 1988 on Megaforce Records, but distributed by Atlantic Records, making it the band's major label debut. While this album may not be as raw or as fast as their debut it's a heavy and technically proficient thrash album and, quite frankly, a masterpiece of the tail end of the storied '80s thrash scene. By 1988 most thrash bands had either abandoned their thrash roots altogether or were in the process of it. Yet here was Testament ripping it up with one of their best offerings. I'd go so far as to say that if not for bands like Testament who took thrash to new and more technical ground the thrash scene of the '80s would have petered out much sooner.

Recommended Track: "Disciples of the Watch"

64. Venom – Welcome To Hell

Welcome To Hell is the debut album from England's Venom, originally released on Neat Records in 1981. There was really nothing like Venom up to that point. The closest relation was probably Motörhead. But take Motörhead, crank them up another couple notches and add in some blatant Satanic imagery/lyrics and maybe you get a close approximation of Venom. It's well documented that Venom helped create what we know today as black metal. But you could argue they did just as much, if not more, to help facilitate the arrival of thrash metal, speed metal and death metal. Tracks like "Witching Hour" are the perfect Petri dish for the embryonic stages of thrash and death metal. There's no denying that Venom had a huge impact on what would become the storied second wave of black metal, but chalking them up as "first wave black metal" and moving on really doesn't do them or this album justice.

Recommended Track: "Witching Hour"

63. Judas Priest – Killing Machine

Killing Machine was originally released in late 1978 on Columbia Records and is the band's fifth studio album. Because their label was still promoting their previous album, *Stained Class*, also released in 1978, it was decided that this album wouldn't be released in the U.S. until early 1979. To add to the confusion the album's name was changed to *Hell Bent For Leather* because the label didn't like the "murderous implications" of the original title. The band addresses this album by the original title, and so will we. The album that followed this one, *British Steel*, is considered by many to be their big breakthrough, where the quintessential Judas Priest "metal" sound was formulated. On the contrary, that album was where they perfected their sound. Where it started was right here, including the change in look as evidenced by the photos on the back cover. A true early metal masterpiece if there ever was one.

Recommended Track: "Hell Bent For Leather"

62. Emperor – In The Nightside Eclipse

Norway's Emperor would release their debut full-length album, *In the Nightside Eclipse,* on Candlelight Records in 1994. To say that it had a huge influence on the burgeoning black metal scene is a massive understatement. This album showed the world that not only could you make a black metal record with some seriously grim production but also one with exceptional musicianship. The little flairs they would add - for example synths or spoken word passages - were absolutely brilliant and completely groundbreaking at that time. The black metal scene at that point was often marked by bands simply trying to play faster or have nastier production than anyone else. In 1994 there were few bands like Emperor, and even fewer who could match their stellar musicianship. Anyone looking for an avenue into the world of extreme black metal could do a lot worse than to start with this album.

Recommended Track: "I Am the Black Wizards"

61. Iron Maiden – Somewhere In Time

Somewhere in Time was Iron Maiden's sixth studio album, originally released in 1986 on Capitol Records in the U.S. (EMI in Europe). It came off the heals of the amazing one-two punch of *Powerslave* and *Live After Death* so fans were expecting another dose of epic, sweeping compositions. Instead the band couldn't internally agree on the band's direction and what would emerge was an album not everyone in the band stood behind (specifically Bruce Dickinson who has zero writing credits). This is not to say that this album is some sloppy mess. On the contrary, this is still classic Iron Maiden. Once again Dave Murray and Adrian Smith prove why they are arguably the best guitar duo in metal history, and this was also the first album Maiden added guitar and bass synths to the mix. It's an album that successfully bridged the gap from where they began the 1980s to where they would finish them.

Recommended Track: "Wasted Years"

60. Carcass – Symphonies of Sickness

Symphonies of Sickness was the second full-length album released by England's Carcass. They originally released it at the tail end of 1989 through Earache Records. There's no denying the first Carcass album helped lay the foundation for modern day grindcore (and goregrind if you consider that a stand alone genre). This album, however, begins the band's progression towards a style more akin to death metal. The furious blast beats are still there. There are points where they still play it faster than the speed of light. But it really has more of a death metal tone to it. There are segments where they break it down into slower, sludgy chunks. There's also more melody to these songs (as much melody as a goregrind band can manage) than the first album. Regardless of how you want to classify it there's no denying that it's one of the better extreme metal albums of the late 1980s.

Recommended Track: "Exhume to Consume"

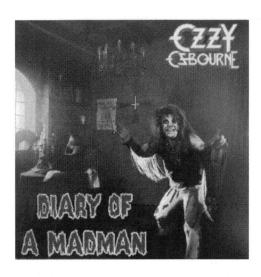

59. Ozzy Osbourne – Diary of a Madman

Diary of a Madman was originally released on Jet Records in late 1981. It was Ozzy Osbourne's second solo album and the final album he released with the great Randy Rhoads on guitar, as Rhoads would be killed in an airplane crash while touring for this record. Is this the heaviest album on this list, or even in the Top 100? Absolutely not, but between Rhodes' amazing guitar work and Ozzy's trademark vocals, this album doesn't need to be overly heavy to impress. It had a much more "metal" sound compared to the first album, which maintained the hard rock ethos of Osbourne's previous band. Tracks like "S.A.T.O." and the title track are phenomenal displays of the magic Rhoads and the rest of the band could weave. If this had to be the last recorded material Randy Rhoads left us with, it has done his legacy proud.

Recommended Track: "Diary of a Madman"

58. King Diamond – Fatal Portrait

There are very few front men in the metal universe as iconic as King Diamond. Whether it's the face paint or the falsetto vocals, the concept albums or the stage shows that unfold like Gothic theater, King Diamond has been a name that every metal fan knows. After a brief but storied run with Mercyful Fate, this was his namesake band's debut album. Mercyful Fate's initial time together was relatively brief and when the band dissolved three-fifths of the members – King Diamond on vocals, Michael Denner on guitar, and Timi Hansen on bass - would go on to form King Diamond. They would add Mikkey Dee on drums (he would later go on to join Motörhead in 1992) and Andy LaRocque on guitar. In 1986 they would release *Fatal Portrait* on Roadrunner Records, setting in motion the second phase of the legend of King Diamond. This is the one King Diamond album that doesn't form a complete concept record, yet the individual songs on here are some of the best they would record.

Recommended Track: "Charon"

57. Blue Cheer – Vincebus Eruptum

Released in January 1968, *Vincebus Eruptum*, was the debut album from San Francisco's Blue Cheer, originally released on Philips Records. Most people who are familiar with Blue Cheer discovered them through their cover of Eddie Cochran's "Summertime Blues", which went all the way to #11 on the Billboard charts. But despite the one hit wonder status this has brought them in the mainstream media, their contributions to the metal world go far beyond. There were no bands like Blue Cheer in 1968. '68 was the "Summer of Love." It was filled with hippies singing anthems about free love and taking on the man, yet here came these three dudes who decided they were going to play as loud and aggressive as humanly possible. What they lacked in technicality they would make up for in volume and a raucous style akin to no one else at the time. True pioneers of the proto-metal movement and a band that the entire metal world owes a debt to.

Recommended Track: "Doctor Please"

56. Napalm Death - Scum

Scum is Napalm Death's debut album, originally self-released by the band but given a proper release through Earache Records in 1987. The amount of talent that plays on both sides of this record is mind-boggling. Side A features the likes of Justin Broadrick (Godflesh, Jesu, etc.), while Side B features the talents of Bill Steer (Carcass), and Lee Dorrian (Cathedral). Both sides feature the amazing Mick Harris on drums. While early crust bands like Amebix had a huge influence on this band, so did the heady punk rock of acts like Crass and Discharge. This band in their earliest stages was as much anarcho-punk as they were anything else. There were very few bands playing it this extreme when Napalm Death first blasted off, and they've since launched a million copy cats who've given rise to one of the most popular and polarizing sub-genres in all of metal.

Recommended Track: "Human Garbage"

55. Iron Maiden – Seventh Son of a Seventh Son

Seventh Son... was the seventh studio album from Iron Maiden, originally released in 1988 on Capitol Records here in the U.S. and EMI in Europe. Partly because of the heightened use of synths this album had a distinctive prog rock feel that previous Maiden efforts did not. However this was also an album which saw a return to form in many ways, including the exceptional vocal performance of Bruce Dickinson. It's the first Maiden album to be a pseudo-concept record, based loosely around the seventh son of a seventh son mythos and the book *Seventh Son* by Orson Scott Card. In fact, based on the concept idea, the enhanced amount of synths, and the overall writing style found on many songs on this album, it would not be unfair to say this is the Iron Maiden record most closely related to the classic progressive rock of the '60s and '70s.

Recommended Track: "Moonchild"

54. Sir Lord Baltimore – Kingdom Come

One review of this album from a famous music magazine of the era actually used the term "heavy metal" to describe it. One of the earliest uses of the term. It was well deserved. *Kingdom Come* was the debut album from New York's Sir Lord Baltimore, originally released in 1970 on Mercury Records. The 'classic' era of Sir Lord Baltimore only yielded two full length records before they dissolved and vanished for over thirty years. But as we've seen so many times before, it's not the quantity of the albums that a band puts out that makes them so essential, but the quality. What set this album apart from not only their other work, but the work of their peers, is the sheer heaviness and intensity it is often played with. These guys were not afraid to turn up the tempo a couple notches, nor were they afraid to tune down and deliver some absolutely crippling blows. When the two elements are combined then you really do have an album that showed some of the earliest flashes of "heavy metal."

Recommended Track: "Kingdom Come"

53. Kreator – Pleasure To Kill

Pleasure To Kill was Kreator's second album, originally released in 1986 on Noise Records. To say that 1986 was a huge year for thrash, and metal in general, would be a massive understatement. This album is one reason why. Kreator's debut was an instant classic, but had the feeling of a band still trying to feel their way around a studio. It was this album that really saw them come into their own and start to fire on all cylinders. The songwriting, the production, everything about this album was tighter than their debut. In terms of influence this is one of the most important metal albums to ever come out of Germany. What we hear is "thrash" but there are so many riffs and techniques lifted from this record and used in death metal releases for decades afterwards. While you could argue that Sodom had a bigger overall influence on the embryonic black metal scene at the time, Kreator's importance to the birth of that beast starts with this record as well.

Recommended Track: "Pleasure To Kill"

52. Bathory - Bathory

Sweden's Bathory, along with Venom, Celtic Frost, and a small handful of other bands, are considered the "first wave" of black metal. However out of all those bands considered the "first wave" of black metal there are really none that carry the true essence of black metal the way Bathory did. Their self-titled, debut album was originally released in 1984 through Black Mark Productions. This first Bathory record is the only album they released that sounded like an unholy mix of Motörhead, punk rock, and thrash. They played it fast and pissed but had a certain aesthetic to their sound that would separate it from pretty much all future Bathory recordings. It's a primal, evil sounding record that has been credited by some sources as single-handedly launching black metal. While that may be debatable, what is not is the influence this album continues to wield today.

Recommended Track: "In Conspiracy with Satan"

51. Rainbow – Rainbow Rising

Rising was Rainbow's second full-length album, originally released in 1976 on Oyster Records (and produced by the legendary Martin Birch who metal fans will know as the knob turner for Iron Maiden and Dio-era Black Sabbath, among others). As phenomenal as the debut record was this album takes on a slightly harder edge. Based on the track "Stargazer" alone this album deserves all the accolades it has received over the years. The overall performance of the entire band seethes metal like few others from that era. While you could argue that both Ronnie James Dio and Ritchie Blackmore had projects that were more important to metal in general – Dio with both Sabbath and his namesake band and Blackmore with Deep Purple – you will be hard pressed to find many bands from the mid to late '70s who had as meaningful of an impact on metal as Rainbow.

Recommended Track: "Stargazer"

50. Death – Spiritual Healing

Spiritual Healing was the third full-length album released by Death, originally in 1990 on Combat Records. It was reissued in 1999 by Century Media when they reissued pretty much the entire Combat back catalog and then again in 2012 by Relapse Records. The musical prowess of the late Chuck Schuldiner is well documented. If you were to look up the definition of "technical death metal" in a musical dictionary there would probably be a picture of Schuldiner in there. He's truly become a legend of the genre and it's not unwarranted. By the dawn of the '90s, Schuldiner's songwriting was starting to become somewhat more melodic and certainly more technical. The lyrical content was moving away from the gore and guts stuff they specialized in on the debut album into social issues of the time. The music reflected that as well. To say that this album was more melodic than the two previous efforts should not be taken as it being less "heavy" in any way. On the contrary, it's still a near-perfect display of pummeling death metal.

Recommended Track: "Living Monstrosity"

49. Black Sabbath - Mob Rules

Mob Rules was the tenth studio album from Black Sabbath, originally released in 1981 via Warner Bros. here in the U.S. (Vertigo in Europe). It would be the first album without original drummer, Bill Ward, and the last album Ronnie James Dio would sing on for a decade. It's well established how important Dio and his magnificent vocal chords are to the history of metal. Tony Iommi and Geezer Butler may very well be the most important guitar and bass players in the history of metal as well. While you might not ever call this album their finest hour together, it has enough absolute gems on it to give it the "classic" tag multiple times over. "Sign of the Southern Cross" and the immensely underrated tracks "Country Girl" and "Turn Up The Night" are some of the best tracks Sabbath recorded with Dio on vocals. The Ozzy lineup will (and should) always be considered the definitive Sabbath line-up, but this record helped cement the Dio-era as completely essential in the formation of heavy metal.

Recommended Track: "Sign of the Southern Cross"

48. Candlemass – Epicus Doomicus Metallicus

Epicus Doomicus Metallicus was the debut Candlemass record, originally released in 1986 on Black Dragon Records in Europe (licensed to Leviathan Records in the U.S.). Think about 1986 for a second in terms of metal. Thrash metal was king. Death metal and black metal were in their embryonic stages. In the mainstream there were the Ozzy Osbournes, the Iron Maidens, and the Judas Priests of the world where things like melody still counted for something. So when Candlemass showed up with slow, sludgy music and soaring baritone vocals, sounding like some weird off-shoot of Black Sabbath, they were unlike almost any other bands at the time. This is the lone album the band would record with vocalist Johan Langqvist, who would be replaced by Messiah Marcolin to form what would be considered the band's 'classic' line-up.

Recommended Track: "Demons Gate"

47. Carcass – Reek of Putrefaction

Reek of Putrefaction was Carcass' debut album, originally released in 1988 on Earache Records. This album takes everything people are taught about music and blows it up in their faces like a watermelon with a stick of dynamite in it. What you have is a band that took death metal and basically played it so frantically that it became almost unrecognizable. So much so virtually no one is calling this a death metal record. If this album doesn't set the blueprint for the modern grindcore scene then nothing does. Throw in the fact they pretty much invented "goregrind" with their ridiculous lyrics culled from medical journals and textbooks, and the original album cover that used autopsy photos. This is a band that really was forging their own blood-soaked path through the metal community unlike any band that came before them.

Recommended Track: "Genital Grinder"

46. Judas Priest – British Steel

British Steel was Priest's sixth full-length album, originally released in 1980 on Columbia Records. An entire generation of metal fans know this record thanks to the heavy rotation of the two singles "Breaking The Law" and "Living After Midnight". This album went Platinum here in the U.S. and still stands as a prime example of NWOBHM. While the band went for less progressive, shorter songs on this album, most likely in an effort to shoot for more radio airplay, what they were also doing was losing the hard rock sound that their first five albums carried in favor for a more metal one. Priest wouldn't go "full metal" until their *Screaming For Vengeance* record two years later. But for a lot of people when you talk about traditional metal, this album is one of the first that comes to mind.

Recommended Track: "Living After Midnight"

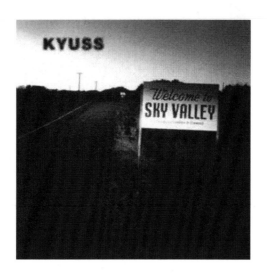

45. Kyuss – Kyuss (Welcome To Sky Valley)

When it comes to stoner rock, California's Kyuss were in a league all their own and this album is their magnum opus. *Welcome to Sky Valley* (as it is often mistakenly called) is the band's third full-length album, originally released in 1994 on Elektra Records. This album was actually recorded a full year earlier than the eventual release date but the folding of their original label, and the revolving door of members (this was the last album to feature drummer Brant Bjork) would force the band to release this album later than originally expected. With that said, the album title, the release date, who quit when, none of that matters once those headphones go on and you start to take this album in. The groove-laden, driving rock contained within is nothing short of a modern day masterpiece. It's the album that launched a million imitators over the decade that would follow, yet none would strike the sonic gold this album would.

Recommended Track: "Gardenia"

44. At The Gates – Slaughter of the Soul

Slaughter of the Soul was At The Gates' fourth studio album, originally released through Earache Records in 1995. For long time fans of the band it was a direct, albeit more melodic, extension of what they had done on previous releases. But for anyone who disliked or was ignorant to Swedish death metal up to that point, it was a revelation. It was an 'in' to a sound they refused to open themselves up to previously, or were honestly ignorant to. This album has been responsible not only for making it acceptable but virtually mandated by the state that all Swedish death metal heretofore have "melodic" in the title and the songwriting. Yet in 1995 it was an absolute ripper of an album that showcased the very best of the "Gothenburg sound" to a tee. Despite some of the questionable "core" acts it indirectly influenced/spawned, one can never overlook the positive impact this album had on the metal world at large.

Recommended Track: "Slaughter of the Soul"

43. Ozzy Osbourne – Blizzard of Ozz

Blizzard of Ozz would be released in 1980 through Jet Records. It featured the highly underrated rhythm section of Bob Daisley (Rainbow) on bass and Lee Kerslake (Uriah Heep) on drums, and of course the guitar virtuosity of Randy Rhoads. The songs on this album run the gamut from hard rockin' jams to acoustic interludes to more intense and intricate tracks like "Revelation (Mother Earth)" and "Steal Away (The Night)." The overall vibe of this album is accessible to the general populace. "Crazy Train" alone has been used in car commercials, at sports arenas, and mainstream rock radio for years. However tracks like "Suicide Solution" (which spawned the famous lawsuit regarding a fan's suicide) and "Mr. Crowley" are fairly dark affairs for the Ozzy pantheon and really showcase Rhoads as a classically trained, metal guitarist. Some of Randy Rhoads finest work is on this album, and for that reason alone this is a must-own for all metal fans.

Recommended Track: "Mr. Crowley"

42. Dissection – Storm of the Light's Bane

Sweden's Dissection had a somewhat brief and bizarre run. After a blistering debut full-length the band signed a worldwide deal with Nuclear Blast Records. In 1995 they would unleash their second full-length album, *Storm of the Light's Bane*. Within two years of the release date though the band would be done, as founder and songwriter, Jon Nodtveidt, would be incarcerated as an accomplice to a murder. However upon his release from prison in 2004, Nodtveidt would reform the band with an entirely new line-up. They would record one album, do some touring in Europe, and then in 2006, Nodtveidt would commit suicide, thus ending the band for good. Dissection somehow seamlessly merged black metal and death metal into this unique brand of extreme music. It held the grimness and Satanic imagery of black metal, yet the technical proficiency of the Swedish death metal scene. It was, especially on this album, the perfect marriage between two of the most powerful and important metal scenes in the world.

Recommended Track: "Where Dead Angels Lie"

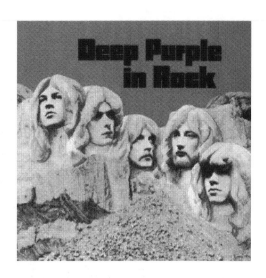

41. Deep Purple – In Rock

Deep Purple in Rock (or simply *In Rock* as most people call it) was the band's fourth studio album, originally released in 1970 on Harvest Records. Their first three albums are pretty solid, if unspectacular. They are a mixed bag of psych rock and that era would culminate in the *Concerto for Group and Orchestra* album, which is exactly what it sounds like. By the time of this recording the band had finally put together the best line-up they were going to have – Ritchie Blackmore on guitar, Jon Lord on organ, Ian Paice on drums, the recently added Ian Gillan on vocals, and Roger Glover on bass. It would be this line-up that would also unleash their best album and an album that had an immense impact on the future of heavy metal. What really hammers home the proto-metal sound on this album is the addition of Gillan on vocals. His potent delivery and screams on tracks like "Bloodsucker," "Child In Time," and "Into The Fire" are legendary. Few albums from that era can be considered direct ancestors of heavy metal in the ways this one can.

Recommended Track: "Into The Fire"

40. Morbid Angel - Covenant

Florida's Morbid Angel are one of the most important death metal bands in the world. Morbid Angel can lay claim to the most technically proficient (and one of the most innovative) guitar players in death metal history in Trey Azagthoth, one of the most intense death metal drummers in Pete Sandoval, and the underrated bass playing of David Vincent. *Covenant* is their third full-length album, originally released on Earache in 1993. Here in the U.S. it was released through Giant Records, which was a subsidiary of the Warner Music Group, thus making it the first death metal album to be released on a major label. While not as flashy or 'thrashy' as the albums that came before it, *Covenant* has stood the test of time. It remains one of the most influential and important death metal albums of all-time.

Recommended Track: "Lion's Den"

39. Testament – The Legacy

The Legacy was originally released in 1987 through Atlantic Records. It's a minor miracle this album ever saw the light of day, between major personnel changes and the fact they had to change their name mid-recording. (They were originally called Legacy before realizing there was a Jazz band that had trademarked the name.) They lost their vocalist, Steve Souza (who would quit to join Exodus) during the writing of this album. Chuck Billy was added on vocals so late in the game there is only one song on the album where he receives any writing credit. Yet they not only released one of the best debut albums in thrash history, but simply one of the best thrash metal albums of the '80s. While the Bay Area had already produced some giants of the metal world by 1987, Testament was able to stand out from the crowd right from the get-go and the influence of this album is still felt today.

Recommended Track: "Over The Wall"

38. Metallica – Ride The Lightning

Ride The Lightning is Metallica's second full-length album, originally released on Megaforce Records in 1984, and reissued by Elektra Records later that year after the band's contract was bought out. It's the last album that would see former guitarist, Dave Mustaine, get a writing credit (for both the title track and the instrumental "Call of Ktulu"). Despite the fact this album received virtually no radio airplay outside of your local college station, it still managed to peak at #100 on the Billboard 200 album charts. When all was said and done it would wind up being certified Platinum six times over, an amazing achievement for any album, but especially poignant for an album as heavy as this one. *Ride The Lightning* was the perfect bridge between the raw thrash of their first effort and the more progressive style they favored on the two records that immediately followed. It also happened to be the album that got them signed to a major label and set in motion heavy metal history.

Recommended Track: "Fight Fire with Fire"

37. Obituary – Slowly We Rot

Slowly We Rot was originally released on Roadrunner's R/C imprint in 1989. After five years, two name changes, and what seemed like an endless amount of demos, Obituary had finally arrived on the scene with an album that was brutally heavy. Not only was it heavy, it was sludgy - sludgy in a way that really no other death metal record had ever achieved prior. Obituary added an entirely new dimension to this still relatively new death metal genre. Obituary, especially on this record, literally sounded like they were crawling out of their graves from deep inside a Florida swamp. It was amazing then and it still is so today. Obituary has written some of the greatest death metal songs ever composed. A ton of those came off of this record. Easily one of the best death metal debuts in the history of the genre.

Recommended Track: "Slowly We Rot"

36. Judas Priest – Defenders of the Faith

For me, as great as those early Judas Priest records were, the period between roughly 1978-1984 represent quintessential Judas Priest. This album was the last one released during that timeframe. *Defenders of the Faith* was the band's ninth studio album, originally released in 1984 on Columbia Records. Nine albums in and Priest was still delivering the goods. (Pun intended.) This album picks up where its predecessor left off. High octane, powerful heavy metal played with an extra sharp razor's edge is the order of the day here. This is easily one of the best albums Priest would produce after shifting their sound from their rock n' roll roots to the full-on heavy metal we know and love today. Every track is played with a dark lining surrounding it like a shroud, which makes this one of Priest's heaviest efforts to date.

Recommended Track: "Freewheel Burning"

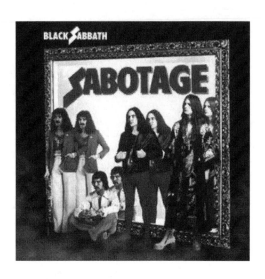

35. Black Sabbath - Sabotage

Sabotage was Black Sabbath's sixth studio album, originally released in 1975 on Warner Brothers here in the U.S. During the writing and recording the band was battling some serious legal troubles as they were being sued by their former manager. While the anger over what they were experiencing may have added to this album's overall heaviness, the hurt and confusion of it all also comes across in the writing process. This is the first Sabbath record where Ozzy Osbourne (admittedly in his recent autobiography) started to lose interest in the recording process. His performance doesn't necessarily suffer because of it, but you can see the cracks of the eventual split start to form on this record. While it was somewhat of a drop off from the first five it's still one of their better efforts and remains an early metal classic.

Recommended Track: "Thrill Of It All"

34. Dio – The Last In Line

Is there any voice that seethes heavy metal the way Ronnie James Dio's voice did? The man could sing names out of the phone book and make it sound like some ancient invocation of demons. *The Last In Line* was the second Dio album, originally released in 1984 on Warner Bros Records. Obviously the strength of this album begins and ends with the title track, which is one of the single greatest songs in metal history. But that's not the only classic track on this record by a long shot. Tracks like "We Rock", "I Speed At Night" and "Evil Eyes" are all some of the best tracks Dio recorded with his namesake band. Truth be told when I'm discussing metal with someone and they say they don't like Dio I stop listening to them. This album is one of many reasons why. It's nothing short of being an absolute classic of traditional metal.

Recommended Track: "The Last In Line"

33. Bathory – Under The Sign Of The Black Mark

Under the Sign of the Black Mark was the third full-length album released by Sweden's Bathory, originally in 1987 on New Renaissance Records here in the U.S. This album was the absolute perfect collision of two sonic worlds Bathory subsisted in. The raw, stripped down, lo-fi brutality of the first few records melded with the beginnings of the epic songwriting style that would dominate their "Viking metal" albums later in their catalog. If you don't like black metal Bathory is a tough pill to swallow. Band mastermind, Quorthon, wrote abrasive, violent music that did its best to bring the atmosphere of hell itself alive inside your stereo. Yet this band went on to almost single-handedly influence an entire generation of musicians that would become the modern day black metal scene.

Recommended Track: "Enter The Eternal Fire"

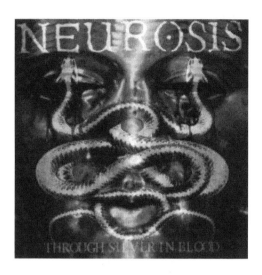

32. Neurosis – Through Silver In Blood

There is no band in the world that has been as influential to heavy music over the last 25 years as Neurosis. This is the album that started their ultimate dominance of the underbelly of the music industry. *Through Silver In Blood* was originally released through Relapse Records in 1996. At that point in time there was virtually nothing like it. There are a million imitators now, but there is still nothing like Neurosis. This album took all of the bizarre soundscapes and mysticism of their previous efforts and extrapolated them over a full album's worth of material. Yet they somehow also managed to exude a heavier and more brutal sound than they ever achieved prior. Look no further than the combination of the tracks "Rehumanize" and "Eye" or "Locust Star" for a perfect example. Every Neurosis album is best listened to front to back however, and none more so than this one.

Recommended Track: "Eye"

31. Angel Witch – Angel Witch

England's Angel Witch began their journey in the late '70s and by the end of the decade they had a record deal with Bronze Records, who would go on to release their self-titled, debut album in 1980. To put this in perspective, this album came out one month prior to Iron Maiden's first album. Yet while Maiden would go on to a long and fruitful career, Angel Witch would basically self-destruct not long after this album's release. However, the greatness of this record rises above all of that and firmly places *Angel Witch* amongst the greatest albums of its era. There's a reason that many people feel this album had the biggest impact on the formation of thrash metal out of all the NWOBHM contributors. It wasn't because they played it faster or heavier than everyone else, they just simply knew how to take their sound to dark places, and it paid off. A true gem from an era that had more than its fair share.

Recommended Track: "Angel Witch"

30. Mercyful Fate – Don't Break The Oath

Denmark's greatest metal export is not a topic that is up for discussion. Mercyful Fate have been, since the early '80s, one of the most influential metal bands of all-time. *Don't Break The Oath* was Mercyful Fate's second full-length album, originally released in 1984 on Roadrunner Records. *Don't Break The Oath* was an album that saw Mercyful Fate experiment just enough to make sure it had a discernibly different sound than the preceding *Melissa* album. Yet, at the same time, it still maintained, and even expanded on how downright evil their sound was by exploring the dark side of melodic and progressive elements. Call it first wave black metal, traditional metal, call it whatever you want, as long as you call this album 'classic' at some point in the discussion.

Recommended Track: "Night of the Unborn"

29. Slayer – Show No Mercy

Show No Mercy was originally released through Metal Blade Records at the tail end of 1983. As far as early thrash records go it's a classic. As far as Slayer records go it contains tracks that are still considered fan favorites to this day, including "Black Magic" and "Antichrist". However, this album, although easy to define as a classic in the Slayer pantheon, has a distinctly different sound from future releases. The play-it-as-fast-as-you-can mantra they would use for most of the '80s wasn't completely in play yet as this album leans much more heavily on melody and an early '80s thrash blueprint. With all of that said it's very easy to see why the black metal scene has taken a particular shine to this album. It's not a stretch to say that this is one of the first truly extreme metal albums. From here Slayer would build their legacy of brutality, eventually forsaking the somewhat melodic for the outright spastic.

Recommended Track: "Black Magic"

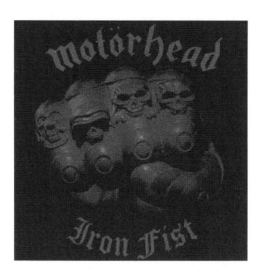

28. Motörhead – Iron Fist

Iron Fist was the fifth studio album released by Motörhead, originally seeing the light of day in 1982 via Bronze Records. Although it is sometimes not compared favorably to its predecessors, and the band themselves have come out saying they weren't fond of the finished product, there is no denying this is one of their more potent offerings. By 1982 Motörhead had toned downed the punk rock side of things and gone 'full metal.' Yet songs like this album's title track were still filled to the brim with a sneering, punk rock aesthetic. It's the type of album that keeps the head banging from start to finish. Simply put, Motörhead was one of the most bad ass bands the planet has ever seen. Their influence on so many genres is immense, and this album holds a special place in the history of thrash metal in particular.

Recommended Track: "Iron Fist"

27. Iron Maiden – Iron Maiden

Iron Maiden are icons of the genre who deserve every ounce of praise heaped upon them. This is where it all began. Iron Maiden's self-titled, debut album was originally released in 1980 on EMI Records in the U.K. and Capitol Records here in the States. This is the first album we are seeing from Maiden to feature original vocalist Paul Di'Anno. While Maiden's sound was truly cemented with the addition of Bruce Dickinson, these first two Maiden albums with Di'Anno are, in their own right, phenomenal. It may lack the production the band desired, but the rawness of this album added to its effectiveness. It's the grittiest and starkest record Maiden would ever release. It's a powerful shot to the arm of a scene that was still quite nebulous. A groundbreaking debut if there ever was one.

Recommended Track: "Iron Maiden"

26. Death – Scream Bloody Gore

It's hard to argue that Death's debut album, *Scream Bloody Gore*, wasn't one of the earliest, if not the earliest, example of modern day death metal. It was originally released through Combat Records in 1987 and was the culmination of a long and interesting journey for founder and band leader Chuck Schuldiner. By 1987 there was a bevy of albums that had begun to take thrash metal to new and extreme heights. But Schuldiner had recorded about 6,000 demos (o.k., maybe not that many) between 1984 and 1987, many of them widely circulated. So even though their debut album didn't officially hit until later in the decade, Schuldiner can still lay claim to writing some of the earliest examples of death metal. Once he resettled in San Francisco (temporarily, as he would relocate back to and stay in Florida after this record) and teamed with drummer Chris Reifert (later of Autopsy and Abscess) Schuldiner would piece together an album that helped set the stage not only for death metal sonically, but also visually and lyrically.

Recommended Track: "Zombie Ritual"

25. Judas Priest – Stained Class

Stained Class was Judas Priest's fourth studio album, originally released in 1978 on Columbia Records here in the States. It is, without a doubt, their most underrated effort on so many levels. It also marks a ton of 'firsts' for this band that would take on this sort of butterfly effect on this history of metal. First and foremost this was, up to this point, the heaviest and darkest record they had ever recorded. It's also, coincidentally, their best produced up to this point. With crisp production and songwriting that no longer drifted sometimes aimlessly in and out of these prog and blues rock passages, you could argue that this is Priest's first true "metal" record. Their sound would take a bit of a step back to their earlier ways on the next record before really going "full metal" by the time the '80s rolled around. But this was where metal thirsts were first fully quenched with this band. It has stood the test of time amazingly well and should be considered a must own for all metal fans.

Recommended Track: "Saints In Hell"

24. Celtic Frost – To Mega Therion

To Mega Therion was Celtic Frost's first full-length album (technically second in the U.S.), originally released through Noise Records in 1985. Thrash metal, death metal, black metal, even sludge and doom metal to a certain extent, owe this band a massive, massive debt. This album took the sludgy bits from the first release and ran them through a vat of hot glue to produce an album that just crushes skulls from beginning to end. Celtic Frost are widely considered to be one of the founding fathers of black metal. That might be more true about their first album than this one. But it's hard to listen to a song like "Dawn of Meggido", with the bombast of horns and exaggerated drums mixed into this serpent-like riff and not hear the influence a track like that had on so many well-known second wave black metal bands. Their career would go on a pretty bizarre arc after this album, featuring material that was both classic and...not so much. But there's no denying this album's place in the metal history books.

Recommended Track: "Circle of Tyrants"

23. Black Sabbath – Heaven and Hell

Heaven and Hell is the ninth studio album by Black Sabbath, originally released in 1980 on Warner Brothers here in the U.S. It was, and possibly still is, the most "metal" album Sabbath had ever done. That is to say the music on this album was in line with what was going on in the metal world in 1980. Instead of trying to re hash their "sound" Sabbath chose to take influence from the modern scene and completely perfect it in a way no one had before. Part of this is obviously because Ronnie James Dio has exceptional range and depth to his voice. While Ozzy was, and still is, perfect for Black Sabbath, he lacked the ability to do with these songs what Dio wound up doing. As Tony Iommi was quoted as saying the difference between the two is that Ozzy "sung with the riff" where Dio sang "across" it. This album is so classic (and so damn heavy at certain points) because the entire band was re-energized and their performance shows it. Tony Iommi, especially, is lights out on this record, penning riff after classic riff.

Recommended Track: "Heaven and Hell"

22. Megadeth – Peace Sells…
But Who's Buying?

Peace Sells…But Who's Buying was Megadeth's second full length album, originally released through Capitol Records in 1986. I think we are all well aware of what Dave Mustaine's former band was doing in 1986. While Metallica was releasing what many still believe is their magnum opus, Megadeth was really just getting started. Their debut album was a raw, aggressive blast of unbridled thrash metal. But it also lacked the songwriting chops of future releases. This album would set the bar very, very high, not just for Megadeth but for the thrash scene as a whole. The rest of the world was on notice. This album is chock full of material that's so filled with vexation, with pure rage. It's very tangible. You hear all the time about athletes playing with a chip on their shoulder. I think Dave Mustaine, at the height of their creative output, was writing music with a chip on his shoulder. The entire album is a classic from beginning to end, worth revisiting as much as possible.

Recommended Track: "Good Mourning/Black Friday"

21. Venom – Black Metal

This band, and specifically this album, had such a monster impact on the metal world. Here's a brief list of bands that have covered Venom songs over the years: Slayer, Mayhem, Obituary, Vader, Sigh, Unleashed, Dimmu Borgir, Cradle of Filth, Macabre, and about a million other bands. You picking up what I'm putting down here? *Black Metal* was Venom's second album, originally released through Neat Records in 1982. It is easily their most "famous" and recognizable album, and obviously gets credit for coining the phrase "black metal" which an entire generation of Scandinavian musicians would adopt. Venom were easily the most extreme and evil sounding outfit to come slithering out of the NWOBHM scene. Listen to this album compared to what bands like Saxon, Priest and Maiden were releasing in 1982. It's dirtier, nastier, and less produced (for a reason). Venom sounds like those band's degenerate brother, you know, the one that always wound up in prison.

Recommended Track: "Black Metal"

20. Dio – Holy Diver

Holy Diver was originally released in 1983 via Warner Brothers. Alongside Ronnie James Dio, it featured fellow Black Sabbath alum, Vinny Appice on drums, former Rainbow bassist Jimmy Bain, and Vivian Campbell on guitar. Prior to this album RJD was already a household name in the metal world. His work with Rainbow and Sabbath would see to that. But it wasn't until the band bore his name that he truly became the focal point of the project. From this point forward the name, Dio, would become synonymous with heavy metal in a way few names have since. It also helps that Dio and his band had the chops to back it up. While the music on this album is more accessible than anything he had done before, it was also, in certain ways, some of the most powerful music Dio would help write. While Dio never achieved super stardom with mainstream America he would go on to become a god amongst men in the metal world, and this album is a huge reason why.

Recommended Track: "Shame on the Night"

19. Black Sabbath – Sabbath Bloody Sabbath

Sabbath Bloody Sabbath was Black Sabbath's fifth studio album, originally released through Warner Brothers and Vertigo Records in 1973 (technically New Year's Day 1974 here in the U.S.). After basically three plus years of non-stop action the members of Black Sabbath had some quit (and a lot of cocaine) in them. When they finally regrouped main songwriter, Tony Iommi, was a dry well of ideas. So they left L.A., where they went to record, and wound up in a supposed haunted castle back in the U.K. Perfect setting for a Black Sabbath record because the first song penned was the epic title track and from there Sabbath would emerge with their most innovative effort to date. Strings, synths, keyboard, you name it they threw it on this record. The band took their compositions and stretched them in ways they never had before. This was a band at the height of their experimentation and innovation, and it stands as the last front-to-back, truly classic album of the original line-up.

Recommended Track: "A National Acrobat"

18. Iron Maiden - Powerslave

Powerslave was Maiden's fifth studio album, originally released in 1984 on Capitol Records here in the U.S. (EMI in Europe.) The obvious attractions for a lot of people with this record are the two singles – "Aces High" and "2 Minutes To Midnight" – which have remained live staples for the past 30+ years. It also contains two of their longest and most inspired efforts of the time in the title track and "Rime of the Ancient Mariner". The rest of the album isn't lacking either. For example a track like "Flash of the Blade" is an absolute gem, underrated in every way possible. Did you know that this was the first Maiden record to have the same line-up as the previous record? True story. It shows as Maiden not only start to take their sound in a slightly more experimental direction, but the finished product is focused and sharp as a razor.

Recommended Track: "Aces High"

17. Slayer – Hell Awaits

As phenomenal as their debut record was, it wasn't until this album that Slayer truly came into their own as the dominant force they would be known as hence forth. *Hell Awaits* was Slayer's second full-length album, originally released in 1985 on Metal Blade Records. This album lays the groundwork for everything that came afterwards. One of the hallmarks of this album, as noted by several musical sources, is the propensity for Slayer to cobble together longer and more technically inspired songs than on previous efforts. Several songs take twists and turns in structure that Slayer never really explored prior, and this new sonic proficiency combined with Slayer's propensity for dastardly atmospherics rendered it a knock-out punch.

Recommended Track: "At Dawn They Sleep"

16. Motörhead – Ace Of Spades

Ace of Spades was Motörhead's fourth full-length album, originally released in 1980 on Mercury Records here in the U.S. and Bronze Records in the rest of the world. These guys started clogging up the U.K. charts with the release of the title track as the album's first single. It was, and still is, the most iconic song they have ever released. So recognizable and so deadly. But as great as the title track is, *Ace of Spades* is actually a gem of a record, front to back. It's also an album that continued to move the band away from their punk roots to a more "rock 'n' roll" sound. Motörhead's name is often invoked when discussing the earliest days of thrash metal, and arguably no album they released had a bigger impact on that burgeoning scene than this one. It's a rollicking affair that seems to never age.

Recommended Track: "Ace of Spades"

15. Black Sabbath – Vol. 4

Vol. 4 was originally released through Warner Brothers in 1972 and was the fourth full-length album from Black Sabbath. It was originally intended to be titled "Snowblind" but the cocaine references were a little over the top for their record label who changed the album title without the band's consent. There have been theories that the band's overt drug use aided in giving this album a sense of dread that shrouds the whole thing. Drugs or not, there is a palpable sense of doom that hangs thick in the air on each track making this one of the heaviest albums the '70s ever produced. Songs on this album have been covered by the likes of Cathedral, Entombed, Overkill, Coalesce, Converge, Ministry, Sleep, Black Label Society, Brutal Truth, Sepultura, Iron Monkey, and Bongzilla, just to name a few. To say that this is one of the most influential metal albums of all-time is a complete understatement. The fact it includes two instrumentals and a piano-based ballad, leaving it with only seven tracks of actual heaviness, is even more impressive.

Recommended Track: "Snowblind"

14. Celtic Frost – Morbid Tales

Depending on where in the world you live this could be considered the highest ranking EP on the list. *Morbid Tales* was originally released in Europe in 1984 through Noise Records as a six-song EP. However on the first U.S. pressing, released through Metal Blade, the label added two songs off the *Emperor's Return* EP – "Dethroned Emperor" and "Morbid Tales" – to make this album a full-length. (In 1999 this album was reissued with all six tracks from the *Emperor's Return* EP included.) Celtic Frost were never darlings of the music journalist pool. In fact they were brushed off by a lot of journalists who just felt their sound was too extreme. Yet the sheer volume of genres and bands littering the bowels of the metal underground to claim this album as an influence is quite mind-blowing. Black metal, death metal, doom, thrash, etc. All of it owes a debt, one way or another, to the mighty Celtic Frost.

Recommended Track: "Into the Crypts of Rays"

13. Possessed – Seven Churches

After some highly touted, well-circulated demos, and an appearance on one of those classic Metal Blade comps, Possessed released their full-length debut in 1985 via Combat Records. *Seven Churches* has been called a lot of things – groundbreaking, the first death metal record, the missing link between thrash and death metal, etc. One could believe that all of it is absolutely true. Due to their geographic proximity, Possessed has been lumped into the Bay Area thrash scene. One would first need to acknowledge though that Possessed were faster, heavier, nastier, rawer, and eviler than any other band to ever come out of the Bay Area thrash scene. When this album hit in 1985 there was little like it at the time. Possessed weren't without their own influences. Venom and Motörhead were fast and raw, and Celtic Frost were heavy as sin. But no band combined all of those elements in the way Possessed did. Their legacy runs extremely deep into the cavernous metal underground.

Recommended Track: "The Exorcist"

12. Iron Maiden – Piece of Mind

Piece of Mind was the fourth full length album Maiden produced, originally released in 1983 via Capitol Records here in the U.S. It's the second album with Bruce Dickinson on vocals and the first to feature Nicko McBrain on drums. It's also an album that features some of their most recognizable songs, specifically "Flight of Icarus" and "The Trooper". If the previous album was a transition album from the Paul Di'Anno era to the Dickinson era, then this album is the first album really written with Dickinson and his vocal style firmly in mind (pun intended). The average song begins to grow a little longer in length and this album starts to see the band take some songwriting chances they hadn't on previous records. Despite contributing to three tracks on *Number of the Beast*, you could also argue this is the first album that Adrian Smith starts to really flex his songwriting muscles. It's the album that established them as master storytellers, and still stands as an absolute landmark of the genre.

Recommended Track: "Sun and Steel"

11. Black Sabbath – Master Of Reality

This album changed the course of music history. By the beginning of 1971, Black Sabbath was starting to blow up. They saw their first real chart successes with the *Paranoid* album, and the title track was a Top 5 hit in the U.K. It would have been real easy for them to go the way of so many other bands and begin writing radio friendly singles and songs that would have been a blatant attempt at a wider audience. Instead Tony Iommi and Geezer Butler down-tuned even further and what they came away with was the heaviest record that had ever been recorded up to that point. *Master of Reality* was the third full-length Sabbath album, originally released in 1971 through Warner Brothers here in the U.S. It's really hard to argue with the notion that no record prior to this one emulated what we now consider things like doom and stoner rock the way this one does. When we think huge, meaty riffs, bass lines that are like a grizzly bear walking upright, and drums that are controlled chaos, *Master of Reality* is the first album to make it all 'go to 11'.

Recommended Track: "Lord of This World"

10. Metallica – Master of Puppets

Master of Puppets was Metallica's third full-length album, originally released in 1986, their first offering officially for Elektra Records. It is considered by many reputable sources as not only the greatest thrash record of all-time, but possibly the greatest metal record of all-time. It was the first thrash record ever certified Platinum and since then has gone Platinum six times over. Songs from this album have appeared in major motion pictures. The legacy and influence of this record have never been in doubt. It's also the final record to feature Cliff Burton, one of the greatest bass players in metal history. For millions of kids getting into metal at this time it was somewhat of a life-changing experience. This record had everything – killer riffs, intricate songs that despite their length held your interest, angry, poignant lyrics, rad album artwork – it was the total package then and remains so to this day.

Recommended Track: "Battery"

9. Megadeth – Rust In Peace

Rust In Peace was Megadeth's fourth full-length album, originally released in 1990 on Capitol Records. The fact that it was released in 1990 makes it the highest ranking album from the '90s on this list. It's also an album that literally helped save thrash metal, or at least staved off its inevitable decline. By the end of the '80s there were so many pretenders out there and most of them had major label record deals thanks to the success of bands like Megadeth and Metallica. Even Metallica had started their downward decent at this point. Then this album came out and it was literally like an atom bomb, just laying waste to everything in its path. A thing of beauty, wrapped in some of the sickest guitar playing ever recorded. One of the most brilliant and technically proficient metal albums you will ever hear, and still one of metal's most influential pieces.

Recommended Track: "Holy Wars...The Punishment Due"

8. Mercyful Fate – Melissa

After the release of a highly sought-after EP, Mercyful Fate would sign to the brand new Roadrunner Records label and release their debut full-length album, *Melissa*, in 1983 (via Megaforce originally here in the U.S.). Mercyful Fate starts with King Diamond. He's not only one of the most recognizable figures in the history of metal but his vocals are absolutely unmistakable. Really though the true strength behind this band and this album is the twin guitar attack of Hank Shermann and Michael Denner, the most underrated guitar duo in metal history. This album is especially important, not just because it introduced the world to a killer band, but because the material on this album would be used to help launch a myriad of genres and offshoots. Behind King Diamond and four amazingly underrated musicians this band succeeded in creating an album that, still to this day, sounds as heavy, as eerie, and as downright sinister as it did over 30 years ago.

Recommended Track: "Into the Coven"

7. Judas Priest – Screaming For Vengeance

Screaming for Vengeance was Priest's eighth full length album, originally released on CBS Records here in the U.S. in 1982. The beauty of this album is that it's not only one of their best selling albums, it also happens to be one of their heaviest. While the big radio hit off this album that propelled a huge portion of sales is not a particularly heavy track ("You've Got Another Thing Comin'") and the album did feature other tracks that kept in line with what appeared on the *Point of Entry* album, the overall vibe is about as metal as you can get. "The Hellion/Electric Eye" is a metal masterpiece but it's not even the best track on the record as that distinction gets battled out between "Riding on the Wind" and the title track. The entire album is a showcase for just how amazing Rob Halford's vocal range could be while the guitar duo of Downing and Tipton are at the absolute top of their game.

Recommended Track: "Riding on the Wind"

6. Iron Maiden - Killers

Killers was Maiden's second full-length album, originally released in 1981 on EMI Records (Capitol Records here in the U.S.). It is, of course, the last album to feature Paul Di'Anno on vocals and the first album to feature Adrian Smith on guitar. Two huge developments that would not only affect the history of this band, but really the history of metal in general. There's a grittiness to the first two albums that they polished away after Di'Anno left the band. This album maintains a nasty edge to it from start to finish, and that tenaciousness in style gave birth to some of the most underrated songs this band ever wrote – "Wrathchild", "Murders in the Rue Morgue", "Drifter", "Purgatory", and the title track. The entire band delivers a brilliant performance. I challenge anyone to find another record written at this time that was as stout in production, execution, and presentation as *Killers*. It stands as not only one of the greatest albums to ever emerge out of the NWOBHM scene but one of the greatest metal albums of all time.

Recommended Track: "Murders in the Rue Morgue"

5. Black Sabbath - Paranoid

Paranoid was the second full-length album from Sabbath, originally released in 1970 via Vertigo Records (January of 1971 here in the U.S. through Warner Brothers). It stands as one of only two Sabbath albums to ever top the U.K. album charts and the title track is the only song they ever recorded that cracked the Top 20 on the U.K. charts. Here in the States it's gone Platinum four times over and cracked the Top 15 on the U.S. album charts. It stands, still to this day, as their most popular album. The title track, "War Pigs" and "Iron Man", along with "Fairies Wear Boots" have been concert staples for the last 40+ years. But it's not just album sales that make an album influential. What makes this album so great is it still sounds so phenomenal. "Iron Man" might contain the greatest guitar riff ever written, certainly the greatest opening to a song ever penned. Meanwhile, hidden gems like "Hand of Doom" and "Electric Funeral" are just as good, if not better than, the tracks that grab all the headlines. It can not be understated how important and influential this album wound up being.

Recommended Track: "Iron Man"

4. Slayer – Reign In Blood

Reign in Blood was Slayer's third full-length album, originally released in 1986 through Def Jam (and distributed by Geffen originally). It was shorter, faster, heavier, meaner, and more malicious than anything they had ever recorded before or since. Only three of the ten songs on the original pressing crack the three-minute mark and the entire record clocks in at just under a half hour. But in 1986 that was the most frenzied and, at times, frightening half hour you could spend with a record. Not only did Slayer blow away all the competition with this record, but they in turn became one of the biggest influences on the entire metal world, even more so than they may have been with their two previous efforts. Death metal, black metal, and especially thrash owe this record a massive, massive debt.

Recommended Track: "Altar of Sacrifice"

3. Metallica – Kill 'Em All

Kill 'Em All is Metallica's debut and was originally released in 1983 via Megaforce Records. To say that *Kill 'Em All* is rawer and more harrowing than anything else they've ever done is an absolute understatement. The vocals are almost unrecognizable compared to the near baritone 'Yeah-Yeahs' that Hetfield spews today. The songs are faster and heavier, and even Lars seems to find a place to compliment the music on this album. This is the album that launched one of the most successful careers in the history of metal. There needs to be some respect given for that, especially knowing the ridiculous circumstances this album was recorded under. When you think of thrash metal, when you think of the quintessential albums of the genre you should be thinking about this record. No other Metallica album represented thrash metal the way this one does and it did it at a time when thrash was still in its infancy.

Recommended Track: "Jump in the Fire"

2. Iron Maiden – The Number Of The Beast

The Number of the Beast was Iron Maiden's third full-length album, originally released in 1982 via EMI. As everyone is well aware, it's the first album to feature the mighty Bruce Dickinson on vocals. It also happens to be the final album with Clive Burr on drums, and his dismissal from the band certainly couldn't have been due to his playing on this record because he's exceptional. This album was really a bridge between the Di'Anno years and the subsequent Dickinson era. It is the absolute best of both worlds. The more progressive elements of future records would meet the rawness of the first two albums and wed in sonic perfection. It's not a mystery why Iron Maiden still chooses to fill their set with at least half of this album every night on tour. Some of the greatest songs in metal history appear on this record. *The Number of the Beast* would be Iron Maiden's first album to go to #1 on the U.K. album charts and has sold over 14 million albums worldwide.

Recommended Track: "The Prisoner"

1. Black Sabbath – Black Sabbath

It starts with the pitter-patter of rain. A lone bell chimes in the distance. Then with the crushing reverberation of a handful of notes, heavy metal music as we know it today is born. Black Sabbath released their debut album on February 13, 1970 in the UK through Vertigo Records. (June 1 in the U.S. through Warner Brothers.) It is widely accepted by several reputable sources to be the demarcation line between hard rock and heavy metal. The unholy womb from whence heavy metal came crawling out of. The Blues were often considered the "Devil's music" but in reality this is where music fans would start to wear the proverbial black mark. It's not just the lyrical content or the inverted cross on the inside of the original album sleeve. No, this album seethed a kind of malicious intent, a kind of bewitching ethos that no other album had ever delivered before. Black Sabbath was more than just some meaty, down-tuned Blues riffs. They were darker and more malevolent than any other band in the world. This is where it all began…

Recommended Track: "Black Sabbath"

II. Examining The Body

Albums By Year

Year	#of album
1968	3
1969	1
1970	8
1971	3
1972	1
1973	1
1974	1
1975	2
1976	3
1977	1
1978	4
1979	4
1980	9
1981	7
1982	10
1983	11
1984	20
1985	29
1986	23
1987	37
1988	29
1989	26
1990	24
1991	34
1992	25
1993	34
1994	25
1995	28
1996	24
1997	34
1998	35
1999	20
2000	18
2001	14

Albums By Year Cont'd

Year	#of album
2003	14
2004	9
2005	11
2006	10
2007	13
2008	12
2009	5
2010	7
2011	9
2012	12

Albums By Decade

1970s	28
1980s	201
1990s	283
2000s	122

Albums By Country

USA – 317
UK – 109
Sweden – 87
Norway – 35
Germany – 24
Canada - 23
Finland – 15
Switzerland – 11
Netherlands – 10
Brazil – 7
Denmark – 7
Australia – 4

Albums By Country Cont'd

Greece – 4
Austria – 3
Belgium – 2
Japan – 2
Poland – 2
Czech Republic – 1
Ireland – 1
Portugal – 1
Spain – 1

Albums By Label (6 or more albums)

Relapse – 62
Metal Blade – 50
Roadrunner - Roadracer - R/C – 48
Century Media – 38
Earache – 33
Combat – 22
Noise – 20
Nuclear Blast – 18
Warner Bros. – 16
Candlelight Records – 15
Peaceville – 14
Megaforce – 13´
Osmose – 11
Rise Above – 11
Columbia – 8
EMI – 7
Neat – 7
CBS – 6
Elektra – 6
Music For Nations – 6
Victory Records – 6

Top Albums Per Year

1980

Motörhead - Ace of Spades
Black Sabbath - Heaven and Hell
Iron Maiden – Iron Maiden
Angel Witch – Angel Witch
Ozzy Osbourne - Blizzard of Ozz

1981

Iron Maiden - Killers
Black Sabbath - Mob Rules
Ozzy Osbourne - Diary of a Madman
Venom - Welcome To Hell
Saxon - Denim and Leather

1982

Iron Maiden - Number of the Beast
Judas Priest - Screaming For Vengeance
Venom - Black Metal
Motörhead - Iron Fist
Witchfinder General - Death Penalty
Diamond Head - Borrowed Time
Raven - Wiped Out
Twisted Sister - Under The Blade
Anvil - Metal on Metal
Manowar - Battle Hymns

1983

Metallica - Kill 'Em All
Mercyful Fate - Melissa
Iron Maiden - Piece of Mind
Dio - Holy Diver
Slayer - Show No Mercy
Ozzy Osbourne - Bark At The Moon
Witchfinder General - Friends of Hell
Manowar - Into Glory Ride
OZ - Fire In The Brain
Raven - All For One

1984

Celtic Frost - Morbid Tales
Iron Maiden - Powerslave
Mercyful Fate - Don't Break The Oath
Dio - The Last In Line
Judas Priest - Defenders of the Faith
Metallica - Ride The Lightening
Bathory - Bathory
Voivod - War and Pain
Anthrax - Fistful of Metal
Trouble - Psalm 9

1985

Possessed - Seven Churches
Slayer - Hell Awaits
Celtic Frost - To Mega Therion
Bathory - The Return......
Kreator - Endless Pain
Destruction - Infernal Overkill
Amebix - Arise!
Carnivore - s/t
Megadeth - Killing Is My Business...
Trouble - The Skull

1986

Slayer - Reign In Blood
Metallica - Master of Puppets
Megadeth - Peace Sells...But Who's Buying
Candlemass - Epicus Doomicus Metallicus
Kreator - Pleasure To Kill
King Diamond - Fatal Potrait
Iron Maiden - Somewhere In Time
Saint Vitus - Born Too Late
Possessed - Beyond The Gates
Cryptic Slaughter - Convicted

1987

Death - Scream Bloody Gore
Bathory - Under The Sign Of The Black Mark
Testament - The Legacy
Napalm Death - Scum
Celtic Frost - Into The Pandemonium
Sodom - Persecution Mania
Carnivore - Retaliation
Mercyful Fate - The Beginning
Anthrax - Among the Living
D.R.I. - Crossover

1988

Carcass - Reek of Putrefaction
Iron Maiden - Seventh Son of a Seventh Son
Testament - The New Order
Metallica - ...And Justice For All
Slayer - South Of Heaven
Death - Leprosy
Bolt Thrower - In Battle There Is No Law
Danzig - Danzig
Napalm Death - From Enslavement To Obliteration
Destruction - Release From Agony

1989

Obituary - Slowly We Rot
Carcass - Symphonies of Sickness
Bolt Thrower - Realm Of Chaos - Slaves of Darkness
Terrorizer - World Downfall
Morbid Angel - Altars of Madness
Bathory - Blood Fire Death
Repulsion - Horrified
Testament - Practice What You Preach
Kreator - Extreme Aggression
Sepultura - Beneath The Remains

1990

Megadeth - Rust In Peace
Death - Spiritual Healing
Deicide - Deicide
Danzig - II - Lucifuge
Entombed - Left Hand Path
Obituary - Cause of Death
Slayer - Seasons In The Abyss
Hellhammer - Apocalyptic Raids 1990 A.D.
Exhorder - Slaughter In The Vatican
Cannibal Corpse - Eaten Back To Life

1991

Cathedral - Forest of Equilibrium
Carcass - Necroticism - Descanting the Insalubrious
Morbid Angel - Blessed Are The Sick
Entombed - Clandestine
Atheist - Unquestionable Presence
Autopsy - Mental Funeral
Death - Human
Paradise Lost - Gothic
Dismember - Like An Everflowing Stream
Unleashed - Where No Life Dwells

1992

Kyuss - Blues For The Red Sun
Darkthrone - A Blaze In The Northern Sky
Amorphis - The Karelian Isthmus
Bolt Thrower - The IVth Crusade
At The Gates - The Red In The Sky Is Ours
Asphyx - Last One On Earth
Eyehategod - In The Name of Suffering
Deicide - Legion
Obituary - The End Complete
Exhorder - The Law

1993

Morbid Angel - Covenant
Rotting Christ - Thy Mighty Contract
Eyehategod - Take As Needed For Pain
My Dying Bride - Turn Loose The Swans
Dissection - The Somberlain
Blasphemy - Gods of War
Sleep - Holy Mountain
Mercyful Fate - In The Shadows
Cathedral - The Ethereal Mirror
Neurosis - Enemy Of The Sun

1994

Kyuss – Kyuss (Welcome To Sky Valley)
Emperor - In The Nightside Eclipse
Amorphis - Tales From The Thousand Lakes
At The Gates - Terminal Spirit Disease
Mayhem - De Mysteriis Dom Sathanas
Acid Bath - When The Kite String Pops
Rotting Christ - Non Serviam
Darkthrone - Transilvanian Hunger
Samael - Ceremony of Opposites
Fu Manchu - No One Rides For Free

1995

Dissection - Storm of the Light's Bane
At The Gates - Slaughter of the Soul
Kyuss - ...And The Circus Leaves Town
My Dying Bride - The Angel and The Dark River
Opeth - Orchid
Deadguy - Fixation on a Co-Worker
Cathedral - The Carnival Bizarre
Celestial Season - Solar Lovers
Absu - The Sun of Tiphareth
The Gathering – Mandylion

1996

Neurosis - Through Silver In Blood
Eyehategod - Dopesick
Satyricon - Nemesis Divina
Cryptopsy - None So Vile
His Hero Is Gone - Fifteen Counts of Arson
Acid Bath - Paegan Terrorism Tactics
Bethlehem - Dictius Te Necare
Deadguy - Screaming With the Deadguy Quintet
Converge - Petitioning The Empty Sky
Type O Negative - October Rust

1997

Emperor - Anthems To The Welkin At Dusk
Electric Wizard - Come My Fanatics...
Enslaved - Eld
His Hero Is Gone - Monuments To Thieves
Brutal Truth - Sounds of the Animal Kingdom
Coalesce - Give Them Rope
Fu Manchu - The Action Is Go
Immortal - Blizzard Beasts
Borknagar - The Olden Domain
Assück - Misery Index

1998

Nasum - Inhale/Exhale
Coalesce - Functioning On Impatience
Opeth - My Arms, Your Hearse
Amon Amarth - Once Sent From the Golden Hall
Nebula - Let It Burn
Exhumed - Gore Metal
Marduk - Nightwing
Clutch - The Elephant Riders
Soilent Green - Sewn Mouth Secrets
Converge - When Forever Comes Crashing

1999

Neurosis - Times of Grace
Coalesce - 0:12 Revolution in Just Listening
Emperor - IX Equilibrium
Dillinger Escape Plan - Calculating Infinity
Immortal - At The Heart of Winter
Spirit Caravan - Jug Fulla Sun
Black Label Society - Sonic Brew
Darkthrone - Ravishing Grimness
Botch - We Are The Romans
Morgion - Solinari

2000

Iron Maiden - Brave New World
High On Fire - The Art of Self Defense
Cephalic Carnage - Exploiting Dysfunction
Electric Wizard - Dopethrone
Agents of Oblivion - Agents of Oblivion
Exhumed - Slaughtercult
Goatwhore - The Eclipse of Ages Into Black
The Mystick Krewe of Clearlight – The Mystic Krewe…
Nasum - Human 2.0
Isis - Celestial

2001

Pentagram - First Daze Here (The Vintage Collection)
Opeth - Blackwater Park
Emperor - Prometheus: The Dsiscipline of Fire & Demise
Converge - Jane Doe
Clutch - Pure Rock Fury
Neurosis - A Sun That Never Sets
Impaled Nazarene - Absence of War...
Pig Destroyer - Prowler In The Yard
Absu - Tara
Anaal Nathrakh - The Codex Necro

2002

Immortal - Sons of Northern Darkness
High On Fire - Surrounded By Thieves
Amon Amarth - Versus The World
Opeth - Deliverance
Reverend Bizarre - In The Rectory...
Satyricon - Volcano
The Red Chord - Fused Together In Revolving Doors
Cephalic Carnage - Lucid Interval
Mastadon - Remission
Bloodbath - Resurrection Through Carnage

2003

Sleep - Dopesmoker
The Locust - Plague Soundscapes
Cult of Luna - The Beyond
Integrity - To Die For
Daughters - Canada Songs
Aborted - Goremageddon
The Black Dahlia Murder - Unhallowed
Agalloch - The Mantle
Ed Gein - It's A Shame...
Watchmaker - Kill.Fucking.Everyone

2004

Marduk - Plague Angel
Pig Destroyer - Terrifyer
Amon Amarth - Fate Of Norns
Enslaved - Isa
Pagan Altar - Lords of Hypocrisy

2005

Witchcraft - Firewood
Rotten Sound - Exit
Buried Inside - Chronoclast
Opeth - Ghost Reveries
Belphegor - Gaotreich – Fleshcult

2006

Celtic Frost - Monotheist
The Sword - Age of Winters
Dissection - Reinkaos
Pentagram - First Daze Here Too
Ihsahn - The Adversary

2007

Neurosis - Given To The Rising
Electric Wizard - Witchcult Today
Witchcraft - The Alchemist
Skeletonwitch - Beyond the Permafrost
Baroness - Red album

2008

Blood Ceremony - Blood Ceremony
Amon Amarth - Twilight of the Thunder God
Mythical Beast - Scales
Rotten Sound - Cycles
Testament - The Formation of Damnation

2009

Coalesce - OX
Baroness - Blue album
Goatwhore - Carving Out The Eyes Of God
Woods of Ypres - Woods IV: The Green Album
Black Pyramid – Black Pyramid

2010

Horseback - The Invisible Mountain
Triptykon - Eparistera Daimones
Electric Wizard - Black Masses
Watain - Lawless Darkness
Wodenstrhrone - Loss

2011

Rotten Sound - Cursed
Blood Ceremony - Living With The Ancients
In Solitude - The World, The Flesh, The Devil
Graveyard - Hisingen Blues
Red Fang - Murder The Mountains

2012

Horseback - Half Blood
Witchcraft - Legend
Royal Thunder - CVI
The Devil's Blood - The Thousandfold Epicentre
Christian Mistress - Possession

Top Albums 2013-2016

2013
Blood Ceremony – The Eldritch Dark
Ulcerate – Vermis
Demon Lung – The Hundreth Name
Vastum – Patricidal Lust
Amon Amarth – Deceiver of the Gods
ASG – Blood Drive
Carcass – Surgical Steel
Clutch – Earth Rocker
Eight Bells – The Captain's Daughter
Lycus – Tempest
In Solitude – Sister
Primitive Man – Scorn
Sea of Bones – The Earth Wants Us Dead
Secrets of the Sky – To Sail Black Waters
Immortal Bird – Akrasia
Darkthrone – The Underground Resistance
Exhumed – Necrocracy
Watain – The Wild Hunt
Inter Arma – Sky Burial
Cathedral – The Last Spire
Skeletonwitch – Serpents Unleashed
Oranssi Pazuzu – Velonielu
Nails – Abandon All Life
Inquisition – Obscure Verses for the Multiverse
SubRosa – More Constant Than the Gods

2014
Eyehategod – Eyehategod
Ides of Gemini – Old World New Wave
Indian – From All Purity
Agalloch – The Serpent and The Sphere
Triptykon – Melana Chasmata
Pallbearer – Foundations of Burden

2014 Cont'd

Sabbath Assembly – Quaternity
Secret Cutter – Self Titled
Lord Mantis – Death Mask
Bask – American Hollow
Blodhemn – H7
Myrkur – Myrkur
Obliterations – Poison Everything
Torch Runner – Endless Nothing
Usnea – Random Cosmic Violence
Wormwood – Wormwood
Krieg – Transient
Panopticon – Roads To The North
Dead Congregation – Promulgation Of The Fall
Winterfylleth – The Divination Of Antiquity
Martyrdöd – Elddop
YOB – Clearing The Path To Ascend
Goatwhore – Constricting Rage Of The Merciless
Mayhem – Esoteric Warfare
Electric Wizard – Time To Die

2015

Paradise Lost – The Plague Within
My Dying Bride – Feel The Misery
Immortal Bird – Empress/Abscess
Lament Cityscape – The Torn
Murg – Varg & Bjorn
Obsequiae – Aria of Vernal Tombs
Panopticon – Autumn Eternal
Tribulation – The Children of the Night
Valkyrie – Shadows
Secrets of the Sky – Pathway
Crown – Natron
Crypt Sermon – Out of the Garden
Gospel of the Witches – Salem's Wounds
Vastum – Hole Below
Voices – London

2015 Cont'd

Marduk – Frontschwein
Abyss – Heretical Anatomy
AEvangelist – Enthrall To The Void Of Bliss
Grave Ritual – Morbid Throne
Magic Circle – Journey Blind
Christian Mistress – To Your Death
Dead In The Manger – Cessation
Maruta – Remain Dystopian
Mgla – Exercises In Futility
Skepticism – Ordeal

2016

Neurosis – Fires Within Fires
Cult of Luna & Julie Christmas – Mariner
Bethlehem – Bethlehem
Waldgeflüster – Ruinen
Inverloch – Distance | Collapsed
Blood Ceremony – Lord of Misrule
Dead Register – Fiber
Eight Bells – Landless
Asphyx – Incoming Death
Anagnorisis – Peripeteia
Hemelbestormer – Aether
AnaalNathrahk – The Whole of the Law
Lament Cityscape & Theologian – Soft Tissue
SubRosa – For This We Fought The Battle Of Ages
T.O.M.B. – Fury Nocturnus
Testament – Brotherhood of the Snake
Worm Ouroboros – What Graceless Dawn
Ghoul – Dungeon Bastards
Vanhelgd – Temple of Phobos
Abbath – Abbath
Ulcerate – Shrines of Paralysis
Borknagar – Winter Thrice
Chthe'ilist – Le Dernier Crepuscule
Dark Funeral – Where Shadows Forever Reign
Darkthrone – Arctic Thunder

III. Index

Made in the USA
Lexington, KY
05 June 2017